Contents

and for those who want to relate their own experience to the collected wisdom of many of today's brightest business leaders.'
Paul Walsh, *Management Today*

'. . . the best connected man in the business world.' *Guardian*

'He takes us on a breakneck tour of the hot topics of business in 2007 . . . the contributors of the book are impressive and interesting, and the book barrels along at such a pace, with such enthusiasm, that we are breathlessly carried along . . . *On Leadership* is a profoundly hopeful read – informed by the almost palpable joy Leighton feels in inspiring and leading others.' *World Business*

'The best management book I've read in a long while . . .' **Chris Blackhurst, City Editor,** *Evening Standard*

'Leighton has chosen to consult an impressive selection of friends and colleagues about the subject, and chuck in his own thoughts in a jaunty narrative. His cast is first rate, and his access to A-list business leaders striking . . . for a selection of conventional wisdom on business leadership, and a sense of what is being discussed in the first-class lounges of the world's airports, you could do no better than to read this book.' *Financial Times*

On Leadership

Allan Leighton began his career at Mars Confectionery where he rose to become group marketing director before leaving to join the loss-making ASDA supermarket chain. There he was credited with turning what he once described as a basket case into a highly successful company that was sold to US retail giant Wal-Mart for £6.7 billion in 1999. When he left his position as president and chief executive of Wal-Mart Europe he famously coined the phrase 'going plural' as he took on non-executive positions at a string of companies, including lastminute.com, Leeds United, Bhs, BSkyB and Selfridges.

Allan is currently Chairman of Royal Mail Group and Race for Opportunity and non-executive director of BSkyB and George Weston, as well as deputy chairman of Selfridges & Co.

Teena Lyons has spent most of her career as a financial and consumer affairs journalist. She spent seven years as retail corres-pondent at the *Mail on Sunday*, breaking a number of high-profile news stories and regularly interviewing the most important business leaders in the sector. She has also written for a number of other national newspapers including the *Daily Telegraph*, *Daily Mail* and *Sunday Mirror*. Teena is a regular contributor to a range of consumer and trade press magazine titles, including *Cosmopolitan*, *Woman* and the *Grocer*.

Praise for *On Leadership*

'*On Leadership* is immensely readable. It will provide a welcome resource for those wanting to tell others stories about leadership

On Leadership

Practical Wisdom from the People Who Know

ALLAN LEIGHTON

with Teena Lyons

BUSINESS
BOOKS

Published by Random House Business Books 2008

2 4 6 8 10 9 7 5 3 1

First published in Great Britain in 2007 by
Random House Business Books
Random House, 20 Vauxhall Bridge Road,
London SW1V 2SA

www.rbooks.co.uk

Addresses for companies within The Random House Group Limited can be found at:
www.randomhouse.co.uk/offices.htm

The Random House Group Limited Reg. No. 954009

A CIP catalogue record for this book
is available from the British Library

ISBN 9781905211449

The Random House Group Limited supports The Forest Stewardship Council (FSC), the leading
international forest certification organisation. All our titles that are printed on Greenpeace
approved FSC certified paper carry the FSC logo. Our paper procurement policy can be found at:
www.rbooks.co.uk/environment

Mixed Sources
Product group from well-managed
forests and other controlled sources
www.fsc.org Cert no. TT-COC-2139
© 1996 Forest Stewardship Council

Typeset in Antiqua by Palimpsest Book Production Limited,
Grangemouth, Stirlingshire

Printed and bound in Great Britain by
CPI Bookmarque, Croydon CRO 4TD

*To Annie, Rebecca, Jay,
Rob, Bertie and Rosie*

Acknowledgements

I'd like to thank ex-*Mail on Sunday* business journalist Teena Lyons for the sterling support she gave me in helping write this book. Also Christine, my personal secretary for over fifteen years, who had the unenviable challenge of arranging interviews with the sixty busy men and women who shared their thoughts on leadership. Quite an achievement!

At Random House, Gail Rebuck for spurring me into capturing my thoughts in the first place and Nigel Wilcockson who has worked so hard in overseeing the project.

My appreciation of course to all those who kindly gave their time to share their valuable insight into what it takes to be a great leader.

Finally I'd like to thank all the people I've worked with over the years – whether it be a checkout operator, postman or -woman, chairman or chief executive – all of whom have taught me so much about life, business and myself.

All my royalties from this book will be donated to Breast Cancer Care.

Allan Leighton
June 2007

Introduction

Among the many things that have happened to me in my thirty or so years in business, two events stand out particularly clearly in my mind. The most recent occurred in April 2002, when I became chairman of the Royal Mail. In taking on the role, I was, of course, only too acutely aware of the mess that the Royal Mail had got itself into – it was haemorrhaging money at a rate of knots. I also knew that, almost before I did anything else, I needed to do something about its name. Back in March 2001 the Post Office holding company had changed the organisation's name to Consignia in an ill-fated attempt to reflect the quickly changing nature of the business. Yet it was clear that at the core of the Royal Mail business was pride in its association with the Crown – after all, this was a business that could trace its roots back to Charles I. Everyone I spoke to hated the new corporate name of Consignia, not least because it meant nothing at all. By contrast, staff and customers had really valued the fact that the Mail was 'Royal' because there is hardly anything called Royal these days and few organisations that display the Queen's crown. In marketing terms 'Royal' is a hugely powerful image.

I got the message – the Royal Mail was all about its heritage, which was Royal and British, a fact reflected in its uniform and red livery. The core idea was that it was much more than just a company. I knew it would also give me a quick win on taking the chair to reverse the unpopular change and ditch the Consignia name for good; and a quick win is very useful for any new boy. It would help to prove to critics, fed up with lacklustre service, that we really meant business.

When I summoned the advisers there was much shaking of heads. They told me point-blank that such a change would take at least six months. We needed permission for the change from the Queen and this was a lengthy process. But I wanted action now. Fortunately, I've worked with Prince Charles a number of times on Prince's Trust projects, and so I felt able to contact him and tell him what I wanted to do. He was hugely enthusiastic and added that he thought it would be particularly appropriate in the Golden Jubilee year. This meant that the change could be announced virtually overnight – instead of having to wait up to a year for various advisers to follow things through. I think we were all glad to consign Consignia to the flames.

The other event in my career that I remember particularly clearly came some three years earlier – on Monday, 7 June 1999, to be precise. It began in the departure lounge at Heathrow airport, where I was waiting for my Concorde flight to New York with a baseball cap pulled low over my eyes, praying that no one would recognise me.

That Monday, ASDA, of which I was CEO, and DIY-to-electricals conglomerate Kingfisher were supposedly just days away from signing a deal that would create a new force in European retailing. We had agreed the £18 billion merger in April. The details were all but finalised. Proposals were at an advanced stage for an international chain of out-of-town hypermarkets combining ASDA's food expertise and its George fashion brand with Kingfisher's Comet electrical chain and Superdrug beauty stores. All was going according to plan.

Except, here I was on my way to Bentonville, Arkansas, to talk to Wal-Mart.

The trip had been arranged in enormous secrecy in a series of calls between myself, my colleague Archie Norman, Wal-Mart's chairman Rob Walton and the then chief executive David Glass. ASDA had had strong links with Wal-Mart for years, ever since I was hauled into an office in Bentonville so that management could give me the once-over and find out why I was taking so many pictures of their stores. Indeed, Archie and I had copied so many of Wal-Mart's ideas, that there was a widely held view that ASDA was simply a British version of the US giant and that a deal was inevitable. Now it was crunch time. Given the Kingfisher situation, they had to make a move to prove they were really serious.

Wal-Mart's counterattack had been under discussion for months. The moment the Kingfisher deal was announced in the Spring, David Glass had called in Wal-Mart's bankers, Wasserstein Perella. The brief was simple. Wishbone (Wal-Mart's code name for itself) wanted the bankers to come up with a way of taking over Apple (Wal-Mart's code name for ASDA). However, they wouldn't make a hostile move; it was not their style. Now time was running out.

For my part, I had for some weeks felt the Kingfisher deal was wrong. I just thought it wouldn't work. With the benefit of hindsight, I think we'd underestimated what a great business ASDA was. Perhaps, after the years of struggle, which saw thousands of redundancies, a wage freeze and store closures, we could never quite believe the business was prospering so well. ASDA was a great prize for a takeover, but we thought we had to merge or find another way of maintaining the momentum, and that's when Kingfisher came along.

What made me most uneasy was just how different our teams were. An enormous culture clash was quite apparent. At every meeting, for example, we would turn up with three people and they would arrive with an army. Kingfisher had three investment banks and we, because we were trying to save money, had just one. We would meet and, when there was an issue, we'd make a decision. Kingfisher would go away to cogitate and ask their advisers. Everyone on the ASDA team came back from such meetings less motivated than when they'd left the office.

So, there I was, bound for the USA, looking as casual as I could with my heart and mind racing. Ironically, despite my clumsy attempts at disguise, a number of other businessmen hurrying to New York that morning recognised me and came up to say hello. I even found myself sitting next to my close neighbour in Yorkshire, the Earl of Harewood, who seemed slightly bemused by my outlandish baseball cap and dark glasses. I need hardly have bothered. As we landed at JFK airport a few hours later, an announcement boomed over the public address system:

'Would Mr Leighton of ASDA, being met by the Wal-Mart jet, please make himself known to the cabin crew.'

Although my cover was well and truly blown, remarkably, and luckily, no one made the connection. Three hours later, when I arrived at Bentonville airport in the baking heat, a battered pick-up truck screeched to a halt beside the private jet. Climbing out of the driver's seat, with a broad grin and an outstretched hand, was Rob Walton, casually dressed in jeans and a checked shirt. It felt the most natural thing in the world to fling my bags into the back of the truck, climb in the cab and chat about the Arkansas countryside as we sped along.

Within hours we'd come to an outline agreement and Rob and his senior executives were planning their own trip to the UK to look at our ASDA stores. On Wednesday, 9 June, even as Kingfisher chief executive Sir Geoff Mulcahy was phoning Archie Norman to ask if anything was going on, Wal-Mart's Lear jet was landing at Leeds-Bradford airport. To allay any concerns, we put out the story that they were American investors. By Saturday, the deal was done.

Intuitively, I didn't think the Kingfisher deal would work. The spirit of ASDA and its team, everything we had spent almost a decade building, would have been diluted. We had worked hard to recruit the best brains who easily understood the culture and could make things happen. We had an incredible team at every layer of the organisation. After copying the Wal-Mart model so diligently, we didn't want the business to go to the wrong place.

It was not an easy decision. After announcing a transaction of the scale of the Kingfisher deal, most people would have stuck with it, even if it felt wrong. But we simply wanted to do the right thing. Arguably, the deal with Wal-Mart dramatically changed the destiny of all concerned. Kingfisher never really recovered and, although ASDA has seen some tough times since, it has hugely benefited from its association with Wal-Mart.

'Urgency is energy'

'What you don't know you can learn'

These two incidents – rebranding one company, selling another – couldn't have been more different. Looking back on them, though, I realise that in both cases, when I was trying to decide what to do, I ended up drawing on lessons I had learned earlier in my career, either directly or from someone I respected. In the case of Consignia, for example, I knew that one quality leaders I admire have in common is knowing when to act decisively, and if there was ever a time to do so it was with a company that at the time was losing £1 million a day. Effective leadership inevitably means taking decisions – and often pretty tough ones at that. Good leaders have to have the drive and ambition to lead from the front. They don't accept the necessity of always doing things the same way simply because no one else has bothered to see a different path. They continuously search for improvement, often in the face of some fairly vocal criticism from the outside.

I'd learned this – often the hard way – earlier in my career. Over the years I have also seen or read about others who were good at acting decisively. Rupert Murdoch, for example. I'm very aware that his detractors claim that he is a gambler who randomly backs his hunches. And I know that they're eager to point out the times when it nearly went wrong – such as in 1990 when he was driven to the brink following the merger of the Sky satellite TV company with its rival to form BSkyB. Yet I also know that he had the last laugh: today BSkyB continues to announce record profits. His decisiveness and intuition have built the world's most powerful media empire on the back of owning just one evening newspaper in Adelaide, Australia. I have always found his views and experiences very helpful.

Gut instinct is another leadership quality you have to rely on, and something I just had to take seriously in the case of the ASDA–Kingfisher merger. Although reason was telling me one thing, my gut instinct was telling me something entirely different. From experience I knew that gut instinct can often be right and that there is a whole range of leaders who can trace their success in business to this key ability. Sir Philip Green, for example, is brilliant at predicting market trends. He really understands and knows his product. He instinctively knows whether something is going to capture the customer's imagination or if it won't. In the conversation I had with him for this book, instinct was one of the topics I quizzed him about, and he described how heavily he relies on it. 'When my team hang up all the product for review,' he told me, 'I can immediately say if I don't like it. It's just the things you see. Say we have the pick of forty toy dogs for Bhs and they say, "Right Philip, pick one". I say to the buyer that the eyes are too close together, or I don't like the face. You don't know why it is the wrong colour red or blue, but you know. Then you get it in and it sells out. It's feel and gut instinct. You get to know things that are instinctively not right.'

I'm very aware that when leadership ideals are stated in simple, bold words – 'be decisive', 'obey your gut instincts' and so on – these injunctions can often seem rather empty, despite the fact that they may be true. It doesn't take a genius to work out that a leader needs to be decisive, so just stating the fact isn't particularly useful. But I've always felt that when you hear these qualities discussed by figures you respect, or they emerge from stories and anecdotes you hear, they have a way of becoming more concrete, more persuasive and, in practical terms, more helpful. This is the reason why, in this book, I haven't set out to write some generalised theory of good management and leadership, but to show these principles at work through my own experiences and through the words and deeds of a whole range of people I particularly admire.

I have been lucky in that during my thirty-year career at Mars, ASDA and then 'going plural' – building up a portfolio of directorships and chairman's posts across various industries – I have worked with and learned lessons from many of the world's best-known and most respected business leaders. There have been plenty of time, hands-on experience and top role models to help me consider just what qualities are required to make a great leader. And because I wanted to explore in their own no-nonsense words what it takes to lead a successful business, and to compare it with my own experiences, I have talked to more than fifty of the business world's greatest authorities, and set them the 'twenty-minute test'. Working on my belief that you get more done in the first twenty minutes of a meeting than if you sit together in a room for twenty hours, I invited each of these top businessmen and -women to spend just twenty minutes talking about their views on leadership.

Inevitably, I've also drawn heavily on my own experiences. A large proportion of my working life has been spent at two companies: Mars, where I was for eighteen years, and ASDA, where I stayed for eight. I never thought I would leave the first, let alone the second, but following ASDA's sale to Wal-Mart in 1999, I decided that I didn't want to be CEO any more. Initially, I had the idea of working less and maybe doing two or three things instead of one. I had to explain this to the press, though: it was important to me that it didn't look like I had been fired and I knew people would find my action difficult to understand. So I said I was 'going plural'. It was the first thing that came into my head, and the phrase has since taken on a life of its own. I was offered a number of opportunities and in the end I took executive and non-executive roles with a number of firms, including Bhs, Dyson, lastminute.com, Scottish Power, Leeds United, Cannons, Wilson-Connolly, BSkyB, Business in the Community and the Royal Mail. This career path has also given me the space I need to look constantly at other potential opportunities that will make use of my previous experiences. I have, for example, many times been linked with possible bids for J Sainsbury, Marks & Spencer and many others. What has excited me about all the businesses I have signed up to has been the differences between them. They'd all experienced extreme ups and downs, and I was interested in helping them prosper. And yet, despite their diversity and their very different histories, I've found that what I've learned in one company I can often apply to another.

Take 'communication', for example, which is a quality many business people think they are brilliant at, but most are not. All my experience has taught me that leaders have to make sure that the way they communicate, both internally and externally, really works. And, not surprisingly, to communicate you need to get close to your team.

I discovered this the hard way very early on in my career when I was selected to be on the leadership programme at Mars and was informed that I was going to start off on the Maltesers line in Slough as a production manager. On my first day the factory manager told me that he did not really have much time for the leadership programme and that my one task was not to screw anything up. The only word of advice he offered was to listen to what the charge hand told me.

I was then handed a brush and told to sweep up any Maltesers that fell off the line. I spent three exhausting hours with that brush chasing little balls of chocolate as they rolled around the factory floor. My success rate was dreadful, and I still remember the bemused expressions on my colleagues' faces as they observed the new boy who had been handpicked for supposedly greater things.

Eventually, my humiliation complete, the charge hand stepped forward and told me the secret: tread on the Maltesers before you sweep them up. It was an embarrassing way to learn that 'operators know best' and that getting close to them is key.

When I joined ASDA as marketing director in 1992, the company was a basket case. On my first day at ASDA House in Leeds two things immediately stood out – the office structure and the floor plan. This told me a lot about the company culture. Directors sat in one area of the building, known as the 'directorate', and the quality of their office and furnishings was determined by their position in the hierarchy. It was archaic. I hadn't sat in an office for years – Mars had been strictly open plan. I was completely thrown when I was shown to my separate office. It was miles away from anything interesting, I didn't know what was going on and there was no one around. I immediately decided that I wasn't going to sit in an office. I picked up my papers and went to sit with my team in the marketing department. Very soon we decided to knock down all the walls in marketing and very soon the whole of ASDA House was open plan.

At one level, this is an easy lesson to learn, but nothing taught

'If you insist on perfection make the first demands of yourself'

me it more forcibly than seeing just how bad things were at ASDA. When I later joined the Royal Mail, I made absolutely sure that accessibility was a top priority. My 'Ask Allan' scheme generates 400 emails a day from colleagues. They vary from 'Can I get voluntary redundancy?', 'My manager is beating up on me' and 'Did you know this is the latest scheme that has been introduced and we all think it is mad?' to 'It's raining and my pouch leaks'. The emails are all answered within an hour, and I try to do at least half of them personally. People ask me how, or even why, I do that. The answer is that it's an incredibly powerful tool for knowing what's going on. It's great radar and probably as important as anything else I do. I can fix the problem, email back that it's been fixed and the recipient will probably then tell twenty people. That's a huge payback.

To say that the same issues crop up in all businesses is not to say that there is a one-size-fits-all solution to them. Apart from anything else, human nature being what it is, different people are inevitably going to have very different approaches. Philip Green's response to an early set-back in his career, Rupert Murdoch's way of dealing with the hostile reaction to the appointment of his son as CEO of BSkyB, or Stuart Rose's approach to turning around M&S aren't what every leader would necessarily have done, or indeed the only way of doing things. But it's fascinating when you hear the stories such leaders have to tell, how certain recurrent strategies and thought-processes are so often in place. And it's these recurrent strategies and thought-processes that fascinate me.

My starting point for my exploration of leadership is those imaginative mavericks, the entrepreneurs – the James Dysons of this world. They have to embody such key qualities as determination and persistence to get their businesses started, and the successful ones display these qualities in spades. So they offer fascinating non-textbook examples of how to lead from the front and how to keep going. Normally, of course, the aspiring entrepreneur is the very small mouse in the elephants' playground and getting started in a marketplace dominated by large organisations can be tricky. In order to build the new hotel at Heathrow's Terminal 5, Surinder Arora, a business figure I admire hugely, had to pitch his company, which at the time had a balance sheet in millions, against an established hotel group that counted its funds in billions. James Dyson was up against huge multinational companies that regarded his ideas as eccentric. But both these people had what it took to succeed.

Of course, running companies that are already well established poses challenges and problems all of their own. So, having looked at entrepreneurial start-ups, I go on to look at existing businesses, including ones that are struggling – an abiding interest of mine, not surprisingly given my experiences at ASDA and the Royal Mail. Certainly, I'll never forget what Archie Norman and I faced when we joined ASDA. It was some mountain to climb, but I knew that there were certain things you have to do: you have to go back to basics; you have to understand the product that you're taking to market; and you have to know that market inside out. That means getting out there at the sharp end as soon as possible and as often as possible. I think Adam Crozier, when he joined me at the Royal Mail from running the Football Association, was a bit surprised to find himself at a sorting office at 4.30 am on his first morning preparing to make a delivery with an equally surprised postman, but it's actions like that that get you close to both product and customer.

And this inevitably leads me on to talk about people. It may sound trite, but it's absolutely the case that businesses are above all things a collection of people, so my conversations with other business leaders dwelt on this topic at considerable length. I would wholeheartedly agree with Sir Terry Leahy, the CEO of Tesco, when he talks of 'hiring the best and making them champions', and with Fred Smith, the founder of FedEx, who uses a sporting analogy to make the same point: 'If you want to win football games, you can't hire eighty-pound skinny lads to play.' In regard to people, my watchword would be teamwork and how you create it and nurture it. For the business leaders I've spoken to, it's an overwhelming priority.

As, of course, is communicating your message – to your customers, your investors, your team. It probably accounts for around 25 per cent of time spent in the job nowadays. When I started out it was probably just 5 per cent. Plus, in this information age the business leader has to be adept and prepared to operate in the full glare of the 24-hour media spotlight – a trial for everyone. One of a company's most important assets is its reputation. Having a good reputation is like a line of credit at the bank that a company can draw upon if it has a problem. The way a corporation is portrayed in the media has an impact on recruitment, on its ability to attract new customers and maintain the loyalty of existing staff and customers, and, of course, on the share price.

No business gets anywhere without the moneymen. They control its lifeblood, and they can help it to the next level or pull the plug at a moment's notice. But there's more to it than that. With the best financial advisers you get an invaluable and objective healthcheck. These are people who can take an outsider's impartial view and help you isolate what you could do better and, very often, what you shouldn't be doing at all. Take David Mayhew, for example. He is the chairman at JP Morgan Cazenove, and I've drawn on his advice for years. I've also drawn on his wisdom, as well as that of other financial figures I respect, in the course of this book.

And then there's the government. Now, not every leader has to deal directly with government, but everyone is affected in some way by our rulers' activities, even if it's just the regulations that they put out and under which everyone has to operate. The government has a huge part to play in so many areas of corporate life. For most business leaders the government's worst offences are not deep matters of principle. Most shameful in corporate eyes is an elected official's need to court short-term political popularity with little regard to or appreciation of the long-term consequences for business or the economy. In democratic government it's the same the world over. None of the normal business rules apply.

Businesses have to deliver on a quarterly basis forever, whereas politics has to deliver over an election timescale. Company leaders are increasingly alarmed that successive political initiatives, ostensibly, for example, to prevent boardroom abuses, show an obsession with form over substance. The truth is that the interests of politicians and business leaders are not aligned. Politicians are interested in reporting and observing due process, not with taking controlled risks, opening markets or running business intelligently for profit. The argument that business has in its favour is that ultimately the competitiveness of a country and its ability to earn a living on the world stage are in its hands.

It's business that creates economic stability, not the government. It's business that generates the wealth and the value that enable the government to invest in other areas. It seems totally appropriate in a book such as this that due attention should be given to the complex relationship between business and politics. Apart from anything else, it serves to show that business does not operate in a vacuum, that companies are involved in a wider world that may well have a different set of priorities and issues but that has to be listened to.

From all I've just said, you might think that leadership is a very worthy and serious undertaking, but I do want to stress that leadership is, above all, great fun, and leaders need themselves to have a great sense of humour and the ability to laugh at themselves and not take themselves too seriously. The tasks they face are challenging. Anybody who doesn't believe that running a business is a 24-hour, seven-day-a-week task from when they join until the day they leave is not going to do very well. There isn't a day, not even Christmas Day or family holidays, when anyone in this group of top businessmen is not thinking about their organisation, worrying about it, and thinking about how they can make it better.

So fun is fundamental. If it weren't fun there would be no point in pushing yourself to the limits. Fun enables you to get things done that you otherwise couldn't do. It takes a lot of the stress away too.

'Fun is a factor in performance'

The need for an injection of fun was another of my first and most memorable lessons. When I became a Mars area manager at the relatively young age of twenty-two, I mistakenly adopted a rather serious demeanour that I believed more fitting to my elevated management role. I was put in charge of a large group of sales associates in the North East. They had been around a long time and they were both tough and good. And, there was I, the serious-faced rookie trying to show them what to do. It was obvious that the sales figures were a disaster, so, after three months of successive drops in performance, I gathered them together at a local hotel to give them a 'rollicking'. I can still remember the fifteen very unimpressed faces sitting around the table staring into their steaming mugs of tea, waiting for the inevitable from the lad at the head of the table.

Undeterred, I drew heavily on my previous training to launch into my set-piece speech. It went something like: 'I have been here for three months and for three months we have missed our targets. It is a disgrace and unacceptable and everyone should be really thinking about why it has happened. Each one of you should be ashamed because you are experienced guys. If you people cannot get it right we are going to have a big problem.'

Then, just as I had learned on my management training course, I paused for effect. Triumphant about my excellent use of the pause, I picked up my tea, missed my mouth and poured the whole mug of warm liquid down my shirt and tie and into my lap. Everyone burst out laughing as I sat there covered in tea, trying to muster as much dignity as I could in the circumstances. But, in an instant, the whole atmosphere changed. The whole relationship changed and our way of working changed. What's more, so did the sales figures. We went on to beat our targets consistently.

Maybe my favourite piece of wisdom on leadership is from the book *The Wit and Wisdom of Forrest Gump*:

If you go to the zoo, always take something to feed the animals, even if the signs say 'Do not feed the animals'. It wasn't the animals that put them signs up.

It's true. Every day we metaphorically decide what the 'animals' want. We don't talk to the animals enough, we don't ask the animals enough questions and we don't listen to the animals enough. We just think we know what to feed them. The companies who don't do that, but who ask the 'animals' what they want, are the ones that work and succeed. I have spent my life going around companies fixing them when they've gone wrong. When I review why they went wrong in the first place it always brings me back to this: the zookeepers didn't ask the animals what they wanted; they just stuck up a sign. Every time I think about leadership I think about *Forrest Gump*.

Chapter 1

Getting Started

The entrepreneurial touch

In the early 1970s I left the job I'd done for five years after school and decided to buy and sell on my own. I had a £20,000 bank loan to get started. One day, I was offered something I wanted to buy for £100,000. I called my mum and told her I had this great opportunity. She suggested I see the guy at the bank in Southampton Row we'd always used. When I told him about the deal and how much I wanted he flatly refused. He even said, 'Do I look that stupid?'

I called my mum and told her that I needed this money for just four weeks. She called the bank up, gave them some security and they drew up a banker's draft to lend me the money. On my way home I just thought that this is not how it should be. So I went to see someone I knew who had a big old warehouse in Edmonton. I explained the situation. He took me into his office and gave me £100,000 in cash in a cardboard box. I drove straight back to Southampton Row and asked to see the manager, but was told he was busy. I simply knocked on his door and walked in, got his wastepaper basket from under his desk and put £100,000 cash in it. I said, 'That's you repaid and I won't be banking here any more.' My family had been with them for thirty or forty years.

A few years ago that same manager phoned me up, would you believe, asking for a job. 'Can I be of any use?' he asked. I admit to enjoying telling him that he was probably of no more use now than he was twenty-five years ago.

The speaker is Sir Philip Green, and he's describing his early days as an entrepreneur. It's a typically forthright story, and it shows some of the qualities that have made him so phenomenally successful. In just one anecdote he displays his total self-belief, his single-mindedness and his refusal to take no for an answer.

Had he been born a hundred years ago, an entrepreneurial leader like Sir Philip would have been fêted as a famous innovator. Nowadays he and his ilk have to settle for more transitory recognition, such as creating one of the hottest stock market debuts ever or securing an entry in the *Guinness Book of Records* for the highest sales per square foot of retail space or raising millions for charity. They may even get fêted for changing a nation's highly

LEADERSHIP LESSONS
› Absolute focus.
› Learn from people.
› Don't complicate things.
› Have the respect and trust of staff.
› Be reliable.

Sir Philip Green, Arcadia and Bhs

entrenched attitude to what's on its dinner plate. In fact, four of the entrepreneurs I spoke to while writing this book have won just such accolades and more besides.

In my view, modern entrepreneurs are no less significant than their counterparts in the Industrial Revolution. Like their predecessors, they've all started with a great product, a few pounds in their pocket and sufficient self-belief to enable them to knock on people's doors, often hundreds of people's doors. There are plenty of failures along the way, but those who have made it after years of dogged hard work have transformed whole markets and changed forever the way things are done. Entrepreneurs have a determination and drive to succeed like no other people I've met. They identify closely with their business and feel compelled to drive it relentlessly and get things done. Because they started from scratch and had to do everything for themselves, from VAT returns to emptying the bins, they can identify closely with every area of the business. Indeed, many have to force themselves to let go of the minutiae of running the company to concentrate on what they're good at – vision and strategy – the reason they began the business in the first place. They never feel as though they've achieved their vision or at least once they've achieved one target they set out on another. Sir Philip believes that being first generation in a business you set your own goals and your own targets. 'When you make a £1 million you think that's great since you never thought you'd get to £1 million. Then you get to £10 million.' Some people think that they might as well call it a day at that point, but I, along with Sir Philip and other leaders, tend to think it's the time to really get going because there are other things you want to do. You drive yourself to do better. Contrary to what many people think, the money isn't really the driver. You just wonder if it can be done, and the money follows as a result.

'I am lucky because I have a memory like an elephant. It drives people around me mad. I can go back to a meeting three months later and I will remember that there was a pink dress I didn't like hanging three dresses from the end of a row. I can remember exactly how many we sold of any item in which week'

Sir Philip Green, Arcadia and Bhs

Entrepreneurs may seem special cases. After all, they've 'invented' something, and not many of us can claim to have done that. But actually, anyone can learn from them, because they demonstrate, often in a particularly highly developed form, most of the qualities that all leaders need, whatever the nature of their business or their position in the company.

Never say never

It almost goes without saying that entrepreneurs and other leaders love a challenge. They are driven by a manic need to succeed. They measure success in many ways, such as money, recognition, fame or power. But more than that, if you tell them it can't be done because no one has ever done it before they light up. They *need* to make it happen. They exude a sense of confidence and determination, and if all the odds are stacked against them, then it's even better.

'No dreams, no future'

Allan Leighton

Surinder Arora offers the perfect example of this. Despite his success at building up the largest independent hotel chain in the UK in just seven years, he has never once considered sitting back to enjoy his success. Years before planning permission was granted to build the new Terminal 5 complex at Heathrow, Surinder decided that he would be the one to build and operate a five-star hotel there. He knew that this would mean being pitched against the might of established and far more financially secure brands, but he didn't let that put him off. His persistence means that Arora has the only hotel at the new Terminal 5, in a 600-bedroom joint venture with Accor's Sofitel brand. As he told me:

> It's a £4.5 billion project, the largest construction project in Europe, so when BAA started looking for a company to manage their hotel, it felt obvious that they needed to go with a major brand; but I had started dreaming about this hotel at least two years before BAA even began asking for people to bid for the concession.
>
> I knew that Arora was more than capable of building and running the hotel, but we didn't have the worldwide presence of an established brand. I went to some of the major international companies and asked if they would give us a franchise on their top brand. They all said no, they would never franchise their top brand. They reasoned that if they gave a franchise to someone and they made a hash of it, this would affect the brand worldwide.
>
> I didn't give up. I identified two companies with no presence

at Heathrow, one was Hyatt and the other was Sofitel. I rang Hyatt in Chicago and was told to talk to their director in Europe. I begged this director to listen to my proposal, offering to meet him anywhere in Europe. But he was not interested. This was completely contrary to my philosophy: I believe that when any opportunity arises, one should always at least have a look at it.

And quite right, too: there are legions of stories about managers missing opportunities to sign the Beatles and so on. Perhaps the best one is the apocryphal story of the salesperson selling the first machine gun to a general fighting a battle with bows and arrows. 'Go away,' said the general. 'Can't you see I'm busy fighting a war?' If someone goes to the trouble of working an idea into a suggestion, in my experience it's always worth looking into it.

When Surinder spoke to Accor Sofitel their reaction was much more positive. They said that they would love the opportunity to work with him, but they added that they wanted to manage the hotel themselves, because they'd never franchised the brand before. Surinder just wouldn't accept that: *he* wanted to run it. When I asked him why he didn't just give up at this point, his reply was that it simply never occurred to him. He invited Accor Sofitel's senior directors to come and see his operation. They looked round the hotel and then, for the next couple of months, without Surinder's knowledge, they paid a number of mystery guest visits. About three months later they came back and said that, although they had never franchised their brand in Europe before, they had faith in Arora and wanted to work with them. The Arora bid was that Arora would own, build and manage the hotel, under the Sofitel name.

Starting from a shortlist of twelve companies BAA got the bidders down to just Marriott and Arora. Everyone in the industry

> If you want your team to respect you, respect them first.
> If you work hard you can achieve anything.
> Constantly seek out challenges.

Surinder Arora, Arora International

thought Arora would struggle to complete a hotel in time, that involving a comparatively small player in a £4.5 billion terminal was too risky and that Marriott would win the contract by virtue of their sheer size. But Surinder reckoned he had one or two things in his favour, in particular long-lasting and very strong relationships with his bank, accountants and lawyers:

> The only thing I could offer them was to introduce them to my bankers. The senior directors and advisers at BAA met them and asked if we had enough money to build the Terminal 5 hotel. The banks said we had. They asked what would happen if we overran by £10 or £20 million. The banks said, 'No problem.' BAA then asked for a performance guarantee, so, if Arora folded, the banks would come in and finish the project. The banks said they normally wouldn't do that, but were so confident in this case that they would give that guarantee. That was crucial to the deal. BAA and its advisers were looking at the strength of financial guarantees and through our long relationship with our banks ours even outgraded Marriott's.
>
> A few weeks later I was in Scotland. I had had a pleasant and absorbing lunch at Loch Lomond with friends. So absorbing that it wasn't until we were driving back to our hotel at 5 o'clock that I

realised that I had had no signal on my mobile phone all day. When I checked my voice mail it was full of messages. Everyone had been trying to contact me to tell me the news. One of the messages was from BAA's advisers saying they had some news I might just want to hear. I felt like stopping in the middle of the road to cry. It was brilliant. It's something that will live with me forever.

The sheer enthusiasm of an entrepreneur such as Surinder is infectious and hugely motivating. In fact, I reckon that the main difference between one entrepreneur who goes on to run a multi-million pound conglomerate and one who is still in their garage tinkering with their would-be world-beating concept is precisely this determination and persistence. The successful one is prepared to get up again and again when they are knocked down. If they are prepared to get their hands dirty and have the utmost faith in their business and huge reserves of self-confidence, the odds are in their favour. They don't waste their time daydreaming about success. They get an idea and act swiftly.

This persistence has to go hand in hand with a strong sense of self-belief. Entrepreneurship is not for the faint-hearted. If you don't have an unwavering, total belief in yourself and a determination not to let anyone, or anything, dispel it, you simply won't make it. You have to pursue your own principles, follow your intuition and do what you think is right. Good entrepreneurs see an opportunity but, more importantly, they actually take it. There are loads of opportunities arising all the time, but only some people have the courage to have a go at them. You do have to push yourself to do things that you haven't done before. If an entrepreneur doesn't have the courage to take a leap into the unknown, you'll never hear of their business. In fact, most entrepreneurs have been moulded by at least one failure.

Failure is born out of risk and being prepared to break the rules.

All the entrepreneurs I can think of show these qualities in spades – none more so than Jacqueline Gold, who joined Ann Summers as an office junior midway through her A-level year and subsequently transformed the business into a multi-million pound concern. When she started, the chain, which was owned by her father, boasted just two stores 'filled with the dirty mac brigade'. Jacqueline hit upon the idea of selling sexy lingerie and sex toys at private parties, because many women just didn't want to be seen in the shops. But she was told dismissively by one member of the board that it wouldn't work because 'women aren't interested in sex'. Such a response could easily have put her off. After all, it's easy enough to be bullied when you are starting out in business; even more so when it's a controversial business such as Jacqueline's. But she relentlessly pursued her idea, eventually building a sales force of 7,500 women as party organisers. Her tenacity has seen her named as Britain's most powerful woman by countless women's magazines and even lauded in *OK!* magazine as 'the woman responsible for bringing sex to the high street and liberating thousands of women between the sheets'.

LEADERSHIP LESSONS
› Unique selling point (USP) is incredibly important. Keep going back to what it is that sets a business apart from the competition.
› Recruit dynamic and entrepreneurial people. Don't go for the safe option.
› Initiate change on a regular basis and be totally in tune with the trends.

Jacqueline Gold, Ann Summers

The way she sees it, much of Jacqueline's success has arisen from the fact that, throughout her career, she has repeatedly pushed herself out of her 'comfort zone' in order to take on new challenges and deal with new situations:

> There's a saying that there's nothing more to fear than fear itself and that always did well for me. An entrepreneur is a free spirit. They base their decisions on gut feeling and intuition. That can require a lot of confidence. Personally, I'm not how anyone expects a businessperson to be because I'm quietly spoken and not at all in your face. But I've always, always pushed myself outside my comfort zone at every opportunity, right from the start. I still vividly remember when I first advertised for party organisers and stood in front of an audience of bemused strangers at the Strand Palace Hotel in London to talk about my concept.
>
> People often believe that the main quality of an entrepreneur is being prepared to take risks; but I prefer to call it courage. When I look back over my career, the decisions I've made have all been born out of courage and self-belief. That was particularly important in my business, which was obviously very controversial when I began, certainly much more so than it is now. Many people may have seen the potential of where I was going but wouldn't have pursued it for fear of negative opinion and adverse media reaction.

This self-belief is particularly important because most entrepreneurs meet with initial scepticism. There are, after all, a thousand reasons why something might not work, and probably only one or two why it might. Moreover, for many people it's almost a gut reaction to be suspicious when presented with something new. Inventor and entrepreneur James Dyson speaks from deep personal experience when he says:

One of the things I have noticed is, when someone has an interesting idea that breaks the mould, it upsets people. In many companies the person with ideas is even seen as a crank. Since they encounter a lot of cynicism from everyone telling them it'll never work the people with the ideas tend to get snuffed out.

His constant mantra is that Dyson is about breaking rules, not inventing them. He argues that his company has a unique spirit that drives it to make things happen against all the odds. It's this philosophy that has shaped his style of leadership and fosters the inventive talents of his staff. 'Getting rid of that cynicism about new ideas,' he says, 'is terribly important if a company is to succeed. When someone has a good idea I say, "that's great". I don't reject it; I look at it. It is about praising people who have good ideas and protecting them because ideas are fragile things.'

He illustrates this belief in encouraging ideas and not accepting the status quo with an account of one particular

---

LEADERSHIP LESSONS
› Never, ever give up.
› Make it very clear what you are doing and
   why you are doing it, publicly and internally.
› Sometimes you cannot make a big leap but
   only lots of little improvements. In the end
   it adds up to a big improvement.

James Dyson, Dyson International

innovation that was made at Dyson a while back. In itself, the innovation wasn't an earth-shattering one. It was simply a decision to start putting Dyson's helpline number at the top of all their machines. But it symbolises a very different mindset from that which you find in most companies.

This was an idea from someone in the call centre who asked, 'How do people know how to get in touch with us?' The stock reply was that the customer should look in the instruction manual for our phone number. 'But,' said the persistent worker, 'they'll probably have thrown that away, so why not print the number on the top of the machine?' The obvious answer was that customers might think that the number was prominent because the machine was likely to break down. We decided to ignore that for the moment, put the number on the top and got it out to the shops. Our competitors sniggered at us but, a year later, were all copying us. There were ten very good reasons why we shouldn't have done it and just one why we should.

James's story leads me to another point about successful entrepreneurs, and one that may seem initially surprising: they care about teamwork. This may appear odd if you have too strong a picture in your mind of the lonely genius working away in the hut at the end of the garden. But the fact is that, the moment things get going, a team is essential. For some this can prove an insuperable challenge, and the result is that they remain forever more in their garden shed. But others recognise that they can't do it all on their own, even if they do have a winning idea or a fantastic product. In fact, they often prove particularly good at working with others because they care so much about what they're doing that they want to create an environment in which everyone buys into their vision.

For Perween Warsi, dubbed 'Britain's curry queen' after she turned a small business making finger foods from her Derby home into a major UK food business, the analogy is family. 'People are a main pillar of my palace,' she told me when I interviewed her. 'I have always had to make sure that they were right. From the very beginning, when I had six ladies working at home, we were like family and we're still like family. Some of them have retired, but quite a few of them are still with me.' For Perween, 'The challenge is to maintain that culture as you grow.'

It does get difficult, but you depend on your senior team and your management to keep that culture in the business. When you bring in new people as the business grows, they must be people who buy into your vision and values, because that's where misunderstanding or misalignment can creep in. I am constantly thinking about how we can keep the team engaged and really understanding the direction of the company. If you don't constantly think about that, then it won't happen.

As far as she is concerned, a team can make or break a fledgling business.

Brent Hoberman, co-founder of lastminute.com, takes a similar view. He argues that an entrepreneurial start-up is a collective thing, where everyone must feel that they're all in it together, and where the company head must have an overarching ambition to succeed if the team is to buy in to what the company is about. He believes that passion shines through in terms of motivating staff. If you are passionate and excited about the business and are prepared to do everything yourself, you'll be fun to work

LEADERSHIP LESSONS

The company's competitive position rests on
    three things:
› Its customer base – which you need to get the
    best products.
› Its technology – at lastminute.com £20 million
    a year was spent on it.
› Its brand name.
Anyone can do one – few can do all three.

Brent Hoberman, co-founder lastminute.com

with as you go through the scary first period of trading. As he
explains:

> **Anybody could tell that Martha [Lane Fox, lastminute.com's
> co-founder] and I were passionate about lastminute.com
> and were on the same wavelength. We also gave people a lot
> of responsibility; very important in motivating them. Letting
> them do a lot more than they would in other jobs and throw-
> ing them in at the deep end is very appealing to the right
> person.**

Naming names

So far I've talked about the personal qualities that entrepreneurial
leaders need to embody. But, of course, they are also faced with
some rather more practical concerns as well. Not least of these is
choosing a company name. If you think of many of the businesses

that have become familiar to us all – Carphone Warehouse, Easy Jet, holiday autos, lastminute.com, Richer Sounds – they all have compelling names. They tell you at a glance everything you need to know about the company. To misquote the well-known Ronseal advertising slogan, these are businesses that do exactly what they say on the tin.

lastminute.com, for example, is just what it says. Probably the best known of the 1990s e-commerce set-ups, it is more than just a source of late holiday bargains. It's the ultimate lifestyle resource for people who are cash rich and time poor. When founders Brent Hoberman and Martha Lane Fox launched it in 1998 it was a model unique in its marketplace, giving tour companies an opportunity to sell volume that they otherwise wouldn't have been able to offload. But what really got it off the ground was its name: simple, straightforward and implying to the customer pretty much everything it's taken me several dozen words to explain.

Brent Hoberman knew straightaway that lastminute.com was the right name for the company, and he was utterly unwilling to compromise on it:

> We were initially called lastminutenetwork.com and raised the first £600,000 of venture capital money on that name. But that wasn't the name we wanted. A brand is not built on compromise and lastminute.com was *the* name. Unfortunately, a German entrepreneur already had the lastminute.com domain. I called him five times and on the fifth time he said 'yes'. It was just a couple of months before the launch and we paid £16,000 in two instalments of £8,000. It was the most amazing deal and a big moment.

Just under a decade earlier, Charles Dunstone was in the same position as Brent and Martha: he had a great idea for a company, and he needed a name to go with it. His idea was to bring mobile phones to builders and plumbers, and he wanted a name that would not only convey that, but also reflect his policy of choice and low prices. He came up with Carphone Warehouse, even though there wasn't a warehouse in sight. It was a huge success, and Charles reaped the rewards. Much later, he agonised over whether he should change the name to reflect the company's increasingly wider audience and product range. Eventually he decided – rightly in my view – that the name had become just too powerful and well known to be tinkered with.

So often people setting out in business think it's very creative and clever to come up with a name like 'Monster Dragon', but it just confuses their potential customers. The successful entrepreneur, by contrast, knows how important it is to create an immediate sense of brand and brand values through their company name. It's something that other business leaders can forget too easily, especially when they are managing a long-established business. The fact that people seriously thought at one stage that it was a good idea to change the Royal Mail's name to Consignia shows just how wrong

LEADERSHIP LESSONS
› Create a team that gels and a vision that everyone can believe in.
› Ensure a common sense of purpose throughout the organisation.

Charles Dunstone, Carphone Warehouse

things can go when focus is lost and the essential attributes of a company are forgotten. After all, the Royal Mail had spent over 200 years developing a brand franchise based on its powerful name. Yet at the stroke of a pen they called it something else that didn't mean anything to anybody. Why the hell would anybody want to do that? If, on top of that, the company is unsuccessful, as the Royal Mail was when it was renamed Consignia, then you have got an even bigger problem. The name becomes the focus while everyone ignores the inherent problems of the business.

Company names and brand names are an essential part of what makes any business tick. New businesses, as I've said, have to start off on the right foot; established businesses with strong brand names have to protect them at all costs. It is, quite rightly, a preoccupation for big companies such as Marks & Spencer, Tesco and Virgin, and should be for a company of any size. In fact, in my world, the chief executive or president of a company is actually the chief marketing officer who is responsible for protecting and developing the brand.

The number one rule when seeking to protect the integrity of a brand is not to put anything under that brand name that does not add value. One of the big issues when people think they have a winning brand is they often spread it too thin, diluting the equity of the core brand in the process. As soon as you try to put nuts in a Mars Bar, it is not a Mars Bar any more. By contrast, the great thing about a Mars ice-cream is that it looks like a Mars Bar, it tastes like a Mars Bar, and it adds something to the brand.

Rule number two is to protect the brand legally. Anything elsewhere that smacks of copying the brand and its essence must be stamped on immediately.

Fiddling around with silly new names for good brands is a daft thing to do. It's not a mistake any good entrepreneur would make.

Show me the money

Simultaneously with having to find a suitable company name, entrepreneurs, of course, have to raise money. It's not easy, but in recent years there has been good news on this front. Despite the silly season of the dotcom boom era when everybody thought the internet was the billion dollar answer to everything, there is, if anything, more money available for investment today. When the heady euphoria of the online era was at its height, I predicted that 80 per cent of the companies involved would go pop, but that it would be a great thing for the Great Britain Plc talent bank. And it was. A lot of people had to learn very quickly about business in a way that had never happened before. There were many broken dreams and failed business models, but the episode was a positive one for the country, which has benefited from the new breed of young entrepreneurs with big ideas coming through into the business community. Although a lot of money was lost in the 1990s, a lot of good companies were spawned, including Amazon, eBay, Google, lastminute.com and Yahoo. These businesses have become household names, and some have claimed their spot in the league tables of the largest companies in the world, ahead of numerous corporations established decades earlier. Thanks to these monumental success stories there's still a great deal of cash available for good ideas.

It's bizarre to think that it's probably currently easier to borrow

£100 million than it is to borrow £100,000. Would-be backers like to think the idea is so big it just has to be worth a huge punt; if they don't they walk away. Private equity groups can prove an invaluable source of investment for those who can demonstrate a good idea. They're probably not going to give all the funding required, but they may well supply some. And then the true entrepreneur will beg or borrow money from anywhere – their mates, their families. They even sell their prized cars and reduce their personal expenditure to the lowest it can possibly be. Making personal sacrifices to succeed is no problem to the committed entrepreneur and is, I think, a good indication of their commitment to their idea. I've always had a feeling that there should be some sort of government fund to encourage start-ups; but, on the other hand, if they did put one together it wouldn't work because it would take six months to fill out the forms.

Many entrepreneurs, such as Clive Jacobs at holiday autos, start their businesses with virtually nothing – just a desk and a phone. They build it up from a standing start through sheer hard work, long hours and determination. In Clive's case he built the business from zero to a £200 million turnover in seven years in this way. Conversely, Martha Lane Fox and Brent Hoberman, who needed a significant investment from the start to invest in technology, took their ideas and enthusiasm to the money markets and raised £600,000 within weeks of producing their business plan. OK, it sounds easy, but, as I said, at that time investors were throwing money at high-tech start-ups and the pair looked a good bet. It is just as important that the entrepreneur is in tune with the mood of the time in order to raise funds.

Ironically, Martha had initially scoffed at Brent Hoberman's vision to set up lastminute.com. She hadn't believed she could be passionate about technology. But starting out in a 'broom cupboard', her skills at cold-calling airlines, persuading investors and attracting publicity soon made lastminute.com one of the net's best-known dotcom businesses. The result was that they raised an amazing amount of cash and were able to put their business on a completely sure footing. However, one of the things that entrepreneurs sometimes discover when they raise a large sum of money is that their company culture changes as a result, and this can be problematic. While it seems fair enough that in return for the investment a company has to do some proper accounting and tell the City what they are up to, it does change the dynamic of a start-up. Very early on Martha Lane Fox discovered that being a publicly-owned company can interfere with two key issues in the business – teamwork and communication.

> What I found hard was the way I had to change how I dealt with the team. Great leadership and entrepreneurship is a lot to do with performing. I always believed you should get as many people together, as often as possible and tell them as much as possible. Before we changed from a private company to a public company, I used to stand on a desk every Friday to speak to the team. We'd have some cakes and I'd say what had happened during the week. It sent the key messages through the organisation and made people feel very positive. Suddenly I couldn't do things that way in case something got out about a deal.

Since teamwork and communication are so essential to the success of a business, as I discuss later on, this sort of problem can be a very significant one and, badly managed, can damage a company. Its significance can be seen in the fact that several entrepreneurs for whom a more open culture is absolutely essential have eventually opted to buy their businesses back from the City and go private. Richard Branson is one name that immediately comes to mind. In 1986 Virgin was one of Britain's largest private companies, with 4,000 staff. Advised to go public by bankers he took the plunge, despite being told by those close to him that he'd hate losing control. They were right. He ended up feeling stifled by the experience and loathing the fact that his hands were now tied by people who knew very little about his business. And he wasn't helped by the the stock market crash of the late 1980s, which saw his shares halve in value. Two years after the company went to the market he personally raised £182 million to buy all the shares back to keep 'my good name and my freedom', as he put it in his book *Screw It, Let's Do It*.

Imitators beware

I think it's essential in business to be receptive to other people's good ideas, and I'm not ashamed to admit that I've borrowed and copied freely in the course of my career, as I discuss later. The entrepreneur, however, sees the flip side of this. They've spent time developing and understanding their product, and putting systems into place to make sure that everyone else does too; they've set their mission, purpose and values, and promulgated them widely, and they've made sure that everyone in the company knows that continuous change and improvement are the only ways that they'll stay ahead. And then they discover that people are trying to steal their success.

So what do they do? As I've said, imitation in business can be good – indeed essential. But this can be the case only when the ideas in question have been fully formed and shown to work. Entrepreneurial ideas, by contrast, have been formed but not necessarily shown to work, so the entrepreneur has to protect their idea zealously until it has had a chance to grow. An established company has the luxury of being able to keep ahead of imitators by continuously reinventing the model. But entrepreneurs are in a completely different situation, possibly trying to get one single product or idea off the ground. They have to be prepared to use the legal system, daunting and expensive though it is. You can't have people nicking your ideas because they are big ideas. lastminute.com, for example, created something that sold for £577 million. They would never have achieved that value if, in the early days, they hadn't vigorously fought people who tried to copy their ideas and imitate the domain name. James Dyson similarly spent hundreds of thousands of pounds in litigation to protect the Dual Cyclone technology. As he puts it, 'People who invent something, or start new businesses which attack the natural order, will end up upsetting people. It isn't nice fighting things in court, but we won't be pushed over. We'll defend ourselves if we have something to protect. It is not being overly litigious if you sue someone over your patent.'

Entrepreneurs on entrepreneurs

It seems appropriate to end this brief survey of the entrepreneurial spirit by looking at a poacher turned gamekeeper, or rather an entrepreneur turned entrepreneurial investor.

Sir Tom Hunter is a legendary figure in his field. Like many other aspiring entrepreneurs he began with virtually nothing, borrowing £5,000 from his father and £5,000 from the Royal Bank of Scotland. He bought a job lot of shoes and a van and wrote to every retailer in the UK asking for space to sell the footwear. One store said yes almost immediately, and before long he was regularly driving up and down the country to fulfil orders.

LEADERSHIP LESSONS
› Entrepreneurs who want to build businesses of substance and size need to understand what they are good at. Then they can recruit to their weaknesses and build a balanced team.
› With a bit of nurture, education and coaching we can all be a bit better.
› Making mistakes is part of the framework. If people are too scared to make mistakes, there will be no successes.

Sir Tom Hunter, West Coast Capital

His concessions mushroomed, Sports Division was born and within ten years it was turning over £260 million and making a profit of £34 million. He was then introduced to Sir Philip Green, who helped him expand Sports Division considerably with the acquisition of the much larger Olympus sports shop chain from Sears. It was at that point that Tom began his new career as an investor. First of all he spent some of the fortune he had made from Sports Division in Philip's spectacular raid on the Sears empire in 1999. The £550 million deal netted the consortium behind it a £250 million profit within a year by breaking up the business. Today Tom invests in a myriad of different businesses.

The 'Tom Test' is, What's the story? Does it stack up and are you passionate about it? When he sees an entrepreneur with a great idea and he thinks there is a chance it might work, he'll invest some money to get things going. Tom genuinely believes the new entrepreneur should share some of his good luck, remembering how difficult it was for him to get funding. Spotting good businesses is down to the same old stuff – research. What Tom has found though is that, apart from the standard financial research and due diligence, the most important thing is the *people*. There's no substitute for spending time with the people in the business to find out whether they're right or wrong. It's time consuming, but it's vital.

As he puts it:

Since I've become a boring old moneyman, I've had to change from being the entrepreneurial person who said, 'Let's do this or that', to being the person who says, 'Let's find someone else to do it'. Our skill is to look at that someone else, size them up

and give them the framework in which they can excel. When you are taking a portfolio approach, not all your decisions will be good. In fact, failure at some point is inevitable: we make mistakes and will continue to make them. I don't want my people too scared to make mistakes, otherwise they can't make successes.

He's blunt in his dismissal of people who look for excuses or special treatment:

If I find business people blaming lack of opportunity or the government for too much red tape, I have no truck with it. There is somebody out in the Far East with no help, no red tape, who is getting on with it and who will take the meal from your plate, sunshine. A true leader or entrepreneur doesn't keep blaming someone else; they work with what they're given. He or she will say, 'Here is a framework and I will work my way around it.'

I think this perfectly encapsulates the determined quality that, as I've already described, drives the entrepreneurial leader. For the successful entrepreneur it's not about money. Becoming successful requires a lot of sacrifice and commitment, but the true entrepreneur doesn't start a business to make their fortune. If that were their primary motivation, there would be much

'Remarkably, the harder I work, the luckier I become'

Sir Philip Green, Arcadia and Bhs

> '**Most entrepreneurs will say that they have been lucky. But you also have to create opportunities to be lucky**'
>
> Brent Hoberman, co-founder lastminute.com

easier routes to riches for such talented and focused people. Instead, they utterly believe in their business and the entrepreneurial mind is always sizzling with ideas. In fact, ironically, it's often just at the moment when their idea has finally taken off and the business is becoming firmly established, that they decide to move on to something else. If they were ever to retire to a well-deserved mansion in the country, they would instantly set about inventing a different way to rebuild the house. It's in their DNA. It's what they do: once an inventor, always an inventor.

Chapter 2
Keeping Going
The challenges of the day to day

Most of us aren't entrepreneurs. We come into businesses that are well established, and the challenge we face is to keep things going – or, as often as not, to put things right. So, once you've found your desk and the coffee machine on Day 1, what's the next thing you should do? The answer, as is so often the case, is to take a leaf out of the entrepreneur's book.

I got to know James Dyson after reading his autobiography, *Against the Odds*. I was immensely taken with the fact that everybody who joins Dyson makes a vacuum cleaner on their first day and then takes it home so they own one. At a single stroke they know they're in the vacuum cleaner business and can feel inspired and motivated. Most importantly, according to James, it gives his team confidence in the product:

It's a very simple and direct way of getting across what we are. We're not a company. No one outside is interested in our company; people are interested in our product. The fact that

someone has built and assembled a Dyson vacuum cleaner gives them confidence in the machine, helps them understand it and be able to talk about it. I'm sure a lot of people working at some companies don't actually understand the products they sell. They don't know how to take it to bits; they don't know what's inside it. We emphasise to our people the importance of understanding the product, and knowing how it works.

I was working at ASDA at the time I read the book, and found my equivalent of James's technique in the store checkouts. So, from that day on, everybody who joined the supermarket had a day or two on the tills. No matter how fast or slow they were, they at least knew what business they were joining. I didn't stop there. When I took over at the Royal Mail in 2002, I ensured that everybody who joined the company delivered the mail on their first day.

When Adam Crozier joined Royal Mail as chief executive in February 2003 he readily admitted he knew nothing about running a vast organisation boasting 250,000 employees and the worst strike record in the UK, losing an average of 50,000 days every year to industrial action. But he's a great moderniser and marketer

LEADERSHIP LESSONS
› Keep things simple so people understand what the company is doing and why it is doing it.
› People will only change if they see where that change is taking them.

Adam Crozier, Royal Mail

and knew that he was at the beginning of what could be the last of the UK's really big corporate turnarounds.

The first thing Adam did was go back to the shop floor, or the streets to be exact, clocking on for a 4.30 am delivery round in southwest London. This was quite a surprise to a lot of football fans, who recognised their new postman from his television appearances as chief executive of the Football Association talking to luminaries such as the then England coach Sven Goran Eriksson. In Adam's view, it's vital to know what's going on on the frontline:

> I still try and spend at least a day a week with customers and at least another day every week either talking to, or meeting with, frontline people or frontline managers. If you know what is going on with customers and on the frontline, then you pretty much know what is going on in the business. That enables you to run the business better because you are in touch with the real facts rather than just management speak. It is vital to hear these people's personal experiences. That's how you really learn what is going on, not through a consultant's report.

In other words, before you do anything else you need to know in some detail what you sell or what service you supply and its impact on customers. This may sound blindingly obvious, but it's amazing how few leaders take the time to explore their business. Instead, they tend to rely on endless reports and the views of others. Adam, for one, thinks this is completely the wrong approach:

> Managers say, 'I've read the report and the facts are these . . .' I always say, 'No, those are the facts after they have gone through about eighteen filters with everyone's opinions on them.'

I always pop up rather than prearrange a visit, otherwise everything seems to smell of fresh paint and you get the impression they're all incredibly tidy. What you want is the reality. The great thing about our people is that if you do it in a very relaxed way it's very easy to have a conversation about what's happening and what's going wrong.

The fact is that people at the sharp end often know more about the impact of your products and services than anyone else. They can see the problems. In the case of the Royal Mail, for example, they could see that the mail was arriving late to their sorting offices and that the offices were shabby and falling apart. Only by talking to them could we start to get a handle on the size of the problem and the way to solve it. This approach also enabled us to start spreading the word about what it was that we wanted to do, as Adam briefed everyone he met on what he was planning.

Our people meet customers every single day, whether it is behind a counter at a post office or at a front door delivering post. Customers naturally ask questions about what's going on and it's fantastic if they're actually able to answer them there and then. That's a very powerful tool if you can manage it: making sure your people understand the reality rather than just the spin. People will only change if they see where that change is taking them.

So has it worked? Well, when we first started, the company had lost £1.7 billion over two years. It was losing £1 million a day, had negative cash flow and was about three months from not being a going concern. It hadn't hit a quality of service target for ten years, accounted for 60 per cent of all strikes in Great Britain and had the worst bullying and harassment record of any company in the country. Where are we today? Well, we are profitable, we've raised the quality of service and we're beating all the targets. There is still some way to go but we've really turned the whole thing around by keeping things simple so that everyone understands what the company is doing and why it's doing it – and we've achieved this by going back to first principles and making absolutely sure that we understood the nature of our business.

Obviously, not every strategy has been popular and we have upset some people along the way. Indeed, postmen still encounter some highly vocal criticism on the doorstep. But that makes it even more important to talk to them about the issues and constantly engage with them about proposed changes. To take just one example. We got a lot of flak for taking away the second daily delivery. Customers felt cheated. But the reality was that this second delivery accounted for just 5 per cent of the mail yet took up 20 per cent of the cost of the whole service. It may not have been a popular move, but it was a carefully discussed one, and I hope that over time it will be seen to have been the right one.

Of course, as I've already said, ideas such as asking your team to make one of their own products or getting out behind a counter in a store seem simple and obvious once you hear them. But they really do work. Josh Bekenstein of Bain Capital, one of the world's leading private investment firms, is one of a number of people

'Don't find fault with what you don't understand'

Allan Leighton

I've come across who strongly advocate this sort of approach. 'I know a terrific CEO of a company which makes fairly highly engineered consumer products,' he told me. 'He believes that if you are a senior executive and want to try to sell products to people then you have got to try and use your own products. He is an avid user and encourages the team to get involved in bi-monthly design meetings. He feels if he and the senior team stay close to the designers and engineers, it sends a message to the organisation that that is what matters and it matters a lot.'

After I'd read James Dyson's book I wrote to him and told him I thought that getting his staff to build their own vacuum cleaner was such a great idea that I'd copied it. He wrote back, invited me for lunch and eventually I joined the Dyson board as a non-executive. Appropriately enough, the first day I arrived at Dyson's Malmesbury headquarters as a director I built a vacuum cleaner.

Getting your story right

Spend just a few hours in a store or on the factory floor, and you quickly become aware that your team wants to know the answers to two simple but fundamental questions: What are we setting out to achieve? What's the context in which we're working?

To answer these questions, early on after I've joined a company and got to know the shop floor, I spend days working on a maxim that properly describes the mission, purpose and values of the organisation and then I make sure I repeat it at every opportunity. This maxim sets out the core ideologies of a company. It identifies a set of basic precepts that act like a stake in the ground to declare what the company is about.

I hasten to add that this is not the same as what management consultants airily call a mission statement. It is a guiding set of principles, fundamental to the company, that stand the test of time and ideally should never change. Management consultancy mission statements, by contrast, generally don't mean anything. I once took a hundred FTSE 500 mission statements and counted the same twenty-six words in 85 per cent of them. A mission should be all about what we want to do when we grow up – what a company is trying to achieve. The business may never get there, but it doesn't matter as long as you are always edging towards it. The most important thing is that the company should have a set of ideologies based on the following principles:

- The *mission* statement should be for the organisation, by the organisation and inculcated in the organisation. It is what we want to be when we grow up.
- *Purpose* is all about whom we satisfy. Most businesses are about satisfying somebody because if they don't have customers they don't have income.
- *Values* are all about what the business stands for. They are the context in which the organisation operates, the things we do and the things we don't do.

Here's a great expression of value from Sir Ken Morrison, the president of Bradford-based supermarket chain Wm Morrison. His core value is: Nowt in your pocket and proud of it.

Ken explained this to me once and it sounded so simple. He said, 'When I've got my shoppers coming out of my stores with nowt in their pockets and proud of it then I know that I've given them value.' If you go to the Harvard Business School there are fifty-seven pages of text on what value is, but there it is in just one sentence.

As I've said, when I joined ASDA in 1992 it was a basket case. There were a thousand problems to sort out, but one of the first things that Archie Norman and I actually did was to spend days agonising over the wording of ASDA's mission, purpose and values. Eventually we agreed upon the following: ASDA was to be *Britain's best value fresh foods and clothing superstore*.

- *Britain's* because we weren't going to be anywhere else.
- *Best value* because that was the whole history of ASDA – ASDA Price.
- *Fresh foods* because we were useless at this side of the enterprise and unless you are very good at fresh foods then you will not get anywhere in the grocery business.
- *Clothing* because we had the George fashion brand and that made us distinctive when viewed against the competition.

LEADERSHIP LESSONS
› Stick ruthlessly to the business model.
› Protect your company's heritage.

Sir Ken Morrison, chairman, Wm Morrison

- *Superstore* because we weren't going to have any stores less than 40,000 square feet in size.

This context permeated everything we did and played a vital role in creating the brand. In my eight years at ASDA, during which time we turned it around from that basket case into a successful business that we sold for £6.7 billion to Wal-Mart in 1999, we must have repeated this statement a thousand times. Every time I opened a sales conference or indeed any meeting I said it. It drove me nuts, but it had an effect. We drilled it into the organisation.

Mission, purpose, values. These underpin your activities when you start to build a company, and the biggest mistake a company can make is to change these core values. You've probably seen it happen as often as I have – new management sweeps in and says the values were good for then, but they're not good for now, so everyone must move on. The same thing happened at ASDA. People tried to change the terminology around the values, but I was adamant in saying, No, that's what they are and that's the way they're going to remain. Values are not something you write on a piece of paper and then forget about; they are something you live every day. Businesses that want to be great businesses have great values and everyone understands what they are.

'Mission is all about what you want to be when you grow up.'

Allan Leighton

You often find that values are a particular concern of long-standing and much-venerated institutions – and rightly so. Consequently, I wasn't surprised to find in the course of my conversation with the director general of the BBC, Mark Thompson, that this subject was uppermost in his mind. As he put it:

In my world, by far the most important leadership quality is bound up with personal convictions. If you try, even with the best of intentions, to put on an act, it doesn't work. Whether it's because we have so many journalists working for us and they're very cynical, or whether it's because there isn't a straightforward profit motive at the BBC, people really care about where you're coming from, what you believe and what your values are. The most important thing is to be clear about them and to live up to them. It's about faith and belief in what you're doing more than anything else.

In these established and respected institutions it is not hard to work out what the values are – you just need to ask the team,

LEADERSHIP LESSONS
› Constantly tell the story about the vision to anyone who will listen.
› Keep half a pace ahead of events rather than half a pace behind. Once you get behind, it is difficult to catch up.
› If you take a knock, pick yourself up quickly. It is not the hit, but your reaction and recovery time which make a difference.

Mark Thompson, BBC

as Sir Stuart Hampson, the former chairman of the John Lewis Partnership, found when he conducted this exercise in 2005:

> Culture is about understanding who we are. So many businesses do not understand who they are. They are so busy running their business they never stand back and ask what makes them different from anybody else.
>
> What makes our business special? We started by talking to the partners, asking them what they thought and what the partnership meant to them. There were lots of focus groups and interviews and these six very simple statements came out: Be honest, show respect, recognise others, work together, show enterprise and achieve more. They were not words that I had invented, they were how everyone felt.
>
> It is motherhood and apple pie – every one of us should operate those values at all levels, whether you are chairman or whether you are working in one of the shops, it doesn't matter. Those principles apply every day to everything you do. The motivating and unifying effect of having said those are the principles of the business and they characterise our behaviour every day has had a dramatic effect on the way we work together.
>
> Once you have done the exercise, it enables you to say that if anybody does not want to play by these rules then it is goodbye. No matter how good you are at your job, if you don't agree, then you have got to go. That is a very powerful statement and people have left because they don't fit.
>
> Creating a culture and distilling it into a form which everybody can understand, measure and talk about is a hugely unifying force.

Incidentally, John and Forrest Mars steadfastly ran their confectionery and pet food company on values that many would say came from an earlier era, and it certainly didn't do their business any harm. All employees were known as 'associates' and were handsomely rewarded for their dedication with salaries which were three or four times those offered by rival companies. But they were also expected to do their own photocopying, make their own telephone calls and travel economy class on aeroplanes. There were no perks, no executive bathrooms and no reserved parking spaces. Once again, the brothers led by example, always clocking in before dawn and rarely taking holidays. Everyone from the top of the company to the bottom received a 10 per cent bonus for arriving at work on time. I can vividly remember watching senior managers sprinting across the car park to punch their cards and clock in on time.

Imitation is the highest form of flattery

So far I've talked about the importance of looking inwards at your business. But it's equally important to look outside, too, and see what you can learn. The fact is that in the business world there are not many truly innovative ideas that haven't already been tried. Some just work better for one company than they do for others. My view has always been, why reinvent the wheel? Why not learn from your competitors? This, I hasten to add, isn't about slavish copying – the word 'copying' rightly has pejorative overtones, and, in any case, it's dangerous to copy every detail from a rival, because not everything they do will work for you. But learning from others has to be right. It helps you to develop the best skills, products and strategy for your company; I simply can't understand why people so often frown upon it. In my opinion, a good leader looks at what works elsewhere and then interprets what he sees for his own business model.

I will freely confess to copying good ideas shamelessly and I can't go past a rival's store without nipping in to see what they are up to now. When I started at ASDA I would regularly go to the United States and wander around Wal-Mart stores, noting all the chain's tried and tested techniques. On one trip I was stopped from taking pictures by a store manager. He phoned head office in Bentonville, Arkansas, and they invited me in. Once they established who I was and where I was from, it was fine. They let me copy all of their stuff. As soon as I got back to the UK their Roll Back discounting offer, which permanently reduces prices on core items, went straight into ASDA and eventually added £1.5 billion of value.

Allan Leighton

Now, if I am too busy, or in another country on business, I regularly send out my spies to take snaps of a new store or display concept. There is nothing wrong with it. In fact, it is good practice and it should be everyone's priority to know what the rest of the market is doing. It is far more dangerous to get to the stage where you think you've seen it all and no new concept would impress. But I never do. I get new ideas every day from looking at competitors.

Sainsbury's chief executive, Justin King, agrees with me on this. He reckons you can't possibly experience yourself everything you need to have done to be a chief executive at, say, forty. A lot of it has to be stuff that you have drawn from other people. His rule is to keep your eyes open, watch and observe constantly, trading ideas on occasion, taking the best of what you see and moving them on. As he told me:

> On a personal level, there is not a person I have worked with in my life from whom I haven't learned something. Sometimes it's by watching them do bad things and resolving never to do those things myself. Other times it has been by observing them do great things and replicating them when in a position to do so. You have to be a huge sponge and if you are going to progress quickly then it has to be learned. It isn't all going to be experiential. It can't be.

LEADERSHIP LESSONS

› Have absolute focus on the company.
Expensive artwork that once adorned
Sainsbury's office walls has been replaced
with adverts and photos of our colleagues
in store. Columns used to display sculptures
have been cleared to make room to display
awards.
› Encourage one-to-one communication. At
Sainsbury's internal emails are banned on
Wednesdays and all internal meetings axed
on Fridays.
› All staff, even the chief executive, should wear
a name badge. If you know what someone
is called there's a greater chance you might
talk to them.

Justin King, J Sainsbury

The source of inspiration does not just have to be a direct rival
in the market. Alannah Weston, the creative director at Selfridges,
thinks that good ideas come from the most unexpected quarters. She
constantly uses friends in the fashion and art worlds as an unoffi-
cial thinktank when trying to pin down new trends. She also trawls
stores of all sizes around the world for inspiration. She certainly goes
to see competitors, but she also likes to see shops that are not department stores, like the small concept stores in Paris and Milan, or those
in the East End of London. As she is keen to point out, small businesses are often the best places to find real innovation. And if you
don't constantly look at alternative ways of doing things, then the

> 'If the world zigs, we want to zag. We always set out to do things differently, be a bit cheeky, a bit shocking and challenge convention'
>
> Charles Dunstone, Carphone Warehouse

danger is that you will ultimately get stuck. She finds this constant attention to what others are doing refreshing; it cleanses her palate. And by not simply aping what her main rivals are doing, but instead looking further afield, she stays ahead of the game. As she says:

> If somebody is doing one thing, it's often good to do the opposite. There is a whole 'me too' culture in any business, the 'Oh, look at what they're doing, we had better do it too' syndrome. But when someone says to me, 'Have you seen Harrods' windows?' I will say, 'Yes, that's how Harrods do their windows, but not how we do ours.'

I think Alannah's attitude nicely sums up the need to balance confidence in what you're doing with preparedness to learn from elsewhere. It's an art form, and an essential one.

LEADERSHIP LESSONS
› Challenge but don't criticise.
› Know your role and defend your vision.
› The team should present solutions, not problems.

Alannah Weston, Selfridges

Chapter 3
Innovate or Die

Why standing still is never an option

In January 2003 Rebekah Wade became the first female editor of the *Sun*, taking what she said at the time was the 'best job in newspapers'. It is also, by common consent, one of the toughest, the *Sun* being Britain's biggest selling popular daily and famously laddish. Rebekah's mantra is to give the readers what they want. To do so, she has had to foster a hugely innovative culture at the newspaper, encouraging the whole team to come up with consistently witty, attention-grabbing and pioneering stories and headlines. And the way she goes about this is very revealing:

> One of the characteristics of journalists is to challenge people. When we have our conferences to decide what to splash on, I will say something. Then everyone will offer something else. Obviously you can't lead by committee: someone has to take the final decision. But, if you're in the business of hiring people who are extremely clever, who will challenge you and

in some areas will be better than you, two things happen: the business that you are running is successful and, second, you get better.

We meet every morning to discuss our 'personality'. Someone will say, 'Why don't we send a dwarf dressed as a chipolata to sit outside John Prescott's house for a week, just to really annoy him?' And we'll all say, 'Why did no one think of that before; it's clearly waiting to be done.' We dispatch someone to find a dwarf and a chipolata costume. Or, someone on features may talk about a book they've just read called *Future Jihad* by Walid Phares; 'It's fantastic, it's Armageddon. Yes, it is a bit academic, but if we put it in *Sun* words or get him to write a piece for *Sun* readers it would be a fantastic story.'

You can only create that atmosphere when people feel they can say anything and not be laughed at. When the Korea story broke [underground nuclear tests in October 2006] it was obviously a very serious story. Now, the *Sun*, unlike the *Star* or the *Mirror*, has to have credibility. If a big news story breaks, it has to go on page one. We can't really splash on Wayne Rooney having a bad toenail when Korea is doing nuclear tests. Even though we knew it would be a sales disaster zone, Korea had to be the splash. We were all discussing how we could make it appeal to our readers, when someone completely unconnected with the story just walked past and said, 'It's a real problem isn't it? How do you solve a problem like Korea?' Coming at the time of the high profile televised search for a Maria to star in a new production of *The Sound of Music*, it was just perfect. The back bench [the editor, deputy editor and night editor] literally threw their arms in the air and went, 'Thank you!'

› Hire people who challenge you and want your
   job.
› Treat others how you expect to be treated
   yourself.

Rebekah Wade, *Sun*

Rebekah had to create the kind of environment that encourages people to have a go. Had she not done so, the headline genius almost certainly wouldn't have had the confidence to make a suggestion and a great front page would never have appeared. As it was, the *Sun* not only sorted out that day's story but also discovered that they had someone they could tap into whenever they were faced with a difficult headline.

Rebekah's lively account of a morning in the life of the *Sun* suggests that creative meetings cannot afford to be too controlled. I think that's right, and it's something you find other leaders commenting on, too. Alannah Weston at Selfridges, for example, believes in a certain amount of creative chaos, and she reckons she can put a figure on it:

You need to keep 10 per cent chaos at all times. When I first started working at Burberry, I kept complaining because the whole thing was in chaos. Somebody told me then that I would be so sorry when I had fourteen assistants, all kinds of databases and three sample collections, because the magic would be gone. It is so true.

Certainly, this attitude played its part in shaping her time at Burberry, and saw the company through its revival. It's become part and parcel of her approach at Selfridges, too, and she's unapologetic about the consequences:

> When we did our punk event at Selfridges in 2005, everybody on the staff was complaining. They said, 'Alannah you're driving us nuts, it's Malcolm McLaren one minute, Agent Provocateur the next, and there's a drunk in the bar. We can't stand it.' I told them it's punk, it's supposed to be like that! If it were all organised the thing would be a disaster.

This approach to creativity and innovation is not something that you find only among editors of national newspapers and creative directors of retail outlets. It's an essential attribute of every successful company. The fact is that the pace of change today is quick; in fact it's constant and incessant. Customers are impatient and unforgiving, particularly in consumer-facing businesses like retailing or banking. A company doesn't stay the market leader by doggedly carrying on doing what it has always done. To be the best it has constantly to see, or better still anticipate, the market trends, and be the first with the next big idea. Andy Hornby, the chief executive of HBOS, has strong views on the subject:

> You have got to have the courage to do things first in an industry. Sometimes, when you go first, you will botch it up, but, in

'Small minds are the first to criticise big ideas'

Allan Leighton

general, companies that have the courage to come up with ideas and do them first are hugely successful.

We were the first bank to offer high interest on current accounts. At the time other banks were paying 0.1 per cent and we said no, we would pay 4 per cent. Everyone scoffed, yet we went on to gain considerable market share. Having the courage to do things first, even though you are taking a risk, is really important.

You don't have to be in a position of strength. Most often the companies which are in a position of strength find an excuse not to innovate. It is easier just to batten down the hatches. The fact that a company tries to do something first means there is, of course, more likelihood of something going wrong. I always say to my team that I would never blame them for making mistakes, and I mean it.

He adds a very important proviso, though: 'The trick is to do those things first, but not stop doing the basics well.' And I think this is crucial. You can't afford to lose sight of the basics. You have to maintain those elements that are core to the business and its wellbeing and then incorporate those that are simply a manifestation of the times and what the customer's desires are right now. A past master of this was Sam Walton, the founder of Wal-Mart. His tireless ambition to keep Wal-Mart relevant to both suburban and rural areas made the retailer the global force it is today, and no one whom I've ever met had a greater capacity to change things when it was necessary.

One of Sam Walton's successors, Wal-Mart's current chief executive, Lee Scott, nicely describes the balancing act required to stay relevant to customers:

LEADERSHIP LESSONS
› Spend time on the difficult issues.
› Get rid of the blame culture. Never criticise
   people for making mistakes.
› Never insulate yourself from the feedback.
› Be clear about the four or five things your
   company stands for.

Andy Hornby, HBOS

If you're in a country where the upper middle class is doing much better than an opening-price-point customer, you'll only have modest success if you aim your store's assortment at economically challenged people. Your competitors, who are serving the upper middle class and beyond, are going to have extraordinary success. But, how do you layer on that additional business without walking away from that core customer? Well, there's nothing about our culture that says we're only going to serve working-class people. Our culture should really be that we're going to grow the stores that customers want. If we hold on to the idea that the most important customer, and the only customer to have created our growth, is the opening-price-point customer, then we're going to miss a lot of opportunities. How can you create a company good enough for everyone and not too good for anyone? That's the balance.

Since Lee arrived at Wal-Mart in 1979, the business has acquired an ever greater level of sophistication, and that sophistication has been the most significant change in the way Wal-Mart

› If it is better for customers, then that is the
way it ought to be.
› Never accept corporate entertainment, not
even a Coke, from a supplier. The customer
is paying for it.

Lee Scott, Wal-Mart

does business. Things are not clear-cut, so not every store can be
the same. A store that serves a predominantly Hispanic population is different from one that serves a Muslim or African-American
base. Lee sees it as his job to manage through that and serve individual customers in a way that is right for them, based on the two
fundamentals: price and assortment.

Leaping ahead

Where change has been most marked in recent years has been in
those areas affected by – or created by – new technology and, not
surprisingly, those involved in these sectors are acutely aware of
the need to stay in front. Good product or good service is not good
enough any more. Technological change means constantly
enhancing products and working with shorter lifecycles.

In his conversation with me, James Murdoch, the chairman
and chief executive of News Corp Europe and Asia, was very open
about the challenges ahead – and about the need to be prepared
for a future that cannot be predicted. He spent a lot of time on

> 'Decide how much change a company can take and demand as much of it as it can give, but not so much that it ruins the fabric of the organisation. There is a learning curve to getting that right'
>
> Stephen A. Schwarzman, The Blackstone Group

BSkyB company principles and has worked hard to articulate them and drive them through the organisation. He explains:

> Some businesses suffer, and I think this one did, from going in one direction for too long and from having a cult of imperial leadership. It was how things were done at Sky. We wanted to change that completely and create a culture that was much more centred on our customers and innovation.
>
> The value in this business is really in our determination and appetite for change. It's not about preventing competition, or creating impregnable barriers to entry. You can't do that any more with technology moving so fast. The key culture we have tried to get through is this ability and willingness to adapt – the sense that we won't settle for anything other than changing.
>
> People ask me what Sky is going to look like in ten or fifteen years. I say, 'I don't know, but I can tell you that we're good at changing and good at setting the pace.' We're always right on a handful of big bets every few years and that's the value of this business. It's not in my being able to predict exactly what my customers are going to be consuming. Who could do that? It would be folly even to attempt it.

We are only fifteen years old as an organisation. We are different and we are new. Fifteen years ago there were only four channels in the UK. In the blink of an eye we've changed everything and we're going to keep changing it. That's what's exciting.

The terrestrial TV establishment seems to say, 'If only we could stop all this innovation, why couldn't we have just kept our four-channel universe?' The future is not about four channels, or thirty channels, or even 400 channels. It's going to be about 400 million channels. It's going to be ultimate plurality, something that's just going to happen. Setting the pace towards all of that is enormously exciting.

Some people find it difficult to cope with the constant change, he says, but that's not a reason for ducking the issue. 'You have to be able to take big decisions and convince the team that it's the right journey to go on. They may not feel ready, but you just have to cut through that and go on. People find that liberating and then follow.'

Television is one obvious area where technological advances are effecting a transformation that would have been unthinkable

LEADERSHIP LESSONS
› Be inclusive, but at the same time decisive.
› Constantly change and show a willingness to change.
› When everybody says we're crazy, that's when we feel best about our direction.

James Murdoch, News Corp Europe and Asia

even ten years ago. The same is true of newspapers. And, not surprisingly, this is a major issue for James's father, Rupert Murdoch. There's no doubt, for example, that the internet is going to cause fewer daily newspaper readers. Today there are a greater proportion of men under thirty using the internet as a source for news, and there's no sign of this group settling down and suddenly taking up reading a newspaper. This has implications for advertising revenue, too. As long as you have a market economy, with big and small companies wanting to advertise and get their message out, there will still be a huge amount spent on advertising. But a lot of it is going to be diverted from newspapers and the media will become more fragmented.

Some people would find this terrifying, but Rupert Murdoch clearly loves new technology and anything that enables him to open up entirely new markets. His approach shows a passionate engagement with the newspapers that created his empire, and a clear-sighted acceptance of the necessity and inevitability of change. When I spoke to him, he talked generally about technological innovation, and then specifically about how it is affecting, among other things, politics and the reporting of politics:

> The internet will have a huge role in the political process in future. At the last election, people set up websites, usually to oppose something, and News Corporation's MySpace could play a terrific part in the next one. The whole thing about sites like MySpace is that people contribute every word. It can be hugely powerful at spreading stories that otherwise might go unnoticed. For all that, newspapers are still going to be around, very strong and very influential for a long time. In Britain we consider ourselves to have the best quality daily and we certainly have

got the most successful quality Sunday [newspapers]. At the very least we will be the last ones left standing.

Leaping ahead means never putting off until tomorrow what your gut instincts tell you you should do today or, as Marks & Spencer's chief executive, Sir Stuart Rose, more graphically says:

If it looks like a duck, and quacks like a duck, then it is 95 per cent certain it is a duck. You don't have to send it away for DNA testing to prove it is a duck, because by the time you get to prove it is a duck, it has flown away. That is the mentality you need. It is all about speed, pace, reaction time and cost to your business and cost to your profit.

Don't do tomorrow what you could do today. Quite often you know what you want to do, instinctively or through experience. Don't spend too long analysing and checking it when you should actually just get on with it. It doesn't matter what business you are in today, they are all so fast moving that time is advantage or money.

Best beats biggest always

One obvious way for a company to change is to get bigger, and indeed many people assume that to be the best and to please the customer you have to be the number one global player. Much is always made of where a company sits in its particular sector, its relative size and how well it has tackled the international marketplace.

However, in my view, that's not the point. For an organisation to be world class, it doesn't have to be world active. There are companies that just operate in Yorkshire that are world class. They are innovative and brilliant at what they do, but their strategy hasn't automatically involved a quest to expand.

Superquinn founder Feargal Quinn is a shining example here. He never wanted his chain to be the *biggest*. His sole aim was to be the *best* in food. In towns where there were three Tesco stores, Feargal still only wanted one Superquinn. He wanted people to be sufficiently attracted by the quality of that store to drive that bit further. His business philosophy, he told me, was shaped by his early experiences at the Lipton retailer. 'I was told that I must get as much money off a customer as I could because I might never see them again,' he told me. 'That was logical, but my first experience of business had been at a holiday camp where it was much more important to get the regular, long-term, customer to return again and again. That was what inspired me, how do you get customers to keep coming back?'

His first approach was to focus on value for money:

LEADERSHIP LESSONS
› The main task is to bring the customer back.
› The marketplace looks totally different from where the customer is standing.
› If you don't run your business to suit the customers, your customers will suit themselves in the long run.
› Make sure you hear what you don't want to hear.

Feargal Quinn, founder Superquinn

In those days, our competitors were giving much more service than we were. Our competitors cycled to a housewife's house, asked what they wanted and then cycled back with the goods and allowed her to pay at the end of the month. So you got credit, you got delivery and you got personal service, way beyond what we were able to do. At Superquinn we said, no, we don't deliver, we don't do the shopping for you, and we don't give credit. That was the very opposite of service; but what we were offering was a different sort of shopping and lower prices.

However, as the market started to change, he realised that he would have to change, too:

By the 1980s, our competitors were all supermarkets, so we began to give exceptional service. We wanted to wow our customers, so that when they had a choice of where to shop next week, they came to Superquinn.

This successful strategy, then, was founded on anticipating customer needs. Building more stores for the sake of it played no part in Feargal Quinn's thinking.

Surinder Arora is another business leader who has been successful by focusing on the nature of his business rather than simply its size. He built the Arora International hotel and property empire with an estimated worth of £127 million in just seven years after hitting on the idea of setting up accommodation for air crews. The starting point had been developing a row of houses opposite Heathrow into a large-scale bed-and-breakfast operation. From that emerged his first hotel and a deal with BA to accommodate its air crews.

The idea was to be different from every other hotel because, otherwise, why would people come to Arora, when they could go to the Hilton or the Marriott? They had the brand name and a vast global operation and he didn't. He wanted to treat his guests like royalty and his staff like family. His first hotel, which was the first ever purpose-built crew hotel for British Airways, proved to be a challenge in itself:

All the major hoteliers said I'd never make it work. The airlines pay a lot less than normal commercial guests because the crews give you business all year around. The crews don't spend much money in the hotel bars and restaurant or on pay-per-view TV because they're working and travelling the world. More than half their year is spent living out of a suitcase so why would they spend £50 on a meal every night, when they could be spending a fiver? When I came up with the idea of a crew hotel and approached BA they said they loved the concept, but that I had no experience in building or running four-star hotels. They would only do business with me if I brought in Marriott or Hilton, or one of the big names, to run it for me; but I kept doing more research and going back to them. It was my challenge and I took it up. We eventually built the hotel, opened it three days ahead of schedule and under budget. I have continued to strive to be different from every other hotel company. We have to be different, otherwise why would the customers come to us?

'Emotion is essential'

Allan Leighton

Going global

Another route to change is to expand your geographical scope of business, but it has to be said that successfully taking a business overseas is nobody's birthright. America, for example, has long been considered the graveyard of many British retailers' expansion dreams. Sainsbury, Marks & Spencer and Laura Ashley, to name just a few, have come badly unstuck there in the past. Many business giants have learned the salutary lesson that what wows the customer on their home turf, can completely turn them off elsewhere.

In the light of this, my advice to any business has always been to say, 'Yes, go, learn and develop, but don't be somewhere that you don't need to be. There's always the danger of taking the business one bridge too far.'

Every company I know is always best in its own base. Language makes a big difference and British companies are generally not very good at speaking anything but English. If you are chief executive of a company that has expanded into many countries, everyone running those subsidiaries has to be able to speak English – as they do at GLS, the Royal Mail's European parcel business, now the fastest growing parcel business in the world. Each GLS manager in each country has two hours of English lessons every week. At the same time, I'm very aware that unless you live in the country where you're doing business, you won't understand its cultural nuances. Obviously, you can read the papers, watch local television channels and meet potential customers, but it's still vital to have people on your staff who are native to the country and who understand the culture on the ground. At GLS, 80 per cent of strategy is decided locally and 20 per cent is decided centrally, because we understand that there are different markets, at different stages of evolution, within different communities. That's the model that works.

Mars created what I believe to be the best global framework – think global, but act local! It took global brands with a global presence, one name and one brand strategy, and then acted on a country by country basis. Its global business was very successful. I believe that this success was due in no small measure to the fact that they decided the language to be spoken at all Mars subsidiaries was to be English.

Of course, it's easy to see the appeal of going global, particularly given the opening up of new markets in India and China where there is an enormous potential customer base. But, although this is the next global dimension, these markets are not going to be easy places to do business, or to build up a loyal customer following. They're becoming much more demanding, and their primary concern, quite rightly, is what the country gets out of the transaction, as opposed to what the company gets out of it. They're also very different from one another. China is all about low-cost manufacturing and engineering, while India is all about high-tech products and human capital. I know that these markets are going to change the way we all do business, but it has to be said that even successful global companies haven't yet managed to operate in India and China on the same scale that they have managed elsewhere.

And it's not just India and China that pose difficult challenges. Wal-Mart, which has a huge global presence, with more than $300 billion in sales from 6,600 stores in fifteen countries, has discovered to its cost that it's not easy to succeed even in markets that one would assume would prove less problematic than India and

China. Although the company has been lauded as one of the biggest forces in globalisation, with a role 'that flattened the world', according to the journalist Thomas Friedman in *The World is Flat*, it has nevertheless had to pull out of South Korea and Germany.

Wal-Mart's experience in Germany was particularly painful. Here they had eighty-five stores and poured in hundreds of millions of dollars to compete with local discount chains such as Aldi. Customers, however, just stayed away. Wal-Mart pulled out of Germany in 2006 and learned a lesson which chief executive Lee Scott says has shaped the way the company now operates abroad:

> **One of the worst things about life is that you normally get what you deserve. We just did a very poor job in Germany. It wasn't for lack of effort, or for a lack of people who earnestly wanted its success. It's simply a market dominated by hard discounters who do a fabulous job. Our skill is price and when we get into a country where we can't win on price it's a different game.**
>
> **Our experience in Germany made us handle things differently when we bought ASDA and when we went into Japan. At ASDA, we thought hard about how to leverage the Wal-Mart global presence with what was happening locally and how to do global sourcing. Quite honestly, in the case of ASDA, we probably backed off too much. We went from being overly aggressive in Germany, where we spent a lot of money trying to fix things in a short time, to being somewhat too passive. There is a mid-point that most managers never find. Now we are in Japan, I think we are closer to that mid-point.**

I think Lee Scott is absolutely right to say that the problems were internal ones – in other words, it wasn't Germany's 'fault', it

'The best companies are always worried'

Allan Leighton

was Wal-Mart's. They made a poor acquisition, and then any number of errors, such as not understanding the strength of the competition and the power of the major discounters that were already established there. I also suspect that Wal-Mart made one of those classic mistakes that so many companies do when they expand abroad: they forgot the lessons that, often after a lot of pain, they learned at home. In the case of the German experience, the big mistake was not to focus sufficiently on where the stores were sited. One of the basics of retail is that you have to start with great sites. If you don't have those, nothing else will go right. In Germany, quite simply, Wal-Mart didn't do their homework. But they have learned from the experience.

Chapter 4
Coping with Success, Dealing with Disaster

The art of keeping your eye on the ball

Let's assume everything is going well. The company is focused, staff feel motivated and profits are doing nicely. You would think you could relax a little. Sadly, no. It's often when things seem to be going really well that problems can start to occur. Apart from anything else – and somewhat ironically – any brand or business that reaches the top will inevitably run into hard times by virtue of its very level of success. The company becomes a focal point for anyone who has a grievance with the industry, such as suppliers, competitors or dissatisfied customers. They all form an unholy alliance, with plenty of willing ears on the outside and in the media. Moreover, people start to get tired of what you do, and because you're too busy being successful to respond to what's really happening, the rot starts to set in. It's a subject to which Sir Terry Leahy, chief executive of the UK's largest supermarket group, Tesco, since 1997, has given – not surprisingly – much thought:

LEADERSHIP LESSONS
> Talk to staff, talk to customers and, above all, listen.
> Brands don't tire, provided they stay relevant, but you have got to pay attention.
> Execution is more important than having a good idea.
> Everyone is treated with respect – at Tesco there is no fast track.

Sir Terry Leahy, Tesco

Most businesses rise and all businesses fall. That is part of the cycle of life and part of the creative destruction of capital markets. As long as you're aware of that, you can concentrate on making the gap between the rise and fall as long as possible.

It's important that you're never complacent and that you're never lulled into a sense of permanence. Ultimately it's only customers who decide if you're number one, two or three. The business has got to stay as close to those customers as it possibly can. If you stay relevant to those customers and leave no space for them to go to a competitor, you'll probably be OK. If you don't do that, somebody will take your customers and, frankly, they deserve to do so; just as your business deserves to suffer and decline. There's usually a perfectly logical explanation as to why these things happen, although they can be exaggerated by other events such as a recession.

The biggest threat to an organisation always comes from within. It stems from complacency: losing touch with the customer

'Never believe your own hype, or what the press says about you'

Allan Leighton

and losing touch with the outside environment. It is called losing the corporate memory. When a number one brand hits the buffers, its fall from grace can be surprisingly fast. Marks & Spencer, once famed for its 15 per cent share of the women's clothing market and for selling a third of all women's underwear in the UK, had a spectacular slump in the late 90s, shortly after delivering a record £1.2 billion in profits. After that the chain, one of Britain's oldest, most solid names, stumbled from one turnaround strategy to another, really recovering only in the past few years. One thing you can be sure of now is that the architect of its recovery, chief executive Stuart Rose, is not going to allow the chain to become complacent again. He refused to declare a recovery at M&S until January 2007, after months of successive growth, and is determined that his team will not lose focus, despite the admiring remarks of business commentators.

We have to keep moving. If you don't look out of the window every day you find the world has passed you by.

I don't want the troops to think they have arrived at the top of the hill, otherwise they will sit down, take a break and have a cup of tea. We are in shop-keeping and it is a very competitive industry. The customer is the most fickle person on earth and they want everything different tomorrow morning. The trick is not to be a step ahead of them, because you are then too far ahead. You cannot be in line with them either, because then you

are actually behind them. You have to be that quite difficult half step ahead, so that when you come in as a customer you don't quite know why it is just right for you, but it is just right. If I am two paces ahead of you, you don't get it. If I am in line with you I am passé. That is why you can't stop.

The perils of success

So why does complacency set in? One problem, I think, is that when things are going well you start to believe your own publicity and invincibility. And because you're at the top, you become removed from reality. You don't notice the danger signs that are definitely lurking there somewhere. Several people I've interviewed for this book have commented on the risk of this happening. Val Gooding, for example, who became chief executive of BUPA, Britain's biggest private health provider, in 1998, told me that when she joined BUPA after more than twenty years at British Airways she suddenly found that, as chief executive, she became slightly cut off from reality. Once you're in charge, she says, employees often find it very difficult to dispute your decisions. Even if the company culture is open and democratic, they find it difficult to express an opinion – and they certainly very rarely say 'no' to her. So if things are slipping, she may well not hear about it.

Val's solution is to try and stay as grounded in reality as possible, to ignore the hype and the yea-sayers. As she puts it:

You have to try to consciously counteract it. I go out and visit sites, talk to staff individually and in groups, and talk to customers. Sometimes, if I get an irate letter from a customer, I just phone them up. That's remarkably effective. It means you reach out of the cocoon of your organisation and hear the white-hot news direct from the customer. Instead of hearing everyone telling you are wonderful, get people to tell you where you are not.

I have certainly experienced this phenomenon myself. On one level, it's very nice to find everyone around me agreeing with everything I say and questioning little. But, as I've already said, it's dangerous. At the very least it can lead to the classic problem of people taking whatever you say absolutely literally.

When I was at ASDA, we acquired an old, run-down cricket club in Rochdale, which was a great site for a new supermarket

---

LEADERSHIP LESSONS
› Be ruthless with your time – prioritise the top half dozen things you must do.
› Set up 360 degree feedback for your team, with regular surveys getting comments on executives and staff from customers and colleagues. Results should be published and circulated internally.

Val Gooding, BUPA

development. I drove down to take a look, just as the heavy machinery had started to arrive to knock the club down. Donning my hard hat, I caught up with Pat, our builder, and enthused about it being perfect for our needs. I could already imagine the gleaming ASDA logo sitting proudly on top of the new store. It was then that I noticed, behind the idyllic setting, the two massive high-rise flats that were clearly suffering from years of neglect. They looked terrible. I said, 'You know, Pat, somebody ought to paint those flats because they look bloody awful.' I then had a wander around.

Three months later the store had been built and I drove to Rochdale to take a look. As I swept down the hill, the first thing I saw from my car was the flats. They looked absolutely fantastic, painted a rather jaunty bright pink. I met Pat outside and congratulated him, asking which member of the team had persuaded the council to paint their flats. There was a stunned silence and a collective shuffling of feet. Finally Pat spluttered, 'We painted them; you told us to paint them.' The job had cost ASDA thousands of pounds, although, on the plus side, the local council and residents were delighted.

OK, it was what I said, but what I meant was something completely different. I learned then to make sure I communicate as clearly as possible – and make sure that message sent is message received.

Things fall apart

A sense of reality, then, can be one of the victims of success. And if things do start going wrong, truth rapidly flies out of the window. In fact, I would go so far as to say that one sure sign of a failed or problematic company is that no one ever tells the truth or at least the whole truth. This is partly because the failing company has already lost its grip on reality, but it's also because, as things spiral out of control, no one wants to tell the truth. Why? Because, by this stage, if you tell the truth, you are automatically the carrier of bad news. You are going to be blamed for it and typically get your head chopped off. It is not so much that people are starting to become deliberately misleading; it's more serious than that. They are getting into the habit of deluding themselves about their own project in order to represent themselves as successful and convince themselves that anything wrong is somebody else's fault. And, of course, when a company is struggling, people are also inclined to conceal information from senior executives to avoid being found responsible for a problem they could not fix.

Archie Norman, with whom I worked closely for years on the turnaround of ASDA, quickly identified this syndrome at the super-market chain. He found he could not get people to open up and

'If you don't know where you are, your true situation, then you are lost from the outset. You cannot plot a course forward if you don't know where you are starting from'

Sir Terry Leahy, Tesco

━━━━━━━━━━━━━━━━━━

LEADERSHIP LESSONS
› Shareholders should ask to meet and question
    management more often – they don't
    realise the power they have got.
› Take out all the layers of a business. Build a
    company through high-octane motivation.

Archie Norman, Aurigo Management

tell the truth. To him this was a test of his leadership skills. He knew that in the end it would be the people within the company who would find the solution to its problems, but only if he could get to the right people and persuade them to tell him what was actually happening.

At the start things were not encouraging. 'ASDA was a failed company,' he recalls. 'The chairman and chief executive had been fired, the finance director was going to leave and the non-executives didn't understand the business.' He knew that he had to inject a sense of purpose into the company as quickly as possible, and to get people to tell him what was really going on. This was, as he says, quite a challenge:

> In problematic companies, the leader can't rely on the information that is easily and officially available. You've got to go to the frontline, the people who are dealing with the customers, and get them to say things they would never have said to the preceding management or chief executive. Great leaders rarely respect the protocols of hierarchy. Having a drink with a warehouse manager can tell you more about what's going on than all the spreadsheets in the finance department combined.

He describes the strategy he adopted:

When I first went to ASDA I went straight to the stores to see the store managers. I drove myself because I don't like chauffeurs. You have lost half the battle if you turn up in a limo with a chauffeur. As you arrive people will decide not to tell you anything.

Being trained at McKinsey, I always had a notebook. I would meet the store manager, ask how it was going and say, 'Let's walk around, tell me about this, and tell me about that.' Nobody had ever listened to them before, let alone written down what they said. When the store manager starts to confide in you, the truth will emerge.

ASDA's turnaround, then, began with straight talking and a notebook.

When I became chairman of the Royal Mail I found it had an enormous 'ignore the truth' syndrome. Superficially, you would have thought things ought to have been all right, because every year the organisation did an 'opinion survey' where the staff were

'Great leaders, as opposed to leaders who are good for a particular situation, often have an uncanny ability to listen, to smell what is happening, to see things and get people to tell them what nobody else would tell them'

Archie Norman, Aurigo Management

'The mind is best trained in adversity'

Allan Leighton

guaranteed anonymity in return for their honest views. However, what was actually happening with these faceless surveys was that executives were distancing themselves from the results and denying that a problem found commonly in the survey was occurring in their bit of the business. This had been going on at the Royal Mail for years. They had massive amounts of data, but had taken little action.

I sat down and studied the survey results from the previous two years. To the question, 'Do you feel valued by this company?' less than 20 per cent of the respondents said they did. In response to the question, 'Have you been bullied or harassed in the last twelve months?' a quarter said yes. I was starting work at a company where more people felt bullied or harassed than valued. That was the truth and it was a huge problem.

Discovering what's really going on is absolutely essential in the view of Professor Michael Beer of the Harvard Business School, an expert on corporate renewal. He is critical of management that tries to fix things with top-down solutions, calling people who take little account of the rest of the team or their motivation 'silent killers'. 'The ability for people to speak the truth to the senior team cannot be underestimated,' he argues. 'Once you allow the truth to inform power, things will happen.' He elaborates on this view:

> **The number one reason for failure is new leaders coming in with their own ideas and not inquiring. They don't allow others to**

influence their understanding of the situation and stick rigidly to their own set of principles. That comes from the inability to engage people in honest conversations and, in some cases, a lack of appreciation of its importance for performance and commitment.

Honesty is very hard to come by. Good leaders know how to create honest conversations. Whether it is their senior team or key people in the organisation, or whether it is about performance or culture, the conversations have always to be honest. One of the things that has kept GE [General Electric] a great firm was the ability of Jack Welch [the chief executive] to create honest conversations.

In actual fact people desperately want to make their workplace a better place to work. They walk in trying to do their best. What then happens is that many organisations block them from doing so. Good leaders understand that. They always start with the assumption that employees are motivated to do the right thing. There are people in all organisations and systems who are not and they have to go, but the vast majority of people want to do the right thing. Convince them that the right thing is to be open and honest and you're on your way.

Developing a clear direction for change, honest conversation about barriers, diagnosis and action planning is at the core of effective leadership.

One mental exercise I've found useful when checking out the fitness of an organisation and trying to establish what works and what doesn't is to apply the '7 Cs test'. All you have to do is to answer 'good' or 'bad' to the following. Your answers should be immediate, not the result of deliberation and consultation.

How good or bad is your organisation at the following?

- Co-ordination – does it work in a joined-up way?
- Commitment – how committed are people?
- Competence – how competent are people?
- Communication – is the message sent received?
- Conflict management – can people argue and then get on with it?
- Creativity – what are the creative juices like?
- Capacity management – is there the capacity to do a lot of things?

A great company will score six out of seven; a good company, four out of seven; most, when honestly scored, achieve two or three out of seven.

I undertook this rapid-fire exercise when I joined the Royal Mail. At the time the only box I ticked as healthy was 'commitment'. That's the reason I went straight after the postmen to get them on side. The people were the only thing the organisation had in its favour.

Starting over

Michael Beer's book *The Critical Path to Corporate Renewal* became our bible in the initial heady weeks at ASDA. Archie Norman had given me a copy while I was still in shock about just how bad things were, and I hung on its every word as, chapter by chapter, Michael offered his step-by-step guide to revamping companies in a way that would unite staff and motivate them to assist with the recovery process. When I'd finished going through the book it still seemed like we had a long way to go. So, we got on the phone to Michael to ask what he thought should happen next.

Michael flew to the UK to work with us and became one of many academics and respected business leaders who visited ASDA in Leeds to apply their thinking across the whole organisation. I've always felt that it's fantastically useful to get an outside view of where things are working and where things are not. Even when a company seems to be doing fine, a fresh pair of eyes can soon spot and test whether things really are on track.

In Michael's book he analyses six established companies that have gone through fundamental changes and describes what works and what doesn't in corporate renewal. He looks at the many common errors companies make, such as using standard 'one size fits all' solutions to problems, even when they clearly have no relevance to the company in question. Most importantly, he argues forcefully that employees at all levels have to buy into any major corporate changes.

When he came to Leeds, Michael spent a week out in the field, talking to different people in stores. On his return, he ran a session for our top 200 people in our Tomato Room, which was a large space in ASDA House set up to look like a Harvard classroom.

By this time, Archie and I had made a completely reality-based diagnosis of the business, and while it offered an astonishingly bleak picture, it was also, we felt, accurate. Encouragingly, Michael felt that in doing this we had taken the first and most important step. 'One of the most important things I look for is whether people embrace the reality of the situation or if they're in denial,' he told me recently. 'The weakness of most leaders is that they are more advocates than inquirers. In many cases their

'The most difficult thing to open is a closed mind'

Allan Leighton

diagnosis of the marketplace is more accurate than their diagnosis of the internal organisation.'

So what was the next step? Michael had strong views here.

Effective leaders build on what is already there. I know very few leaders who have succeeded by destroying the past. You have to honour the past. For example, I worked with the chief executive of an organisation in Canada which was in real trouble. We collected some data to help them do a diagnosis. One of the key things that came back was that the leader was not honouring the past. People felt completely disconnected and that their identity was being destroyed. That does not mean they needed to continue to do exactly what they did before. Yet leaders must recognise that the identity of people within the firm is critical to the recovery they are trying to fashion. Part of knowing who you are strategically, as well as from a values point of view, is finding a strategy to sustain. Always adapt, but don't destroy.

We took this advice to heart. Knowing that we shouldn't change things with top-down initiatives, we talked to the front-line first and then moved forward unit by unit. One practical consequence of this was that, rather than rushing into rebuilding the company as a whole as quickly as possible, we chose to revamp a couple of stores initially and create them as models for the future. We knew that there are too many other things going on in any given store, business unit or manufacturing plant that vary behaviour or performance. Perspectives change from store to store. One size does not fit all.

Getting back on message

'Culture' is a word that is often bandied about when people talk about companies, and I know that people joining a struggling enterprise are often told at the start that this is something they have to 'tackle'. In fact, they often feel compelled to change the way things have always been done, just to stamp their mark. But it's something you have to be very careful about. In most companies, the culture is deeply ingrained and changing things won't happen overnight. Moreover, if you reckon you do need to change it – and it's generally the case that you do – I'm afraid there's no point in going to the library for clues on how to do it. No one has written a definitive book about how to change an organisation's culture for the simple reason that while you can copy almost everything else in business, you can't copy culture. And the reason you can't copy it is because you can't see it. It's a simple fact that you can't copy what you can't see.

The answer lies in a delicate combination of a third of what you inherit, a third of the new culture you bring to the company, and a third, to be honest, sheer potluck. The share that you bring to the company will be based on the experience and ideas you have taken from elsewhere. The potluck third will tend to come as things start improving. And the third that you want to maintain from

'Radical change indicates failure of management'

Sir Stuart Hampson, former chairman
John Lewis Partnership

the existing company can be discovered by isolating any good elements of the company that are already there. The fast track to achieving this is, as ever, to talk to people in the organisation. My approach involves asking them to forget about the mess the company is in now, but to pick out the good things that they remember from the past and the things that they reckon will work.

When we undertook this exercise at ASDA, we also looked at photographs from the time, fifteen years previously, when Asda was hailed as the best superstore in Britain. The photographs were very revealing. They showed simple ranges, low prices and an obsession with value. The message could not have been more clear. The greatest thing about ASDA had always been the value for money it offered. 'ASDA Price' wasn't just a slogan; it was a way of doing things – 'the way we do things around here'. The advertising agency that had coined the original phrase had come up with the idea from watching and listening to customers. They had found that shoppers would point at the shelves and say, 'That's an ASDA price' if it was a low price. Or they would say, 'That's not an ASDA price' if they thought it was too expensive. ASDA buyers had operated in the same way. They would recount how they would reject a product they were offered because, 'It wasn't an ASDA price'.

What all this showed conclusively was that the culture of ASDA price was not just an advertising slogan. It came from within the business, and that was the element from the past that we not only decided to retain but to move to the forefront of everything we did. ASDA price again became the core of the business. It was a case of 'Back to the Future'.

Richard Baker adopted a similar approach when he took over at Boots. While pondering how to move things forward, he came across an original advertising sign from the company, dating back to 1900. At that time the chain had 250 stores and was a hugely successful and expanding business under founder Jesse Boot. The sign was simple: it declared Boots to be the largest, cheapest and best. It inspired Richard to base the recovery of the high street giant on going back to its roots and the driving idea of affordable healthcare. Looking back on this decision, he recalls:

> There was no debate about what we were about. We were the best in customer care, with the biggest range and choice, and we were the cheapest for goods and value. We also had stores everywhere; the right stores in the right place. It's a simple, clear and consistent strategy that everybody can understand. Once you've got it, everybody's got it. Lo and behold, by sticking with it and getting every piece of that strategy performing, the numbers improve.

In the most successful companies, such as Tesco, the core culture does not change and, indeed, should not. Yes, it does evolve, but that's not the same thing as people coming in from outside and trying to change things dramatically overnight. You could say that culture is 'the way we do things around here'. If it is working, why change it?

Baggy monsters

I've just talked about 'culture' as though it's a single entity within a single company. But, of course, many businesses are an amalgam of companies, and a business that has been on the acquisition trail before the new chief executive joins can present quite a headache. ASDA, for example, had bought a whole host of businesses in the 1970s and early 80s. Most of them were not related to food, such as the Wades and Allied Retailers chains, which both sold carpets and furniture. Then, in 1985, ASDA had merged with MFI, renowned for its flat-pack, self-assembly kitchens. The reason given at the time for these investments was that there was limited growth potential in the grocery industry and that it was therefore necessary to look further afield. However, the acquisitions were a disparate group of businesses that did not complement each other well, had cost a lot of money to buy and thus diverted much needed cash from other areas. Worse still, the management team at ASDA had little experience of these other industries, and grappling with their problems distracted them from the day-to-day running of the core business.

They addressed the problem by selling Wades in 1985 and demerging MFI two years later, bar a 25 per cent stake. But the stock market crash of 1987 thwarted an attempt to sell the Allied group. Inexplicably, they decided to invest in Allied and expand it by buying Maples, a chain of forty-eight upmarket furnishings stores, bought for £26 million in 1989. Despite £40 million for improvements to the Allied Maples 160-store portfolio, the chain lost £13 million in the first six months of 1992.

On top of the disastrous acquisition strategy, ASDA had developed a bureaucratic and hierarchical structure to deal with the various parts of the sprawling company. There were two boards, and top executives were isolated in separate parts of the HQ, away from their teams. The company had completely lost focus. Staff even mockingly referred to the headquarters as the 'dream factory', because management clearly didn't know what was going on or what to do about it.

Consequently, in addition to trying to sort out exactly what the company culture was, there were major decisions to be made about which areas to keep and which areas to let go. When Archie joined he immediately cut the investment programme in Allied Maples, closed a loss-making food manufacturing operation and stopped the store development and refurbishment programme. He then had to tackle the company's sprawling bureaucracy. He took out a layer of management to create one management board and further layers were removed from stores and trading. He also moved a number of executives in an attempt to cut their ties with the past. Once the structure was in place, the department managers made further staff reductions both in head office and in the stores. They reduced head office personnel to 1,300 people, from a previous height of 1,850. Roughly 500, or 10 per cent, of store managers were changed initially, and this rose to 70 per cent over time.

All this was done in exactly the same way as everything else. Archie and I didn't sit at our desks, but got up, walked around, talked to people and found out what they thought worked and what didn't. The changes to the old hierarchies largely came about to support this, to bring a disparate management team together and improve communication in what had been a shambolic muddle. Things were further simplified by creating an open-plan structure and simple broad bands for pay levels.

It was a stressful time. Archie and I were working exhausting hours and we decided we both needed some sort of exercise to release the tension. So, since we were both keen on sport, we formed a directors' football team to play our colleagues. It was a powerful way to cut through the hierarchy, get to know our people and let them know what was going on in the business. I'm sure that some directors, who were not particularly young or fit, thought they had no option but to play or we'd think they were too old and fire them. Indeed, a couple of them looked close to death when we were annihilated in our first match. But we pursued the idea and soon formed the tradition of a game every Monday night. We invited each department in ASDA House to form a team and then the stores started sending in teams too. After the game we would go out for a pizza, a beer and a chat. It was fun and we learned a great deal.

Gail Rebuck is another leader who faced the problem of dealing with sprawling acquisitions when she became chief executive of Random House in 1991. She started a new publishing venture in 1982 with one phone in an office shared with her business partner Anthony Cheetham, who led the fledgling business. Together with three other directors who joined a few months later, they built Century Publishing into a successful business that took over the far bigger Hutchinson and was subsequently bought by Random House.

The Random House business had consistently grown by acquisition and boasted more than twenty imprints when Gail took charge. Each had its own, highly entrenched way of doing things, its own services and its own structure. 'There was no sense of how they might work together,' Gail recalls. 'Although they were all publishing some good books, there was no thought as to how the

› Be 100 per cent committed and passionate about what you are doing.
› Be authentic. To be effective, leaders have to be themselves.
› Walk around to get a sense of what is going on – the odd conversation in the lift can tell you more than a formal meeting.
› If all else fails, follow your instincts.

Gail Rebuck, Random House

business should be structured, or how to gain any economies of scale. The company was losing a lot of money.' Gail's solution was not dissimilar to the one Archie and I adopted at ASDA:

> I decided I would take a hundred days to actually understand the business. Although I had worked in the business and knew one part of it, I didn't know all of it. Of course, I immediately did some of the no-brainer things, such as creating one head of sales. But I left everything else alone. I talked to my senior team and my board, until I had completely figured out in discussion what we had to do.

Gail knew that while her natural instinct was to build consensus, a directional form of management was ultimately required. But she set out from the start to talk to people, to find out exactly what was going on and to engage people intellectually in the process. 'It was still pretty messy,' she concedes, 'but although it was difficult, people understood the intellectual and strategic argument. Our business is full of very bright graduates. In every department there are very clever people. Once we explained it to them, everybody understood and bought into the idea of where we wanted to go. Actually, if you were to say to them, what would you do in my place, they would have said, "Pretty much the same thing."'

Making the unkindest cuts

No discussion about restructuring and repositioning a company can avoid the topic of cost-cutting. Not surprisingly, it's an emotive subject that promotes many contrasting opinions from practitioners and academics alike.

One popular view holds that if a business is going to survive in the long term, ruthless cost-cutting is an absolute essential. An extreme example of this view in action is the 1994–5 restructuring of former Fortune 500 conglomerate Scott Paper in the USA under the leadership of Al Dunlap. Dunlap earned the sobriquet of 'Chainsaw Al' because of his cost-cutting zeal. Declaring from the start that his mission was to increase shareholder value, he axed 11,000 employees, sold several business units, outsourced non-core functions and purged middle management.

The company's market value tripled during Al Dunlap's twenty months in charge, and the operation was consequently seen as a runaway success. But, ultimately, the brutal restructuring had its effect in the company's capacity for sustained long-term perform-ance. Scott Paper was merged with Kimberly Clark, its long-time rival, in a $9.4 billion deal in 1995. You could argue that Dunlap released shareholder value. You could also argue that his strategy ensured that Scott Paper failed to survive as an independent entity.

For Harvard's Professor Michael Beer, Dunlap's failure can be explained through exclusive focus on Theory E (Economic) assumptions about organisation change and lack of balance or integration of this essential strategy with Theory O (Organisation) assumptions about how to improve firm performance. CEOs who lead with Theory E assumptions focus their energies on improving shareholder values through restructuring. They believe change should be driven from the top and that chief executives need not put people, culture and organisational arrangements as a priority. CEOs who employ Theory O strategies for change, on the other hand, believe in the development of the organisation's human potential. Rather than driving change from the top, Theory O strategies for change involve employees in identifying barriers and creating better ways to run the business.

Financial markets drive managers towards Theory E, and often when a company is facing financial crisis there is no alternative. Staff have to be laid off and units closed. However, Theory O shouldn't be ignored. To return the company to sustained high performance, you have to persuade the employees who are left behind to give their all, despite the fact they're probably feeling resentful and scared. The chief executive who wielded the axe has to be an exceptional leader indeed to win this new commitment. Michael Beer views Jack Welch at General Electric as an example of this sort of person:

> **In the short term, when a leader takes over at a company that's in trouble, he has to worry about the financial elements. Jack Welch at GE laid off 120,000 employees and was known as Neutron Jack (Theory E). If he had stayed as Neutron Jack and hadn't begun**

to employ Theory O strategies, I wouldn't be talking about GE today as an example of a great company. In a recovery situation, you need a turnaround artist, who can do the restructuring.

Michael also talks of the dangers of being someone whose only real skill is in wielding the axe. 'If you hire someone with that dimension only,' he says, 'you'd better be prepared to get rid of that leader within a year or two and bring in another one.' He goes on:

Even then it's a dangerous strategy, because he or she will approach the restructuring job in a way that doesn't link effectively to the next stage. It takes a leader who can embrace the paradox, who understands the different dimensions of management that are required for sustainable performance. That is exactly what accounts for the success of Archie Norman and Allan Leighton in reshaping ASDA, which was near bankruptcy in 1991, into a high-commitment and performance company. They restructured but also engaged people at all levels.

The leader who can do this is a pretty rare animal. For most of us, the key is to be someone who is not so arrogant that they can't incorporate other people's perspectives into their own views. In fact, many people I admire are able to take on board other people's views precisely because they're self-confident and so don't feel that they have to pretend to know all the answers or always be better than the people they work with. A good leader will tend to recruit people who will compensate for their own weaknesses, and they're certainly happy to recruit people who they reckon are better than them in particular areas.

'Hire what you don't know'

Allan Leighton

Making cuts, then, also involves trying to keep people on side and preserving a sense of motivation. If things are handled well, if you're upfront about what is going to happen, and if you do everything you can to treat people well and show them respect, then the period of transition will be swifter and less painful. You have to be honest about the future, too. Generally speaking, when you've done the cuts, the first question everyone will ask is, 'Is that the end of it?' The answer usually has to be no, because all good companies are always driving their sales up and their costs down at the same time. To pretend otherwise is to run the danger of eroding trust further down the line.

One person who has had to face all this recently – and in the glare of public scrutiny – is Mark Thompson, who was appointed director general of the BBC in May 2004, after less than three years as chief executive at Channel 4. Prior to that job he'd spent his entire career at the BBC where he'd seen any number of crises and changes. On his return, he was faced with a whole raft of problems, some par for the course, like the issues surrounding the BBC's charter renewal and licence fee negotiations, others unforeseen, such as the problems arising from the aftermath of the Hutton Inquiry into the death of the scientist Dr David Kelly, in which the BBC had been very severely criticised.

Action had to be taken swiftly, and Mark's early decisions included thousands of job losses, a 15 per cent cut in programme budgets and the announcement of a plan to move 1,800 staff from

London to Manchester. Subsequently, following a lower than expected licence fee agreement, he has had to announce a further wave of across-the-board cuts. None of this was easy. But the real challenge now, Mark says, is to motivate the staff who remain, even though it's an uncertain path ahead. As he says:

> If you ask most people at the BBC if they really enjoy what they're doing you get a very high positive response. Do they like making this programme or do they like the team they're working with? Yes, they feel fantastic about it. If, on the other hand, you ask people in a general way what morale is like, they will say that it's terrible. You get an almost political response to the question. People feel the BBC is like a big family and are concerned about the people around them; so these responses about what the BBC feels like as a whole are valid. Although at one level you could say morale is at an all-time low, the paradox is that most people, most of the time, are having a fantastic amount of enjoyment in what they're doing.

No one would pretend that this is a pleasant position to be in, but Mark feels it is essential to be honest with people about where the BBC is going, and also to communicate his underlying optimism about the future:

> My challenge at the BBC is to give the rather unwelcome message that the days of feeling that everything is solid, steady, and your

'Respect is something you give, not something you get'
Allan Leighton

job is never going to change, are gone forever. We're never going to get back to a point where there's more money than you know what to do with and where there are going to be no efficiency savings. You simply won't be able to do things in the same way in five years' time. There is no part of our universe, or in any other media organisation in the UK and worldwide, where anyone should expect their job to be the same even three years from now. The journey we have to go on is not just through a period of uncertainty, the world is now uncertain for good, we have to get used to it.

What I have to try and do is get everyone in the organisation to start looking at these periods of change as periods of creative opportunity. We can do things we couldn't do before. We can reach people in ways we couldn't before. For example, we used to throw all of our content away once we had broadcast it once. Now a lot of it is going to be available to watch and listen to forever. That's a good thing, an amazing change in broadcasting.

As I've said already, job-cutting is a regrettable but inevitable part of business, especially at times of transition or when things have gone wrong. But there are things that a good leader will do to manage it as well as possible. In the first place, they make sure that the cuts are carefully thought through: you don't just axe a few random jobs in an attempt to lower the head count. And you make sure that you communicate not only what you're doing, but the reasons you're doing it. At the Royal Mail, we have had to let 400,000 people go, but all the signs are that morale in the company is much better than before, and I say that even following the strike action of summer 2007. Why's that? It's because there is now a clearer future and a greater sense of purpose.

> ## 'Leadership is a test of courage, not of popularity. To be a good leader you've often got to do some unpopular things'
>
> Richard Baker, Alliance Boots

Of course, I accept that when you're having to make tough decisions like this, you're not going to make yourself popular. But making tough decisions is an inevitable part of being a leader. I would wholeheartedly go along with Richard Baker at Boots when he says:

What I have had to learn for myself at Boots has been courage versus popularity. I never had to do the really awful stuff, like closing stores or lowering head count, at the other two companies I worked for because I wasn't really senior enough. I now believe that the good leader is the one who finds out what's going on and gets on with what has to be done no matter how unpopular it is.

Somebody once said to me that calm seas don't make great sailors and I think that is an accurate summary of how you develop leadership skills.

Chapter 5

The Art of Communication

Why listening with is more important than talking at

In my early days at Mars I thought I knew everything about presentation and communication. I'd been on the training courses and taken all the basics to heart. Now, I just wanted to get out there and prove myself. I was almost speechless with anticipation when, quite early on, I was called into the boardroom to make a presentation. This was my moment. I'd always been a confident person and, after a number of courses on how to present effectively, I felt sure that the legendary Mars brothers would be bowled over by my professionalism.

On the appointed day, dressed in a stiff shirt, tie and smart black suit, just as I had been taught, I went into the only meeting room in the Mars open-plan offices. Full of thoughts and dreams of where this opportunity might take me, I clutched tightly my box of slides illustrating my presentation and my pointer, one of those silver jobs that telescopes in and out.

John and Forrest Mars were sitting at the end of the long boardroom table, with their backs to me, looking out of the window.

When I shut the door, they took no notice of me whatsoever, not even a nod of the head or a murmur of hello to acknowledge that I'd entered the room. One of them was even using a rolled up newspaper to swat wasps.

I wasn't easily put off, so I proffered a friendly good morning. The silence was deafening. Now, despite my cockiness, I wasn't quite sure what to do. There was certainly nothing in the textbooks about this situation. What was the etiquette here? Should I sit down, or wait to be asked to begin? Should I try another good morning, but perhaps louder this time? I decided to remain silent and standing. As the seconds ticked by the only sound was the noisy clock in the corner, the buzz of furious wasps and the swish-thump of a rolled up copy of *The Times*. Finally, after what seemed like ages, John slowly turned to me. With just the slightest trace of irritation, he said, 'Look my friend, if you don't get on with it, we'll never get to the end of the presentation.' He then turned back to his wasps.

Nervously I presented to their backs for 5 minutes, although it seemed like a lot longer. Despite the unusual circumstances I concentrated hard on following my training and used my pointer with what I thought was great effect to talk through each fact on the slides. Then it was over; but still there was no reaction. Once again, all I could hear was the clock, the wasps and the vigorous whump of the now bloodied newspaper. Finally, Forrest got up, walked slowly and purposefully around the table, took my pointer and snapped it in two over his knee. 'I hate these pointers,' he said, and returned to his seat.

It seems brutal even now, but it was a valuable lesson. Trainers teach everyone the minutiae of professional presentations, but miss a vital point. It's far more important to have an actual conversation with your audience, engage with them and understand what they want to get out of the exercise than to attempt to knock them out with well-prepared purple prose. Communication needs to be a two-way street, and the constant flow of ideas back and forth in an organisation is its life blood. Sir Christopher Gent, who turned Vodafone into a vast global business and is now the non-executive chairman of GlaxoSmithKline, is adamant that communication has to flow two ways:

> **You need to influence, motivate and get the desired outcome by what you say, but it's vital that you're a good listener, too. You must understand the constituencies you need to influence, the customers, shareholders, employees or the local communities you serve. You must know their requirements and what they're looking for. You must shape that relationship if you are going to achieve the desired outcome.**

As so often, the Mars approach to things was absolutely spot on, and I think it's worth summarising the Mars recipe for presentations:

- The presentation should be short with loads of context.
- Don't present at your audience, talk with them.
- Don't show off with technology – your audience will concentrate on the big screen, not on what you are saying.
- Please, no revealing point-by-point. Put the whole slide up and get on with it.
- Don't use complex words you would never normally use. Most people will not understand and it will turn them off.
- Understand your audience. The talk should appeal to them, not you.

And when it comes to listening, Sir Tom Hunter, the Scottish entrepreneur, puts his finger on it when he says, 'Bright people want to work with someone who is willing to hear their ideas and solutions.' If you're not prepared to communicate properly, you won't win or keep good staff.

The tyranny of meetings

For many people, meetings are where communication happens. I'm not so sure. I find that taking the time to solve the day-to-day problems of a large concern means I don't have time for endless meetings. I'm always amazed that, when most executives start to plan their diaries, the first thing they do is to commit themselves to so many meetings that they're unlikely to have time to do anything else. I suspect that Martha Lane Fox is on to something when she says that managers very often use meetings as a diversionary tactic instead of getting down to the real issues:

> **Good leaders know when to get into the detail and know when to get out of it again. I often see people who immerse themselves**

'Heads, not clocks, create time pressure'
Allan Leighton

in detail for comfort. They busy themselves with meetings and all the things you need to do daily in a business while being too scared to think 'What could transform this business?' or 'What direction is this business going in five, ten or fifteen years time?' Mind you, in lastminute.com's time frame, it was five, ten or fifteen months' time.

My own view is that people should start planning their time and diaries with activities that keep them *out* of meetings. In my own case, I start off by writing in time to spend in the delivery offices, time in store and time out in the field. Only after thinking about the things that really count do I consider what time I have left for meetings. Not spending hours in back-to-back meetings leaves more time for productive work, such as looking after the customer and listening to the operators. The trick is to make the few meetings you do agree to attend really effective. I'm very aware that I'm constantly under time pressure. It's important for me only to do the things that really matter and spend time on important issues. If I don't manage my time effectively, I won't run the organisation well and I'll then become exhausted and demoralised. I don't need unnecessary meetings.

When I was at Mars I found that they had strong views on how often – and how – to conduct meetings, and I think their views remain spot on. Here they are in summary form:

- You don't need lots of them.
- Those you do have should start on time and finish on time.
- If you can cover the issue in five minutes, cover it in five minutes. If you call the meeting on the basis it will take three hours, do not take more than three hours.
- Meetings should have real pace to them and they should be fun. Everyone in them should be involved.
- To keep things moving don't make the meetings too comfortable. We had stand-up conference tables at ASDA.
- Chairing the meeting is important. It isn't just going through the agenda. As the chairman you must continually force the momentum and move things along.
- Board papers should be sent out in advance for people and they should be read. It is reasonable for the chairman to assume everyone attending the meeting has read them and therefore not have to go through them again.
- Meetings should be interactive, but they are not always about consensus. They are about decisions.
- When a meeting is finished, it is finished.

Incidentally, one very useful trick I've heard from Rupert Murdoch is to use meetings as a way to keep people on their toes. He reckons that he's given so many papers and board minutes to wade through that he may not always have time to read them all. Instead, he will simply flick to, say, page 56 and focus on a detail that no one has really considered. Quite nonchalantly, he will then refer to the item and ask a detailed question. Of course, unless the rest of the executives have taken care to be exceptionally well briefed, they are left open-mouthed and floundering. It's a very clever, effective way to ensure that everyone consistently stays on the ball.

Getting out and about

So if meetings aren't the answer, what is the best way to communicate? My own view is that a much more informal approach is often best, and this starts with being as accessible as possible. I've already said that at the Royal Mail I have an 'Ask Allan' scheme that generates some 400 emails a day. Others I know adopt similar approaches. Andy Hornby, for example, a former colleague of mine from ASDA, tells me, 'Everyone knows that if they send me an email they'll get a reply that day. I'm very rarely in the office, but I'm always on my mobile. People know that if they leave a message, I'll get back to them straight away.' It's a particular challenge for him because, as the chief executive of HBOS, which he became in 2006 at the early age of thirty-nine, he suddenly found himself in charge of 75,000 people. Keeping in touch is quite a logistical challenge when you're talking about – and to – that many people. Andy, however, strongly believes that you have to be seen to be genuinely accessible or, apart from anything else, everything in the organisation will start slowing down. As he says, 'You must never leave people thinking, "Well, I need to clear that with the top guy", knowing that that could take days or weeks.'

Perween Warsi, who in just a few years went from making samosas in her kitchen to running the multimillion-pound S&A Foods empire, has also introduced a series of initiatives to make herself accessible to everyone. The one I like the most is her 'Call Perween' line, which encourages colleagues to call her direct to discuss any issue. When she first launched the direct line a good few years ago, her management team was up in arms. They thought everyone was going to call her and complain about them, but people haven't, not even once. Sometimes they call about issues unconnected with the business, such as how to get their

> 'I don't want everyone to come to head office, I don't like the whole concept of head office. Going out to talk to everyone, not just directors, in their place of work is the only way to truly understand what is going on. That is the way to both support and challenge the business'
>
> Carolyn McCall, Guardian Media Group

son or daughter admitted to a particular school. Other times it's to suggest ideas. In fact, there have been so many good ideas that they now have a scheme called My Bright Idea (MBI). At the end of the year they have a prize day when they award £2,000 for the best one.

For Perween, the welfare of her staff and success in business go hand in hand:

A leader needs the skill or intuition to spot gaps in the market, but also to spot gaps and opportunities internally too. That is

LEADERSHIP LESSONS
> Keep raising the bar and trying for something new and different.
> Make sure everyone in the team understands and buys into the vision.

Perween Warsi, S&A Foods

what keeps you growing and achieving what you want to achieve. The people I work with are like my family. I don't want to know just what is happening at work, I want to know about before and after, too.

Motivating those people is very important. When everything is going well it's easy to motivate people. When things aren't going right, when the market is getting tougher, or when there is pressure on costs and you have to reduce the number of staff, that is the time true leadership shows. Can you keep your people motivated and energised? You need to keep in touch with them, understand their body language – and understand them. Put yourself in their shoes. What must they be going through?

It is because we are so interested in people, and we believe that they are the ones who can make you or break you, that they are constantly on our minds. It's the modern way of running a business. It's not by hiring and firing; it's by helping people to achieve their objectives, because if they succeed, I succeed. My success is in their hands.

I myself find that one very good way to discover what's on people's minds is to go on informal walkabouts. Listening to colleagues doesn't have to mean bounding in with a jacket and a tie accompanied by an entourage of fifteen similarly besuited flunkies who have given the staff a week-long warning that management are coming. That is intimidating and counter-productive. But if you just turn up on the off chance, have a little wander around and relax with people, they'll quickly tell you exactly what's happening. Colleagues just want that opportunity.

Critics of my approach think that there's a danger that all that will come out of this is gripes and negative comments, but I find

'Listening is not a matter you can delegate, no matter who you are'

Feargal Quinn, founder Superquinn

that half the time this doesn't happen, and, frankly, even if it does it's still vital to know where the problems are.

My line is to ask, 'If there are a couple of things I could magic for you, what would they be?' That's when you find out what the real issues are. The subjects that concern people are always on the top of their minds; they carry them around with them. If I ask anyone what are the two things that bug them most about their company or their home life, they'll rattle them off straightaway.

When Richard Baker started as chief executive of Boots in September 2003, he set out at 7 am on the first day and did a lightning tour of three stores. Later that week he spent two whole days at the Loughborough store working on the shop floor. He asked each store team for ways things could be improved and arrived in the office brimming with enthusiasm with a list of twenty-one ideas to work on. Some of the feedback may have seemed superficially trivial. For example, one thing that Richard learned from Paula at Boots in Loughborough was that the tap in the staff canteen had stopped working years before and had never been repaired. But Paula also told him that the health and beauty chain's prices were too high, so much so that even with staff discount many preferred to shop at a competitor down the road.

Richard got to grips with the pricing, which was clearly driving everyone away. He also got the tap fixed, earning some crucial loyalty and respect as well. In his opinion:

In any company, people are the most important thing you have got and this is particularly true in the personal care business. The colleagues who work in store want to do good things for customers. They can earn the minimum wage in any one of fifty retailers, but they're at Boots because they like the company and really get a buzz out of it.

He also points out that mending a broken tap was an important symbol of a wider problem. 'For years,' he says, 'Boots invested any profits in other parts of the group but not in the stores. Everything looked neglected. We reversed this and invested in the stores. Our colleagues saw we were doing the right things and the mood in the company was quickly improved.'

Broadcasting the news

Success is a team game and every leader knows it. This makes them spend a lot of time and effort thinking about and generating team spirit. As usual, it's different for every team, but the key is to find the glue that melds the team together and find totems

LEADERSHIP LESSONS
› Your people are the most important thing you have.
› You've got to let go to grow.
› Go back to the company roots.

Richard Baker, former CEO Boots

that will remind everyone of their goal in making the whole a lot bigger than the sum of the parts. Listening to a well-motivated team is a terrific aid to timely decision-making. Even awards, like businessperson of the year being given to the guys at the top, can act as a motivator for the whole team if you use them well. As John Waples, business editor of *The Sunday Times*, says, 'People need leaders and when they see their leader winning, they get reflected glory.'

Once a year at ASDA we used to do a major set piece for the managers. Archie would do the serious part outlining the numbers behind our progress. My job was to gee everyone up and get them going. I made a rod for my own back by my first rather extravagant presentation, because everyone expected me to go one better each year. For the first event my theme was based on the fact that the whole business turnaround had to be based on increasing like-for-like sales. We had to have a totem of product sales. Now, the biggest selling item in a supermarket is the banana, so I arranged through Fyffes for 600 blow-up bananas to be delivered to the conference. These three-foot long inflatable bananas were then suspended in a big net in the auditorium above the store managers. After I'd made my upbeat speech, I pulled the cord attached to the net and all the bananas fell down on top of everyone. Everybody then had to hold the inflatable and swear an oath of allegiance to the banana.

I know it sounds faintly, if not completely, daft, but at the time it was a very powerful symbol and everybody still remembers it. They all went back to their offices carrying their giant banana and every day it would remind them that the company recovery was all based on increased sales.

Another year I came on stage accompanied by a load of

dancing girls, dressed as an over-the-top rock star and belting out a suitably over-the-top pop song. Again, it may sound completely ridiculous now, but it stuck in people's consciousness, helped, I suspect, by my rather botched entrance. While I was waiting back-stage, behind a revolving door, dressed in huge boots and a wig, dry ice was pumped on to the stage to create the smoky effect required for my pop star entrance. Unfortunately, too much was pumped in too early, and the door unexpectedly span around rather fast. I managed to miss my cue completely and shot out on to the stage in a complete daze, much to the amusement of my audience.

On another occasion I decided to ride a motorbike into the auditorium, in a move inspired by the Shangri-Las' 60s hit 'Leader of the pack'. I had managed to persuade a rather sceptical Archie Norman that this was a good idea, despite the fact it clearly had nothing to do with the conference and I had never ridden a motor-bike before. In rehearsal, as I burst through the paper screen on my Harley-Davidson, I couldn't stop the powerful low-rider and went hurtling off the stage into the space where the audience would have been sitting. Not surprisingly, Archie insisted I attach a chain to the back of the bike for the event proper, to avoid wiping out a swathe of our best people.

'To get the best out of people, lead from the front. If you are there, you are visible and not afraid to be seen working hard, others will follow'

Clive Jacobs, founder holiday autos

Some of the conference totems were endearingly simple, such as giving out a coat hanger to everyone. The message was – no jackets required. I've always hated it when besuited managers either run or visit a store with a load of flunkies and a clipboard. The message was that they had to be more relaxed and to look more relaxed, hence the coat hanger. I also bought everyone a ten-foot long ruler to illustrate the ten-foot rule: nobody was allowed to walk within ten foot of a customer without saying hello.

Years on, those people who are still at ASDA still have their bananas, rulers and coat hangers. And I strongly feel that it's through this sort of very direct communication that you can change perceptions. Make it fun, make it memorable and give everybody a totem to remind them constantly of the key messages. When ASDA was sold we bought the team involved a small silver banana. On it was engraved 'ASDA – 1989 to 1999 – £500 million to £6.7 billion, what price the banana?' It said to everybody, that's how it was done. That's what the banana did.

Totems aren't just a tool for senior managers either. I gave everyone in store a miniature ladder to remind them about our scan ladder scheme, which recorded and rated the speed at which goods were passed through the checkout to help customers get through more quickly. Every colleague, in every store, was told their scan speed from their shift and these were displayed in a scan ladder scoreboard in the colleague areas. The shifts used to compete against each other and there were prizes for the best improvements and the best store. We drove our scan speeds up by a factor of nearly two within months. The productivity gain was massive.

We also introduced the 'Golden Cone' mystery call prize. The golden rule when colleagues in the stores called ASDA House was that the phone had to be answered within three rings, the colleague had to say their name, hello, and ask how they could help. If they couldn't help, they had to take the caller's phone number and aim to solve that problem themselves within 24 hours. Once a month we'd do mystery calls at random, and see who performed well and who didn't. There would always be a winning individual and he or she would be awarded the 'Golden Cone' and, with it, the best car parking spot in the company. They'd drive up to a space usually reserved for the chairman, park up next to the door and walk in. It was a good incentive. It also drove home a powerful message that stores came first.

A totem I encountered at Wal-Mart, and which we imported into ASDA, was the company song. Commentators often poke fun at the Wal-Mart chant, which is regularly repeated in store, at Bentonville and in company meetings. However, I think they're missing the point. It's the sort of thing the Japanese have been doing for years at the start of each day, and I think it works because it fosters an incredible sense of unity and pride. It's not unlike the way in which soldiers sing as they go into battle: the singing, or whistling, or playing of drums signals a sense of solidarity and confidence in their group.

Having said that, I freely admit that when I first heard the Wal-Mart chant my British reserve came to the fore and I questioned whether I really wanted to take part. What changed my mind was an early store visit in Cincinnati with Wal-Mart executives Lee Scott, Rob Walton and David Glass. As always, they arrived at the store unannounced, toured the various departments and then gathered all the shop staff together for a chat. After praising them and pointing out a few areas where they might like to make improvements, they invited the associates to ask them questions.

The whole process was rounded off with a rousing Wal-Mart chant. It was only when I looked around and saw customers joining in too, that I realised just how powerful all this was.

In the view of Professor Earl Sasser at the Harvard Business School, totems are all about stimulating an emotional attachment to the business. The chief executive can't just send a memo to everyone saying, 'Let's have fun'. Antics like the bananas and the dramatic stage shows drive home the message that, yes, we're going to work hard, but we're going to enjoy it too.

And if you think my performances are over-the-top, they are nothing compared to those of Herb Kelleher, chairman of Southwest Airlines in the United States. He is well known for dressing up as Elvis and driving a Harley to company picnics. But that's just for starters. Earl Sasser reminded me recently of one of Herb's more extravagant gestures. It came about when he received a legal document saying that another smaller player in the airline industry was suing them over their use of the advertising slogan 'Just Plane Smart'. The rival, Stevens Aviation, objected that this was too close to their own advertising slogan, 'Plane Smart'.

Herb ordered an immediate investigation to find out more about the other company. It unearthed the fact that the rival chief executive spent a good deal of his spare time lifting weights. Herb Kelleher, by contrast, was known for lifting only two things: Wild Turkey whiskey and cigarettes. Nevertheless, Herb decided to challenge his business rival to an arm wrestling contest to settle the dispute, and the rival accepted. The deal was that whoever won the contest would win the right to use the slogan. A proper wrestling ring was duly set up, along with all of the pomp and ceremony you usually get at a wrestling match. 'Who saw it?' asks Earl Sasser. 'Well, people were there from both Southwest and Stevens Aviation, so their employees saw it. More than that, their potential employees saw it, their customers saw it and their potential customers saw it. It was a huge PR event. Most important was the symbolism. It said, "We're going to do something that's fun; we are going to do it in a non-traditional way and this is how we do stuff." If people are having fun at the top, then the team really starts to feel fun is what it's all about.'

Keeping the message simple

Totems are all about offering powerful, straightforward messages. They're part and parcel of every leader's challenge: to keep things simple. And avoiding unnecessary complexity is an essential part of good communication and so of good leadership. As the entrepreneur Sir Tom Hunter says:

> If you take an incredibly complex situation, it is the leader's job to break it down and simplify it. You must say to your team, 'If we do these three things we've got it cracked.' People will then recognise that, although things are complex, they themselves have a specific and manageable role. They immediately know what they are doing and where they are going.

Rupert Murdoch is a past master of this. So, too, is Sir Philip Green. Philip has an incredible mental agility that enables him to keep things simple and straightforward for himself and all those around him. People who work with him quickly discover that he doesn't like to be surrounded by hundreds of pieces of paper and he doesn't send emails. He once told me that when he does a deal, all the detail will be on a single sheet of A4, and that's exactly what he takes in to meetings. Not that he ever needs to refer much to his A4 sheet as he rattles through the figures showing why a particular multibillion-pound takeover makes sense.

Immersed in the retail business since he was sixteen years old, Sir Philip developed this skill at the age of twelve, when he started helping his mother, Alma, run the family business following his father's death. Alma used her inheritance to branch out into launderettes and self-service petrol stations, a concept that had just arrived from America. Sir Philip worked on the forecourts, cleaning windscreens and changing oil. He says he learned the value of money there; the better the job he did, the larger the tip.

Philip quit school rather than enrol at university and went to work for a shoe wholesaler in the East End. It was there that he honed the mental agility which has been so vital in his subsequent career. He devised a numbering system in which he would have 500 different styles, numbered one to 500. The wholesaler would ask him for a pair of black brogues and he knew instantly they were number twenty-six. Because he did the job quickly he got credit, whereas his colleagues were slow and given short shrift by the wholesaler. Keeping things simple, then, is a mantra with him, and it's part and parcel of his belief in good, straightforward communication:

I don't like absent landlord businesses. I return 98 per cent of the calls I get each day within 24 hours. It is about being accessible, available and deciding where you want to be. By dealing with issues quickly and simply you save a whole load of time. If I say yes, it doesn't mean maybe. If I say no it doesn't mean might be. There is no grey in my world. It's all very black and white. A decision from £1 million to £150 million will take 3 minutes.

You have to know what you want and you have to be focused. The key is for your people to understand how you work. I don't need an hour-long presentation. I always say, do me a favour and get to the end. I don't need the foreplay, let's just get straight to the action.

I do sometimes worry that simplicity is out of fashion these days when it comes to running a business. Complexity rules. I am only too aware that business is not straightforward, but it doesn't have to be that complicated and it can be made easier if communication is kept simple. In fact, I often felt that my role at ASDA was not chief executive officer – CEO – but rather chief simplicity officer – CSO.

Communication vs office politics

Anyone who works in any company of any size will know all about office politics. They may seem an everyday part of life, acceptable even. But there's no doubt that rivalry between departments, turf issues and general distrust between colleagues jeopardise the progress of a company.

> 'Build a reputation for openness, honesty and good ethics in a company. You must have that and do everything you can to stamp out any politics that might be going on behind you'
>
> Rupert Murdoch, News Corp

It's a problem everyone faces. Sir Martin Sorrell, for example, who founded WPP in 1986 and has since built it into the world's largest communication services agency, told me that he reckons the biggest challenge in running any company is to get all the internal communities to stop squabbling and start working together. His own company is not free of the problem, in his view. WPP has seventy operating companies (twelve key ones), servicing clients around the globe with advertising, public relations and specialist communications services. It employs 98,000 people, in over 2,000 offices, in 106 countries. It stands to reason that internal politics will be more pronounced in such an enterprise, which is multi-branded and has grown by acquisition, than they will be in a single-brand company that has grown organically. As he told me:

> Political rivalries inside our own organisation at WPP, and inside our client organisations too, take up an awful amount of time. I often think if we spent 20, 15 or even 10 per cent of the time that we spend sorting out internal issues focusing on our competition, or our clients, we would be an even more successful business.
>
> It can be very difficult. There are diseconomies of scale in our businesses, with the exception of media buying. The bigger

a creative business gets, the more difficult it is to run. If you double the size of a creative department, it becomes three or four times more difficult to manage. That is a central issue for us. When you have two people you have a coordination problem, when you have 98,000 people you can imagine the problem. There are significant economies of knowledge, but that is not the thing that people focus on.

Clients don't care about agency brands. They care about the people who work on their business and provide solutions to their problems. Whereas the people who work inside agencies, and in particular the people who run agencies, worry about the brands because of the issues of turf, territory and ego which bedevil cooperation inside companies. When you have separate tribes or brands, then people want to focus on the tribes or the brands.

So how do you get all the different units within a company to work well together? I don't think there's an entirely straightforward answer. In fact, I strongly suspect that office politics can never be eliminated altogether. However, I do believe that open communication and the setting of clear objectives and context

LEADERSHIP LESSONS
› Persistence and speed are the key.
› Information is available to everybody so freely these days, but it's how you use that information effectively that counts.

Sir Martin Sorrell, WPP

'Negative thoughts spread more quickly than positive ones'

Allan Leighton

can minimise them. The team becomes sufficiently empowered by being treated consistently fairly and by being involved in the strategic process that they don't waste their energies in futile spats.

The tone, as always, has to be set at the top. Leaders have to distinguish between harmless gossip that arises because people are interested in what's going on, and corrosive gossip that undermines morale and saps confidence. No chat at all can't be good. If people haven't got any outlets for their views, work soon becomes a pretty boring place. But destructive chat has to be broken up, because if it's left unchecked it will become malignant and the various layers of management will then turn to permafrost or treacle and become business prevention squads. Good lines of communication – and plenty of it – give people a sense of accountability. When people have this, plus quite a wide spread of control, they don't have time for politics. They're too busy doing the work.

Even more corrosive than office politics are the twin evils of bullying and harassment, and these are things that have to be stamped on straight away. As I have already mentioned, when I arrived at the Royal Mail both problems were rife, and we had to move fast to create an inclusive culture where people felt valued and respected. To show that we meant business we launched a massive anti-bullying and harassment campaign which included a helpline for employees, staffed by trained counsellors, that was open 24 hours a day, seven days a week. Dignity and Respect at Work (DRAW) groups were also established across the business to provide a forum for all employees to raise and discuss local issues. We also devised the Chairman's Diversity and Inclusion Awards, where employees nominate colleagues who they feel have made a difference. Since these were launched in 2005, they have grown in popularity and stature every year – in fact, the members attending have doubled each year from the initial 500 employees who came along. Although we still have lots to do, it has been this sort of inclusivity that has helped turn the Royal Mail from being a loss-making business to a profit-making one.

Chapter 6
Getting the Right Team
Why no one succeeds on their own

Business is comparatively simple but everyone tries to complicate it. Writers on business often agonise about strategy, but in some ways strategy is the simple part. It's responsible for perhaps 20 per cent of why anything works. The tough bit is execution.

The way I think about it is as a pyramid. The top 20 per cent of the pyramid is strategy and the rest of the pyramid is execution. Strategy is important, but it is a compass not a road map. It tells you in which direction you are heading, but the important bit is how you get there. Companies which have great strategies and lousy execution get nowhere. Companies with average strategies and great execution do better. Companies with great strategies and great execution are great companies.

Execution lies in the hands of the people who really run the company – the line managers. Leaders set the context – the strategy – but managers execute. We don't need millions of leaders trying to work out whether we're doing the right thing, but we definitely need a large number of very, very good managers. It's the way to

> 'I don't do it all, I just conduct the orchestra. I say, "Look, there is a hill, you may not think you can climb it, but I am going to show you a way of getting to the top of that hill"'
>
> Sir Stuart Rose, Marks & Spencer

make a company stand out and to ensure that you satisfy your customers better than anyone else. Any company that wants to get ahead has to differentiate itself from the competition by getting better managers than anyone else.

The problem is that while leaders tend to get all the attention, the managers don't. Professor Charles Handy, a former lecturer at the London Business School and author of countless books on management, offered me a nice analogy of this when he described the conductor of an international opera company who faces a difficult leadership challenge. In front of him while he conducts the opera are the prima donnas. Many of them are so grand they don't bother to turn up for rehearsals but, when they do, they need constant attention because they are the stars. In the darkness, down below the conductor, is the orchestra. These talented people are really important and do most of the work. Yet they get little of the glory and stand up just once at the end of the performance to take their bow. Charles ended his analogy by pointing out that so far as the really critical people, the customers, are concerned, the conductor has his back to them throughout the performance. It's alarming just how similar this is to many businesses I know.

'A business needs to be confident in itself to look for talent. A lot of times chief executives don't look for talent because they are afraid to find it, in case they take over, or become too challenging'

Sir Terry Leahy, Tesco

It's particularly alarming because, quite frankly, leaders don't know all the answers. Very often they need advice and good counsel. I've lost count of the number of times the following scenario has played out in front of me. Someone will come to me and ask, 'What are we going to do?' I will say, 'I'll go away and think about it', which I do. Next day, when I say we need a further discussion, the response will usually be 'Oh, we've had a little think about it and we are going to go away and do this now.' Job done.

For Fred Smith, who founded FedEx in 1971, the key to building his courier company into a global giant was finding the right team and bringing together their energies to achieve the company's goals. This was no mean feat when you consider that the company now employs 260,000 people. Fred started out with just fourteen small aircraft in Memphis delivering 186 packages on its first night. Today, FedEx makes 6 million shipments a day, using a fleet of 674 aircraft and serving 375 airports in 220 countries. 'You have to get the right type of folks to do what it is you want to do,' he told me. 'If you want to win football games, you can't hire eighty-pound skinny lads to play. You have got to match up the resources with the goals.'

› Learn from history: the lessons are clear and proven. There are not many new things under the sun.
› When things go wrong, take responsibility. If there is a chance to rectify a mistake, react urgently and strongly.
› The great conquerors of the past treated the conquered well. Remember that when your company makes an acquisition.

Fred Smith, FedEx

Fred also points out that this focus on getting the right people doesn't only extend to the senior team. Everyone in an organisation has a key role to play. Part of the trick is to know who is capable of doing what. 'In any organisation,' he says, 'there are lots of people who can't assume leadership. That doesn't mean they're bad people, just that they're more suited to other areas of the business. The trick is to identify their capabilities before they are put in a position of management or leadership, because you won't be doing them any favours. We have developed a pretty good system to do that. Our rate of failure of putting people in management positions is much less than it was twenty-five years ago.'

Where I think Fred has been very canny is to hardwire into his company a way of ensuring that different types of talent receive their fair measure of reward. He points out, quite rightly, that in the industrial world 'the compensation system only rewards people that go up the managerial track'. His solution?

'In football, when somebody scores a goal, people tend to forget that someone had to pass them the ball in the first place. In business it is the same: always reward the passer of the ball'

Allan Leighton

We built a dual track. You don't have to be promoted to manager, or managing director, in order to make money and do well. You can be an industrial engineer, a scheduler, a planner or a senior IT person without having to go through the management system.

One way to appreciate very quickly just how important every person in a company is is to look at the role of someone like a PA. They're not just helping out their boss; they're also often the public face of the company. Rebekah Wade at the *Sun* reckons you can tell a lot about a person and their business from their PA.

When people phone and leave a message for you and you return their call, some PAs completely blank you. I say, 'Hello, is so and so there?' They say, 'Who's calling?' 'My name is Rebekah Wade.' 'Rebekah Who?' 'Rebekah Wade.' 'Spell that'. 'R.e.b.e.k.a.h W.a.d.e., and by the way *he* called *me*.' 'Did he?' 'Yes, all I'm doing is returning his call.' D'you know, I'm left thinking this guy's a bit of a loser. They're also the same people who have a new PA every month.

She's vocal in her praise of her own PA, Cheryl Carter, who has been working with her for twelve years:

> **Cheryl is one of my best assets. Whether I'm having dinner with MI5 or the Beckhams (it's a broad church at the *Sun*) everyone tells me how lucky I am to have such a great PA. She doesn't just remember names or voices but she probably remembers the names of their partner or their children, or even their dog. Everyone I know has tried to poach her, but God help anyone who does!**
>
> **Although you obviously have to pay market rates for the hours they put in, keeping a great PA is also about loyalty – both ways. If, as has happened, Cheryl says to me she'd like to try her hand at journalism, I say, sure, try it out and see if you can do it. She reads papers all the time and will tell me when she doesn't like a particular story, because she feels part of it. She's not the person who sorts out my diary; she's very much part of the business.**

In my own case, my private assistant, Christine Staveley, has been with me for more than fifteen years. I also have a secretary at the Royal Mail, Rita Williams, and another assistant who has a broader ranging role, Lucy Dare. They know how I work and everybody I know or don't know. That's really important. If people want to get something to me, wherever I am in the world, or whatever I am doing, they talk to them. Their role takes a load of work off me and takes all the noise away of things I don't need to know about, or deal with. This team is a positive filter and has over the years become an extension of my leadership base. For it to work you have to trust them with everything. They have to

> ### 'One person, one chief executive cannot change a company. They have to empower all of their people'
>
> Dawn Airey, ITV

know all about you, your personal circumstances, your family background and so on.

My driver, Don Smith, who has also been with me for fifteen years, is another vital part of my personal team. I'm constantly on the move and need to use every second efficiently, so I need to do a lot of highly confidential work in the car on my phone. A leader has to be able to feel that they can talk about anything in front of their personal team and feel comfortable that it's not going to go any further. It means I can utilise all of my time: if someone else is driving me it's very difficult to have such conversations on the phone.

Hiring the best

So, do you only hire people who have the right qualifications required for the job, or do you hire people who have the right attitude but not necessarily the right previous experience? According to Professor Earl Sasser of Harvard Business School, the latter is usually the best bet. He recommends spotting traits, or life themes, shared by the current best employees and looking for those among job applicants. At its most obvious level this means that if you want to staff a crèche, hire people who like children. To back up this view,

Earl points out that attitudes can seldom be taught, whereas skills can be instilled after someone has started the job. He cites Southwest Airlines as past masters of the recruitment process:

They get lots of applications, because people tell each other that it's a great place to work. Out of 1,000 résumés, they pick forty people and invite them to Dallas for the first stage interview. They put these forty in a large hotel room, seated around the edges. At the front of the room is the person in charge of hiring and development at Southwest, two people from human resources, two flight attendants, and two customers who have given up time from their busy day. The applicants' names are called randomly and they are asked to stand up and describe their most embarrassing moment ever.

You can immediately see how they react to a large group, you can test their sense of humour and their ability to react on the spot because they're picked randomly. Most importantly, the panel is not only watching what people are saying, it's also watching the reactions of everyone in the room. Some people get up, tell a funny story, but others tune them out. Southwest doesn't want them. They're looking for people with empathy.

The philosophy is: 'We hire for attitude, we train for skill.' Out of that group, probably just three people end up being flight attendants. It's a lot of effort, but they have to get the right person to fit the culture.

Earl's other recommended approach is far more simple. Turn the tables and let the right employee select you. Many good sports stores, for example, are staffed with eager young people who know more about the equipment than the manufacturer.

> 'There is an argument for employing somebody with experience so they hit the ground running. I'd rather someone came in with complete naivety, saw what was in front of them and made a decision based on what they see now. Maybe we will make a few mistakes, but at least we are trying something different'

James Dyson, Dyson International

When Archie Norman and I started out at ASDA we wanted to see everybody we hired, even the store managers. We were re-populating the company and had to do that by finding people who would respond to our particular attitude and set of values. We had to really sell the company and our project. We wanted people who were not hung up on status and wouldn't worry about their job description but rather about the contribution they could make. That could be different from week to week. It's very easy to forget when you're recruiting that it's as important that the candidate wants you as you wanting the candidate. You have to sell your company and vision to people, not just go through a selection procedure. After all, nobody swims towards the *Titanic*.

I also think it's absolutely essential to draw from as diverse a range of candidates as possible. I well remember when I was at Mars some thirty years ago being told by the brothers John and Forrest Mars, 'Fifty per cent of the brains of the world are female. And brains have no colour.' I think that perfectly encapsulates why diversity is so crucial. It's not to do with political correctness; it's all to do with getting the best brains together, and I strongly believe that business leaders who fail to recognise this will inevitably suffer, both commercially and in terms of brand reputation. They'll fail to get the best people, and they'll lack the antennae to reach the full range of potential customers. It's worth remembering, for example, that the ethnic minority population of the UK has an annual disposable income of £32 billion.

There are so many moral and business reasons for making diversity a priority, and I think it's becoming increasingly apparent these days that companies that do diversity the best are also the best-performing companies.

Keeping the best

It's hard to believe now, but when Sir Terry Leahy joined Tesco in 1979 he came close to walking out within months. It was only the intervention of a bright colleague that changed his mind – and probably the future of the supermarket chain. Terry was the first member of the marketing department when it was obviously not a valued department. His boss didn't have a marketing background; he was a computer boffin, and Terry ended up in a windowless room, looking at computer printouts. Naturally he thought it was the biggest mistake he'd ever made and spent the first year planning to leave.

'Customer service comes from the heart, not a textbook'

Allan Leighton

'Surround yourself with good, lucky people, and they will make you look amazingly good'

Allan Leighton

Then another person, Keith Clarke, transformed everything. He spotted Terry's potential, spent time with him, built up his confidence and gave him projects to get excited about. That was leadership and it was the only reason Terry stayed.

Terry says he always thinks there is a chief executive buried under a pile of printouts in a room somewhere and I agree. They are anywhere and everywhere. The top person can't seek out all the talent, so there has to be a culture in the business of always looking for good people. Terry himself places a lot of emphasis on seeking out the best people in his company. He'll go into a store and ask, 'How is the talent-spotting going?' Everyone will know what he means. He explains how things are done at Tesco:

> Our company structure is just six levels between someone on the checkout and myself. There's a ladder between every level called 'options'. It's a universal scheme of advancement and everybody in the company knows about it. At any one level, we're looking at one in ten people to be moving to the next level. In a store of 400 people, I want to know about twenty or thirty people who could be a manager, a deputy manager, a section manager or a team leader. In our system, you don't get any points for what you did on the outside. You can join Tesco as a professor, a graduate or with no qualifications at all and we'll bring you in at an appropriate

level. How you get up those levels is down to what you do in the business; nobody glances at your qualifications ever again. People do come from right at the bottom to right to the top.

There's a very democratic quality to that which is very important in life. The bottom fifth of the population has less social mobility than ever. To come into a place like Tesco from a tough area as a sixteen year old and get to the top of the organisation is a tremendous thing. David Potts, for example, who grew up in the toughest part of Manchester, rose to running all of the stores in the UK.

I've recruited thousands of people and have found that one in five of them will be a star; but one in five will be a complete failure. The remaining three will be a mixture. If you start with that attitude it tells you one thing – recruitment doesn't end when people join. Sorting out what you've hired means taking a continuing personal interest in your people and putting up your hand quickly if you get it wrong. If you have the humility to say early on that this person is not right, then you'll save yourself huge amounts of grief. It'll also save the organisation from being populated by mediocrity.

At the same time, you should encourage the good people you want to retain. I'm constantly amazed by the annual appraisal process that most companies run, grading their teams on a scale of 'excellent', 'very good', 'good', 'average', 'below average' and 'unsatisfactory'. People spend hours filling in the forms and where does everybody end up? Average. Eighty per cent of people turn out as average. Would you like to go home and tell your partner, 'I had my appraisal today and woohoo I'm average'? If 80 per cent of people in the company are *average*, why aren't they called *good*?

What does it say to someone who actually does a decent job, to be labelled average? The mid-point on an appraisal should be good. Then, 80 per cent of the organisation are good and they will feel completely different about their jobs.

Constant motivation is crucial. You have to treat your team as champions, not just focus on developing their core skills. Attracting and keeping the best brains is not just a question of paying well, it is about having a stimulating and rewarding working environment. At Carphone Warehouse, for example, Charles Dunstone has invested millions of pounds in creating a fresh, fun atmosphere for his team, both in store and in the company's large West London offices. He knows that he has to create an environment in which staff feel valued (he even took advice from the founders of top restaurant River Café in a well-publicised attempt to improve canteen food at head office). And he knows that people need a stimulating environment, not just a place where they turn up to do their work:

'I see running a company as a bit like having a bank of light bulbs, and they all have to be shining brightly at the same time. It is no good having one corner brilliantly bright, while in another area they are flickering away and in the middle there is one that has gone out and hasn't been replaced for a long time'

Gail Rebuck, Random House

We always talk about whether you're a Carphone Warehouse person or not. That type of person is good team player, is results orientated and makes things happen. He or she is commercially smart and always has the customer in mind; it's only by pleasing the customer that we have a business which will survive.

Carphone Warehouse people laugh a lot and like winning. Winning is hugely addictive for teams and we treat them well, with dignity and respect. We all really believe that we make the world a better place for our customers and the people that work in the business. The culture of the business is informal and collegiate. We're always travelling slightly faster than we can cope with, but everyone knows it's going to be a bumpy ride. It's about creating a common sense of purpose and vision within an organisation. The belief in what we do is one of our greatest assets.

Julian Richer, the founder of hi-fi empire Richer Sounds, is the leader I admire most for the way he treats his people and I have copied his ideas shamelessly. Everyone shares in the success of the company and is rewarded for their hard work. The company has a Rolls-Royce which is lent every month to the best performing branch. He believes that one of the most powerful motivational tools is a simple 'thank you' for a job well done. He also goes further, funding fifteen holiday homes all over Europe for his employees' use. This, and other perks, such as birthdays off work, are designed to create an environment where employees feel valued and are less likely to take time off sick. Like Charles Dunstone, he regards creating a stimulating environment as a major priority:

Keeping the buzz in the business is an ongoing challenge. Motivating the team is not like building an office, or factory, and leaving it at that for twenty years. People want to be motivated and nurtured constantly. As human beings we do want more and more. We started with one holiday home and at last count we have fifteen exclusively for colleagues' use. For a small company we're proud of that investment. It makes an improved quality of life for our colleagues. I also hope that it makes them more loyal, and happier working for us than they would working for any other electrical retailer.

As far as the economics are concerned, the incredibly low rates of theft that we suffer would pay for them several times over. In addition, there are huge financial benefits of reduced labour turnover and absenteeism. If we didn't look after our colleagues we would get poorer service to customers. It's difficult to calculate the cost of that, but it would be significant.

These sorts of programmes are great for staff. They show a sense of fun and, as Julian says, there's a real commercial logic to it. It encourages everyone to become fully involved in the day-to-day

LEADERSHIP LESSONS
› Offer value for money and top quality customer service.
› Employers should mentally, physically and emotionally look after their staff.
› Staff should be motivated to come up with ideas and rewarded if they do.
› Keep it fun.
› Never be complacent.

Julian Richer, Richer Sounds

running of the company. A lot of people pay lip service to looking after their people, but if you don't live and breathe it, it does show.

The power of self-motivation

The revival of ASDA depended very much on the enthusiasm and adrenalin of the team. To maintain the momentum and motivation, everyone was encouraged, and indeed expected, to make improvements without having to be told. The major change programmes were the only initiatives that required approval from the top. Otherwise there was no 'us versus them' culture. We listened to everyone, and we tried not to underestimate how much we could learn from the team at all levels.

I found a similar attitude when I spoke to Stephen A. Schwarzman, chairman and founder of The Blackstone Group, one of the world's largest private equity firms, famed for its multi-billion dollar funds and deal-making prowess. He pointed out that even the newest or youngest person in the firm can have a vital insight, and that giving them scope to express themselves both helps the company and empowers the individual:

My aim is to give people as much latitude as I can, but not put them in a position where they can blow themselves up. That's very destructive to the organisation and the individual. When we're working on a transaction, everyone in the group is invited to critique the project as a potential investment. That critique is done in the same way, no matter how senior the person working on it.

Everyone knows that we're not criticising their work but

LEADERSHIP LESSONS
> Finance is an apprentice business. As the world changes around you, you have to keep adapting, but you cannot stray from the basic principles.
> Exceed your normal capabilities by continuously pushing beyond them.
> Have a zero defect culture. Every number has to be right and every piece of written work perfect.

Stephen A. Schwarzman, The Blackstone Group

trying to help them. We're pointing out the issues they need to work on to eliminate the chance of a significant oversight. Since everyone participates in that exercise and it benefits us all, no one takes it personally. That's a very important principle.

We also let people negotiate deals themselves within certain limits, so they have the sense of mastery and personal growth that's always important to any really capable person. There's a balance to be struck. We give further latitude as people gain experience and achieve success. The key is allowing people to succeed and grow but, at the same time, having sufficient control so that they can't get in trouble. It's a good method, because it hurts no one and helps everyone to help themselves.

As Stephen says, there does need to be a framework in place to control this process. Otherwise things can quickly get out of hand, as Stuart Rose discovered when he took over at Marks & Spencer in 2004:

It was complete anarchy, with devolved responsibility down to the lowest common multiple. You had people who were taking decisions that they were not qualified to take.

Suppose an M&S buyer over-buys by £10 million? I have got 300 buyers – so that is a potential £3 billion over-commitment. That was what was happening before I arrived. We were massively over-committed in stock because nobody was setting simple rules.

Things now are rather different:

Today M&S will give you as much rope as you want to play with and will pat you on the back if you use that rope to your advantage but it will also give you enough rope to hang yourself. What I must not do is give the team enough rope to hang the business as well.

It's clearly common sense not to give anyone too much un-restricted authority, but if you get the balance right the pros of empowering people easily outweigh the cons. And I can't empha-sise enough how important it is to create a culture where mistakes are permissible. If a team doesn't make mistakes, it's pretty certain that they won't be creating successes either. And if you punish failure, you'll create a risk-averse culture, where people believe they'll be hounded if they get it wrong and get little benefit if they get it right. They'll never realise their true potential.

Moreover, just as a good leader can make mistakes and bounce back, so can the whole team, and they can learn valuable lessons from the experience. Many of the most successful companies in history have been prepared to fail again and again when they enter

› There is no Plan B. Get a Plan A – in our case product, service, environment – and stick to it.
› Look for heroes, doers and people who can take the ball and run with it. Then hold him or her up as an example for everyone to aspire to. It is infectious.
› Never be seduced by your own success or believe your own publicity.
› Keep your antennae switched on both in and out of the business, 24 hours a day.

Sir Stuart Rose, Marks & Spencer

a new field. Electronics companies such as Sony and Microsoft, for example, have been vilified for poor products, yet their designers have persisted with version after version until they finally succeed.

James Dyson endured fifteen years of development, 5,127 prototypes and rejection by a string of companies to get his now famous bagless vacuum cleaner to market. Along the way he was ousted from the company he built, sneered at by established players in the market, embroiled in multi-million dollar lawsuits and copied by the competitors who had rejected his idea. He reckons that 50 per cent of his business decisions have been wrong and that 99 per cent of what his research and development department comes up with is a mistake. But he also believes that having a culture in which mistakes are accepted as part and parcel of the process of innovation is crucial:

That is what R&D and running a business is all about and you learn from it. You want people to make mistakes and you want them to take risks. One of the reasons I've always tried to employ graduates, rather than experienced people, is that I don't want staff who live off their past experience. What works today doesn't necessarily work tomorrow. I especially don't want people to come in and say, 'This is what we did before and here's what happened.' In my company everybody feels they're pioneering and that they're making decisions. Surrounding yourself with good people is vital.

Competing aggressively is about making mistakes. Fred Smith of FedEx says you must be analytical about how and why the mistake was made to guard against it in the future:

When you realise that one of your failings, or the lack of an attribute, caused the mistake you have to shore that up with

'It takes iron discipline at the top to stop meddling in people's jobs, thinking that you can do their job better than they can when you should be focusing on skimming across the top of the waves. That is why the people selection becomes incredibly important. You have to develop a great degree of trust. If you can't trust them, then you have made a bad choice'

Fred Smith, FedEx

someone with that attribute who can watch your blind side. People understand that everyone makes mistakes. The old notion of imperial leadership no longer applies.

And, most importantly, says Sir Terry Leahy, try and make all your mistakes ones that you can survive:

> I've never wanted to bet the company. When you place big bets, you get huge leverage, but if one of them goes wrong you could lose the company. Avoiding betting the company does make it harder to grow, but you just have to work harder at other ways of getting growth. In the public sector it's very difficult to make mistakes, because of the very high standards of public scrutiny. People accept no mistakes, even though many more good things might have emerged. That's the good thing about a privately owned organisation: they generally accept that the things that are got right are, on balance, generally more important than the things that went wrong.

'Understand how to interact and deal with people at all levels – after all, profits and cashflow are made by people, not assets or anything else'

Lord Browne

Chapter 7
The Customer is King
Understanding the first rule of business

The voice on the other end of the mobile phone is friendly, but immediately comes to the point. 'Allan, it's Rupert. I'd like to meet with you tomorrow to discuss your joining the board of BSkyB.' 'I'd love to see you,' I replied, doing my best to hide my amazement at the call from this business icon who, until then, I'd never met. 'But I'm going to be in Hull visiting an ASDA store.' 'Fine, I'll see you there,' came the reply. Then he added, 'Is it OK if I get there at lunchtime?'

Rupert Murdoch, the most powerful media baron in the world, immediately put a line through his obviously frantic schedule to walk the aisles of a supermarket in northern Britain. He had made a decision about the BSkyB board and wanted to act on it immediately. His action that day encapsulates everything I admire about good leadership – seizing the opportunity, focusing and getting the job done.

But when Rupert walked into the ASDA supermarket that day, much to the shock of all the store staff who recognised him, the first thing he did was not to bend my ear. Instead he strode over to the newspaper display. Seeing that the *Sun*, the flagship title of his publishing empire, had sold out he picked up his mobile and phoned the then editor, David Yelland.

'I'm in an ASDA in Hull, it's lunchtime and there are no copies of the *Sun*,' he barked. 'Find out why.'

You can only imagine the head-scratching at News Corporation's HQ in London's Wapping. What could Rupert Murdoch, presumed to be safely ensconced in his London base, possibly be doing at a supermarket in Hull counting, or more to the point not counting, copies of tabloid newspapers? But it isn't hard to guess the effect.

You could call this an obsession with detail. And it certainly is. Whenever I visit a store or a depot, I never fail to pick up the phone to the office with a question for the man or woman who is responsible for something that isn't quite right. Not only does it get the problem sorted – and fast – but it also lets everyone know I don't miss a thing. It's also part and parcel of getting things right for the customer.

My first real glimpse into this type of obsession came when I worked for Mars. It was a business founded on core family values, where the founders acted as role models to their people and on a

LEADERSHIP LESSONS
› Keep in touch with the details.
› Get involved.
› Capitalise quickly on changing opportunities.

Rupert Murdoch, News Corp

conviction that product quality was sacrosanct. All this can be traced to Forrest Senior, the inventor of the Milky Way, who helped his father, Frank Mars, turn a moderately successful US-based sweets venture into a multi-million dollar business. The pair fell out when Forrest Senior decided to assert a few of his own ideas, contradicting his father's orders and throwing the factory into turmoil. Forrest Senior demanded one-third of the company, but instead Frank gave him $50,000 and the foreign rights to Milky Way. Eventually, after a spell at Nestlé in Switzerland, where he learned to make European chocolates, Forrest Senior settled in Slough, where he set up a one-room factory making chocolates by night and selling them by day. One of his first products was an anglicised version of the Milky Way, which was a little sweeter than its American counterpart and which he named the Mars Bar.

It was in the UK that the family's guiding principles were truly developed. Forrest Senior paid his associates well, but demanded absolute devotion and dedication. He lectured on quality with the zeal of a preacher and was known to hurl a box of poorly wrapped chocolates across a room. Before their retirement, Forrest Senior's sons, John and Forrest Mars, continued the spirit of perfectionism. Well into my time at Mars we were still all expected to taste-test the pet food. It may not have been the most pleasant of tasks, but it was symptomatic of the family's obsession with getting things right for their customers – including cats and dogs.

Getting your priorities right

It goes without saying that, if you haven't got customers, you haven't got a business. You simply can't be complacent about their loyalty. As the population becomes more affluent and mobile, there are more and more businesses competing for a share of their cash and their heart. A retailer, for example, is not just competing with other stores, but with every other attraction on which the public spends its money, from concerts and cinemas to coffee bars. In fact, the competition for the attention of customers is fiercer than ever before. So you have to listen to them constantly and seek to influence them. This is not so difficult when your business is small but, as it grows, you can lose sight of this essential relationship, distracted with politics at head office or the minutiae of the day-to-day business of running the company. That's why 'management by walking around' is so important. You have to see and hear what is going on. You may chose to turn a blind eye to the problems you spot, because you don't want to address them at that time, but at least you'll know what they are.

Galen Weston, whose retail empire includes George Weston, Loblaws and Selfridges, runs his businesses just as his father, Garfield, and grandfather, George, ran them before him. Apart from being smart and hardworking, the Weston dynasty has one overwhelming trait in common: an addiction to detail. Galen still spends two half days a week visiting his sprawling empire and he has a rather unorthodox way of making sure every detail is just as he likes it. He starts at the back of the store to see what's where and what has been thrown out (as he says, 'If it's not right in the back, then it can't be right in the front'), before going out front.

The first thing I look at is the trash bucket, to see what has been thrown out. The amount of waste tells the story. I once caught a store manager packing trash cans with food so that he could take it home and sell it to friends. It is the most obvious place

to hide stuff. Senior executives often feel too important to go to the back of a store.

When I go into a store, I often follow the buggies and talk to the customers with the store manager. It's best if the CEO or business manager is there too. Believe me, when I ask customers what products they're looking for that they can't find, the answer can be humiliating for the local person in charge. At my best store in Canada, I once spoke to three customers and found there were seventy-five products they wanted which were out of stock.

On a visit, the first thing I always pick up is just the look and feel of a place. Are people turned on? Are both customers and staff moving around? Are they excited to be there? There has got to be life and the smell of interest. I like to see senior people on the floor and I think it's an important example. People like to see and talk to the person whose face is on the cover of the annual report.

Feargal Quinn, who opened his first shop in Dundalk, Ireland, in 1960, when he was just twenty-three, is a similar retail animal, and he was one of the first grocers to understand that customer service would be the main battleground for the

---

LEADERSHIP LESSONS
› Hire good people.
› Listen to the customer.
› Have humility.
› If a store doesn't work, dump it. Don't throw good money after bad.

Galen Weston, George Weston

emerging supermarket industry. In addition to launching the Superquinn chain of twenty-one supermarkets, Feargal has become something of an institution in Ireland. For ten years he was chairman of Ireland's national post office, An Post, and he spent a lengthy period as an independent member of the Seanad Éireann, the upper house of the Irish parliament. In whatever capacity, his number one preoccupation has always been how to ensure people, whether customers or voters, come back again and again.

Along the way, Feargal has pioneered in-store playhouses for customers' children, made-to-order sausages and self-scan shopping. Such was the popularity of Superquinn under Feargal's leadership, before he stepped down in 2005, that many shoppers drove out of their way and past several other competitors to shop there.

Like Galen Weston, Feargal believes that the key to good leadership is accessibility, not just with the staff but with customers as well. Quite often, he says, important changes in the business were implemented as a direct result of listening and talking to customers, and sensing what they wanted:

> Early on we identified that if we were going to give our customers a good experience, and let's remember we are in the experience business not the food business, then we should take the hassle out of what we identified as the most stressful part of the shopping experience – the checkout. A customer is anxious that they will be charged the right price, that they will have enough money, or that something else will go wrong. So we laid on bag packers, we laid on somebody to wheel their trolley out to the car and put an umbrella over their heads if it was raining. People said it would be more expensive but it paid for itself because it generated extra business.

Feargal also emphasises the importance of informal feedback from staff who have gleaned bits of information, suggestions or gripes from customers they happen to have been talking to.

We're not a company that needs to write things down. We used to discuss everything like this at our Monday morning meetings. Once, a man from the Kilkenny branch told his area manager about a customer who said he was confused about the dates on the fresh orange juice. The juice lasts for about 48 hours and they always put the date on it. The customer said that when he opens up his fridge and sees '23 August' he is never sure if it is today, tomorrow or yesterday. It would be far easier, he suggested, if it just said 'Wednesday'. So, we switched to printing just the day on the juice. The customers loved it and the area manager told the Monday morning meeting: by Tuesday it was in all the shops. I told a friend at Sainsbury's about it and he said that sort of change would take them a year. At the time, staff at Sainsbury's weren't told to think. They were told that this is the way we do things.

'There is a lovely Irish proverb which says, "Listen to the sound of the river if you want to catch fish." If you can encourage people to listen to the sound of the river, which is the marketplace, you have a much better chance of having good fishing'

Feargal Quinn, founder Superquinn

This obsession with customer feedback is something you find again and again in successful companies, whatever their line of business. But I think my vote for the best customer service specialist I have ever come across has to go to Julian Richer, the founder of Richer Sounds. Julian began his entrepreneurial career by hiring a chauffeur-driven Mercedes and driving up to the gates of his school, Clifton College in Bristol, to sell cheap hi-fi gear to his friends. He opened the first branch of Richer Sounds near London Bridge in 1978, when he was just nineteen years old. That shop has grown into one of the UK's most successful retail operations and boasts an entry in the *Guinness Book of Records* as achieving the world's highest sales per square foot of retail space. Julian constantly reviews what his customers are getting and what they want, and he has elaborate systems in place for getting feedback at every opportunity. 'We have safety valves at every stage of the customer interface,' he says in his own book on leadership:

On all our receipts there is a short, tear-off questionnaire with just five questions. We ask customers to send the replies to me, at a freepost address. If they don't buy anything but are given a quote they can write to me on the same form. If (even worse) they never got served, but left after standing in a queue, they can still pick up a 'we're listening' card, prominently displayed on the counter, asking them for comments on the service they have or haven't received.

He also repeatedly identifies himself as the company figurehead, in print and photographs, so everyone knows what he looks like and gets the message that he regards himself as fully accountable. In his view:

It is the leader's job to be the public face of the organisation. You don't have to appear in the media every week, but your customers and suppliers should know your name and how to contact you if they have a problem. You should be their guarantee of quality and, if they are unhappy, you must hear about it.

In Richer Sounds' stores there are mirrors with a notice above them, saying, 'This is the most important person in the shop'. It may sound slightly cheesy, but there's no doubt that everybody smiles when they read it. It's an attractively light-hearted way of engaging with customers, and reminds me a little of some of the things we did at ASDA – for example, we staged the first wedding in a store, and a 'Romance in the Aisles' on singles nights. Some of Julian's quirkier ideas have been born of necessity. Early on, for instance, he didn't have enough money to pay for formal security in his shops, so instead he placed a cardboard cut-out of a policeman in each one with a notice, saying, 'Free ride to the police station today for all shoplifters'.

Taking the initiative

It's not all just about listening and reacting. People in business should never forget that they are customers, too. They have daily experience of shops, or entertainment, or some other type of service, and this experience can fruitfully feed back into the mix.

Dawn Airey is a good example of a leader who draws a lot on her own experiences as a consumer to make decisions. She lives and breathes the world of media, having started her career as a management trainee at Central TV, before leaving to head arts and entertainment at Channel 4 and then launch Channel Five (as it was then known). Prior to joining ITV as head of global content in October 2007, she was responsible for more than 500 channels at Sky Networks. What lies behind her much admired commercial instincts is simple: she's a customer too. She recalls that when the ITV network first employed her, and she was plucked from relative obscurity to run children's ITV and daytime, the broadcasting establishment was highly sceptical. They asked how on earth she could possibly know what kids want to watch. Her response was robust:

> Well, I used to be a kid myself and I know what kids want to watch. I take the same attitude with adults. I am a customer. I don't live in a rarefied address. I live in West London and a little village in Oxfordshire. I interact with a lot of people from different walks of life and the media fascinates me, it is an absolute passion. There's a Customer Closeness Programme at Sky, so I used to visit customers' homes with installers, I sold Sky subs in shopping malls and I went to the call centre to hear customers ringing up to buy Sky, or to complain.
>
> I am very conscious and diligent about keeping in contact with customers in a very direct way. Everyone has an opinion about television, which is not surprising because people watch on average 28 hours a week: outside work that's probably the single biggest thing that most people do with their leisure time. So they're bound to be opinionated, knowledgeable and very engaged with the product. I'm actually very fortunate because I'm naturally very inquisitive, so I ask a lot of questions and listen.

› Employ the best people and don't feel
    threatened if they are better than you.
› Leaders should be very self-aware and
    understand the emotional ebbs and flows
    of an organisation.
› No one can predict the future. The only thing
    that is certain is that something will come
    along which no one has thought about and
    disrupt your business model.

Dawn Airey, ITV

At ASDA there were several occasions when I feel we took the initiative in our dealings with our customers. We liked to have out of the ordinary or wacky events because such things have a particular appeal to the British customer and they showed that we didn't take ourselves too seriously. We were also at the forefront of removing the controversial VAT from medicinal products and bringing the price down on toiletries. These were all highly publicised and successful initiatives.

The most memorable ASDA campaign for me, and one that sparked an incredibly positive customer response, came in 1996. Overnight every supermarket had begun to take British beef off their shelves in response to the furore over BSE and the worries about possible links with CJD in humans. We were holding a board meeting at a store in Totton, Hampshire, when we heard about this reaction by our competitors. We thought about it and said, 'No, we're going to throw all the foreign beef off instead.' That night we were the lead story on the BBC's Six O'Clock News. The upturn in meat sales at ASDA was unbelievable. Our share of the British beef and lamb market went up by ten points. It was a controversial time, punctuated by many high-profile claims and counterclaims, but I was comforted by the fact that many experts believed that British beef was in fact safer than the French equivalent. We weren't endangering our customers, and our actions showed that we were very proud to be British. So were our customers, who voted with their wallets.

Saying sorry is never hard to do

Views about customer complaints have changed in modern times. Advances in product quality and high-profile initiatives to promote good service mean that people are much more willing to come forward if a company fails to make the grade. Having said that, the worrying statistic is that around two-thirds of people still don't bother to pursue a complaint, even though the memory of it still sticks vividly with them a year later. The thing to bear in mind here is that that same two-thirds will probably tell at least a hundred people all about their grievance. And everyone knows how powerful word of mouth can be.

This is an issue that has to be grappled with, and, in my view, the only solution is to set up channels to encourage people to

'Give what you want to receive'

Allan Leighton

complain. These can take the form of telephone helplines, pre-stamped customer complaint cards, customer help desks and post-sale telephone calls. At one time I know companies regarded receiving zero complaints as a badge of honour. I, on the other hand, would say that hearing from a fed-up customer is a good thing. It means your listening channels are open and that they believe you care what they think. Of course, leaders want their companies to be perfect, but no matter how hard anyone tries, they'll never quite manage it. If there is room for complaint, and there always is, the essential thing is to resolve the problem and learn from it. Every complaint gives the business an opportunity to improve what it offers customers.

Complaints offer a fantastic opportunity to win increased loyalty from otherwise displeased customers and to improve your relationship with them. Although liability or fault should not be admitted until the full facts are known, the complainant should be listened to in a sincere, sympathetic and courteous way. And, if the company is in any way in the wrong, there should be an apology. Certainly, the customer must never ever feel that they're being put in the wrong. Saying sorry goes a long way.

The team has to be given the authority and initiative to resolve complaints as quickly as possible and should know who to pass them to if they can't deal with them. At the same time, I believe that the member of staff who receives the original complaint should track it to its successful conclusion.

I said earlier that any brand that reaches the top inevitably becomes a focal point for anyone with a grievance, and negative publicity is something that a number of successful companies are faced with. Wal-Mart is a good example in this respect. Its detrac-tors have waged a high-profile campaign against the company over the past few years, alleging everything from unfairness to staff to unethical sourcing of products, plus a fair bit more besides.

In the past, Wal-Mart tended to ignore the brickbats. They operated at an individual customer and associate level and, even when they became larger and were seen to have more of a relationship with society as a whole, they felt that broader criticisms would simply go away. Now, however, under Lee Scott, Wal-Mart are meeting recurring attacks head on. Lee himself has embarked on a media charm offensive, with a crack team of PR experts in the supermarket's HQ aiming to respond within hours to any media criticism. Wal-Mart has set up new offices for community relations, held talks with activist groups about reducing environmental impact and created an internal website called Lee's Garage to improve communication with managers. 'In some ways,' Lee says, 'we felt that the critics had ill will towards the company and wanted us not to be successful; but, for the most part, many of our critics would simply like us to do better.' He goes on to elaborate on this point:

> Many of the environmentalists just want Wal-Mart to be more helpful about their goal of the world becoming more environmentally friendly. As we have listened to them and thought about what we're doing, we have actually created support and found people to help us achieve our environmental goals.
>
> People who are extraordinarily interested in ethical sourcing have a goal not to see Wal-Mart go out of business, but to see Wal-Mart play a leadership role in some of the issues in sourcing around the world. These people have been willing to help us to be better, not to try to do us harm. It's also true in the creation of a diverse workforce, which is certainly in Wal-

Mart's best interests because we have a diverse customer base; there are many people who used to be our critics now working with us to develop our programme to move diversity forward.

Wal-Mart has always had the clear-cut vision 'sell for less', and it's difficult to take on new social perspectives when the one thing that has historically mattered to you is the price of your merchandise. But, here again, by meeting criticism head on and listening to it, benefits can flow for all involved. For example, if you incorporate ethical sourcing into your programme, what you'll find is that you're doing business with better factories and that you're producing better quality items. Often those items are at the same kind of price that you were paying previously because there is now more consistency in dealing with production schedules, removing delivery errors and so on. You've got happier customers, and you've got a better business, too. Sir Christopher Gent at GlaxoSmithKline is another business leader who endorses this way of doing business:

The need to be valued in your community is becoming much more of an issue. There has to be a level of trust, because that trust is your licence to trade. It's absolutely critical in a pharmaceutical business such as GlaxoSmithKline. After all, it's a matter of life or death for the people we care for. This perception of community value is now pretty widely accepted.

He concedes, though, that at present 'there is variable perform-ance in execution' among some major companies in this respect.

The virtuous circle

It's always tempting to think that keeping customers happy and keeping staff happy are two separate issues. But they're not. As Professor Earl Sasser of Harvard Business School points out, they're intimately bound up with one another. His theory, quite simply, is that satisfied, loyal and committed employees produce satisfied, loyal and committed customers who, in turn, drive growth and prof-itability. The rule here is retention, related sales and referrals. If you do a good job the customer will come back to you – retention. If, as in the case of a retailer, the customer not only continues to deal with you, but also gives you a bigger share of their wallet, that's related sales. When the customer tells everyone how good the company is, that's referrals. What's more, if these customers really believe in you, they will become totally attached to you. They'll make suggestions as to how you can improve new products and processes. In short, they will help you with your research and development. They care and have a feeling of ownership of the organisation.

Earl elaborates on this 'service profit chain':

Our simple model says that you have to think about the target market you're trying to reach and get your people to where they are able to serve the customers well.

There are, of course, also negatives to retention, related sales and referrals. The customer might not come back; they could buy less or be negative about the company.

'The balance sheet and the strategy are the hardware of a business which can easily be copied. What can really make a company different is the software, the culture of leadership – how they treat their employees. Treating people as human beings and releasing the potential that everyone keeps secret is what makes a company stand out'

Professor Earl Sasser, Harvard Business School

Most importantly, we discovered that the same indicators applied to employees. It is more of an issue in the States where we have, compared to Europe, more liberal laws on the firing of people and allowing them to leave. But this retention of people is what we want everywhere. Companies need to get more of a share of the employee's mind. You don't want to hire someone to work 35–40 hours a week and just get their body to do a task. If they don't think about stuff, they don't become an owner to the level where it's constantly on their mind. It's important to have share of mind, rather than just share of wallet. You want the team to feel good about it and to tell everyone that this is a great place to work.

The service profit chain starts with a voice, goes to the customers and, if you do that well, you get pretty good results for the shareholders too. They stay with the company because it is producing adequate returns. They might even put more of the company into their portfolio, tell other people about what a good investment you are and make suggestions about how things could be changed.

It's a very simple concept of people, customers and investors. In too many cases companies ignore it and just focus on investors. Then they do things that mess up customers and mess up employees. The leadership chain must treat people as valued resources. It empowers them. It can be an almost spiritual feeling when it becomes more than just going to work and doing their set hours. Everyone wants to get some meaning out of what they do every day.

Chapter 8
Talking to the Media
How to get your message across

In the summer of 1998 it looked as though it was finally going to happen. The potential merger of ASDA and Kingfisher, which had been discussed on and off for years, seemed to be inching its way towards a positive conclusion. Accordingly, early one Saturday morning, Sir Geoff Mulcahy, Kingfisher's chief executive, gave me a ring. He was overwhelming in his enthusiasm to do the deal. 'Let's talk it through today,' he said. 'I'm getting into my car right now and coming to Leeds.'

When Geoff eventually arrived at my house in Boston Spa, after a long drive from London, we held our informal talks in the garden, as it was a gloriously sunny day. The leafy surroundings made a nice change from the sort of venues where I'd spent the frantic previous day, cramming in store visits, a management meeting and marketing review at head office. The talks were pleasant and seemed to be proceeding well. After an hour or so, Geoff got back into his car and drove off, agreeing that we would take things further on Monday morning.

Fifteen minutes later, before we had cleared away the still warm tea cups, my phone rang. On the line with a cheery 'hello' was Jeff Randall, the then editor of the recently relaunched *Sunday Business* newspaper. He came straight to the point. 'I understand Sir Geoff Mulcahy has just been drinking tea in your garden,' he said. 'Are you going to do a deal with Kingfisher?'

It was the call every chief executive dreads – a well-briefed journalist, clearly in possession of the key facts, catches you by surprise. It can easily destroy a potential deal, and in this case it did actually delay things for some months. Neither Geoff nor I had leaked the news of our talks and I'll probably never know who did. Jeff certainly wouldn't tell me: journalists zealously guard their sources. Actually, I suspect things happened quite casually. When stories such as this leak it's often down to a careless executive mentioning just one fact to someone; that someone then says it to someone else; and suddenly it's in the public domain.

A few years ago, if you were a chief executive leading a successful company that was keeping its shareholders happy, you could get away with being a very private individual. Not today. Anyone planning a career at a senior level in business must be prepared for media interest in them and their company. There is now an enormous appetite for rags-to-riches stories or tales of hard-fought hostile takeovers. Even mainstream television is in on the act with a plethora of business-related reality TV shows such as *The Apprentice*, *Dragons' Den* and *Risking it All*. And while it may be hard to identify with visions, concepts or the complex products that characterise many companies, once you wrap ideas around a particular personality, then you've got a story. Every stakeholder, customer, employee, politician and investor wants to know what the person in charge has to say and has a thousand ways of getting information on them, whether through the press, television or via the internet. Jeff Randall, now editor-at-large at the *Daily Telegraph* after a spell as business editor at the BBC, reckons that the appetite among the public for business stories is actually on the increase. If you add to that a point that Rupert Murdoch once made to me – that newspapers have to print everyday, that there are going to be sixty pages, and that no newspaper proprietor is ever going to print an apology saying, 'I am sorry, we only have twenty pages today, as there is not much going on' – then it's clear that more and more space in the media is going to be devoted to business and to the people who lead it. As Jeff Randall says:

> It's become an almost self-fulfilling process. As the papers devote more space to business stories, the general public becomes more aware of who these people are. That familiarity creates a desire for more facts and information. Quite often business can be portrayed as soap opera, and the public locks into that soap opera. They can't wait to know the next stage. The biggest soap opera of recent times was Philip Green and Marks & Spencer. There were daily episodes. Everybody wanted to know what Philip and Stuart Rose were up to today. It was better than *EastEnders* or *Coronation Street* because it was for real.
>
> The story had it all. There were some great characters, plus all the advisers, and, of course, a fantastic brand name. M&S has always had an almost mystical hold over us. It was the perfect soap opera/business story. It was fought out in the press because it was a battle for the hearts and minds of shoppers, as much as anything else. Many of the shoppers were shareholders too. Was it perfect for all the parties involved? No. If they could re-run

> 'In a Plc, your lack of ability to deal with the media can kill you long before the performance of the company'

Justin King, J Sainsbury

the video I'm not sure whether Philip would have had a (much publicised) scuffle in Baker Street with Stuart. But the attention served Stuart quite well.

'Media intrusion' or 'good publicity'?

Cautionary tales about over-exposure in the media abound. Perhaps the most famous victim of his own publicity was Gerald Ratner, who, after joining the family business in 1966, built the Ratners Group into an international jewellery chain. At its peak it was achieving sales of £1.2 billion, but one thoughtless speech to 6,000 directors at the Royal Albert Hall, in which he described a sherry decanter as 'total crap' and poked fun at the fact that his earrings were cheaper than an M&S prawn sandwich, had devastating consequences. It cost him his personal fortune, his job, wiped £500 million off the company value and turned substantial profits into a £122 million loss. Even the name of his family business had eventually to be changed to Signet in a bid to wipe the incident from the nation's memory.

After more than a decade in the business wilderness, Gerald still says that he could kick himself for providing such rich ammunition, and to this day no media commentary about his current business activities fails to mention the 'total crap' incident. But, says Jeff Randall, it was more than just a few ill-considered comments at the wrong time that brought about Gerald's downfall. He had invited the attention by becoming too immersed in the soap opera side of business:

> **Gerald's big problem was that he had become a celebrity. He started to do 'A day in the life of', 'My beautiful home' and all that rubbish. Once you turn that tap on, you're the celebrity, you're the soap opera. Everything you say, therefore, is much more interesting and newsworthy. Gerald went from being some bloke you've never heard of to being that bloke who was on *Through the Keyhole*. There was a very high recognition factor.**

Gerald Ratner is not the only person to have made this mistake. Clive Jacobs of holiday autos fame reckons that he also got burned by inviting too much publicity, though in his case it was a well-intentioned move which grew out of control. He had originally agreed to appear in what was billed an 'educational programme' but the brief subsequently changed after a new producer was brought in and it became a notorious 'fly-on-the-wall' documentary.

I can well understand the temptation, especially when you're desperate for your company to get some publicity, but it seems to be a rule that back-to-the-floor-style documentaries, where company bosses work on the shop or factory floor for an agreed period, finish more careers than they improve. Going back to the floor, or communicating face to face with your workforce, is something you should do naturally; it shouldn't be a stunt for a TV series. The very fact that a chief executive does it for a TV series strongly suggests that they don't do it the rest of the time. You can always tell this when the camera pans around the bemused faces of colleagues. Most important of all, of course, is the fact that you have no control over the final product. The documentary can present you any way it likes.

In Clive's case, he found himself described as 'the most loathsome man on television' following his, albeit unwilling, starring role in the series filmed at holiday autos in 2000 and 2001. At the time, holiday autos was the world's largest car rental broker, with 750,000 cars on its books and hundreds of staff. Clive stole the show, but he also found that reviews drew unflattering comparisons between him and Ricky Gervais's overbearing, jargon-fuelled boss, David Brent, from the hit series *The Office*. Clive was shown berating his customer service team for the volume of irate calls they received and regularly interfering in middle-management decisions. The programme prompted a 40 per cent surge in sales, but, even so, Clive says it was the biggest mistake that he ever made:

> It was heartbreaking. Ultimately, it contributed to my decision to sell the business when I received an approach from lastminute.com. I was poisoned by it and my people were upset because they were very proud about the place they worked. Given my time again I would never agree to it. It so happened the cameras were around at the time when things were a little tricky: we were moving office and my daughter Martha had just been born. I was a bit stressed, but I always lead from the front, so I rolled my sleeves up and sorted things out myself.
>
> The programme completely stitched me up. There's this classic scene where I go into a meeting, and the voiceover says that I've promised to be quiet and listen. Of course, two seconds

later I'm shown interrupting. It was complete nonsense; they edited a two-hour meeting carefully and had a field day.

It really hurt me to read the things people wrote. They were disgraceful; it was spiteful, malicious and very personal. Yet these were people who didn't know anything about me, about what I've achieved or where I've come from. I did get thousands of emails from the public saying they thought it was a great programme and they'd love to work for me, or even see me run the country. But once someone twisted it and likened me to David Brent this image was everywhere. It even found its way into the financial press. How can you compare me to David Brent? He wasn't a businessman. He was a figure in a comedy programme about a little office in Slough, whereas I had built an important business from nothing and was employing thousands of people. Would I trust anybody in media again? Never.

Clive's bitterness shows through strongly here. He evidently didn't realise what a risk he was taking. Jeff Randall, by contrast, has clear and unequivocal views on the dangers of this sort of media exposure:

My advice would be, don't ever do those profiles. Focus on the business. Spend a lot of time explaining the business, what it is

'Good judgement is a result of experience. Experience is the result of bad judgement'

Clive Jacobs, founder holiday autos

you are trying to do and how you hope to get there. Don't do, 'Oh, and welcome to my private life.' It's more compelling to tell a story about a human being rather than a piece of business machinery. But you have to know where the line is. You get some rather flattering profiles in the early stages, but it can very quickly turn into nonsense and in the end into poisonous abuse. A pleasant piece about your lovely home in the south of France can quickly turn into a headline screaming, 'The man who sacked 5,000 lounges by his pool in Nice. How can he sleep at night?'

That's not to say that taking the opposite approach and shunning all publicity is the answer, either. As I've already said, the media is interested in business. They're not going to go away just because you want them to. And since, by the very nature of journalism, most press mentions are reserved for companies in trouble, those company leaders who don't take the time to articulate their views in a public forum, or build a good relationship with the media over a period of time, will find they suffer if the company ever finds itself going through a difficult patch. After all, the moment you find yourself struggling is definitely not the best time to start getting to know sceptical journalists whom you have previously ignored.

The experience of Morrisons' founder, Sir Ken Morrison, offers a textbook example of what I mean. For years he was renowned for his reluctance to communicate with the Square Mile or Fleet Street, preferring set-piece City events based around the annual results presentation. As long as he could point to a track record of more than thirty-five years of unbroken sales and profit growth at the Bradford-based supermarket chain, he felt the need to say very little else. However, the 2002 takeover battle for the rival

Safeway chain, which lined Morrisons up against ASDA, Sainsbury and Tesco, sparked a lengthy government inquiry and suddenly made good public relations a paramount issue.

As the war of words around the Safeway deal escalated, Ken hastily appointed City PR consultants and personally hosted a series of store visits for journalists and analysts. Fortunately, though initially unwilling to get involved, he proved a natural communicator and was adept at getting his message across. The national press wrote glowing reports about the northern-based chain, which many London-based journalists had never previously stepped inside. In May 2004 the *Independent* was still writing about Morrisons' legions of private shareholders, happy to hero-worship the plain-speaking Yorkshire man.

Morrisons' bid was successful but, as the grocer struggled with the integration of the two companies, the media queued up to criticise. The message was clear. As long as Morrisons continued to deliver outstanding results, the City and its commentators were prepared to excuse the eccentricities of its founder. Once things took a turn for the worse, however, Ken had no friends to turn to in the City or financial press. He subsequently became embroiled in a bitter boardroom battle with deputy chairman David Jones. Jones, the former head of fashion chain Next, was far more media savvy and well known among City scribblers. The resultant coverage significantly eroded Ken's power base.

Today, Sir Ken admits that he learned a lot by the experience, but too late:

I don't think I ever had the necessary skills to deal properly with the media. It's not in my nature to be in the limelight. In the past, the only story we had to tell each year was how

we had got a bit better and had increased profits. It was a really simple story that told itself. You didn't need to have enormous skills to do that. It was when we stopped delivering that the problem arose. I've learned an awful lot, but it's late in the day because I'm near retirement. I should have taken it more seriously than I did. Perhaps I was just over-confident. I was never one to get carried away by praise and, frankly, I didn't find the criticism too difficult either. It was just annoying and really bad for morale within the business.

He also makes the important point that charm offensives aren't only about the media:

The biggest stumbling block wasn't the media – the City was not prepared to give us sufficient time. I'd never run the business to please the City.

Alex Brummer, who has been city editor at the *Daily Mail* since 2000 and who has had a distinguished career in business journalism, explains what's going on in cases such as this. 'Journalists do take revenge on companies which don't speak to the media,' he says. 'People who are not communicative reap their own harvest in the end, because the media takes a dislike to them. They say this company is terribly private and refuses to talk to most of the press apart from the *Financial Times*. So the media is always looking for criticism of the way this type of leader runs his companies and so on. We don't want private scrutiny. We want scrutiny of the way they run their business and access to them, that is all.'

'Leadership is about standing up and being counted if something goes wrong. Too rarely do people stand up in the press and say, "Yes, we made a mistake, this is how it went wrong and this is how we are going to fix it"'

Robert Peston, BBC

Most importantly, if something is factually incorrect, a business leader must contact the publication immediately. If they do not flag up the mistake, the article will enter the archives and be used by other journalists as a research tool for future articles – thus repeating the mistake again and again. If the publication agrees there has been a factual error, a note to this effect will be added to the electronic files to warn against future repeats.

Dealing with the inevitable

Even business leaders who are happy to engage with the media have to accept that they can't wholly control the interest there may be or the level of public curiosity. Justin King, for example, who has proved to be a good communicator in a high-profile and at times difficult role at Sainsbury, has found that media scrutiny comes at a considerable personal price. His constant appearances in the press and on the small screen have made him highly recognisable. While he likes nothing more than to get feedback from shoppers on the shop floor and to personally answer letters from his customers, some of the attention, he confesses, he finds challenging:

> There's no doubt that you become public property as a chief executive – sometimes to an unreasonable extent. People now walk up to me in the street when I am in my civvies to talk to me about Sainsbury. They send letters to my home address, even though I'm unlisted. I do think that side of things is deeply worrying. One reason there is a talent drain from public companies and a reluctance on the part of many to become chief executive is that there are things that go way beyond your responsibilities in the job. Politicians inevitably accept the media intrusion as part of the turf. But even they should have the right to absolute privacy on matters that play no part in their political position. I think all this will have a significant impact. You pay a price for it which you weren't aware of when you signed up for the ticket.

I think you have to keep your head when media attention reaches this sort of level. The danger, otherwise, is that it all starts becoming a distraction and you end up doing your job badly. Certainly, this is what I gleaned from Sir Terry Leahy when I discussed with him what it's like running a company like Tesco which, as the UK's number one grocer, features in the business and consumer pages virtually every day. 'It doesn't matter whether we get the media that we deserve,' he says. 'The media is another industry, it has got to do its work and we have got to do ours.' He has the sort of mindset that doesn't get shaken by media interest:

I don't mean to underplay the effect of the media, because our customers and staff read newspapers and they watch television. But it's also important not to overstate the impact of the media – it's just another business selling another entertainment product.

I find that, particularly in our industry, people can weigh what they read against their own experience of working in-store, working with management, working with other members of staff or, most importantly, working with customers. They've got a fairly firm grip on reality and what people are really thinking. Colleagues and customers can read things, but they can also check it out. Customers can read about the supermarket chain, but then shop there every day and form their own views.

Sir Gulam Noon takes a similar view, and feels strongly that colleagues in the business world should not waste too much energy on unwelcome or even negative press. He is probably Britain's best-known Muslim businessman who, as well as donating millions to good causes through the Noon Foundation, has given more than £220,000 to the Labour party since 1997, with the result that he became embroiled in the cash-for-honours row after Tony Blair nominated him for a peerage. Despite the media frenzy, though, he's determined not to be blown off course:

There's an old saying about an elephant walking through the villages of India. The dogs are barking in the background, but the elephant doesn't turn back because he feels he's supreme and so doesn't care. Whatever the objective, business or charity, you mustn't allow negative influences to distract you. Don't waste your energy on negativities. In my life I've made many mistakes, socially and financially. Friends have always told me to correct any mistake that I've made, but in this case [the cash-for-honours controversy] there's nothing I can do. I don't blame anyone for this. When things happen in life, it's how you react that is important. If you react in a negative manner all your life will be bitter. I'm not bitter. I have my business, my friends and my family and nothing else changes in my life. So I'm not sitting in the august House of Lords, so what?

Sometimes, negative publicity actually spurs people on to try to achieve more. Martha Lane Fox is a good example of this. Things for her started going wrong when lastminute.com went public and the share price began to slide alarmingly. She recalls the hostile press coverage and the numerous abusive emails from individual investors. It was a stressful time, but she knew that, first and foremost, she had to remain level-headed:

LEADERSHIP LESSONS
› Pay attention to financial detail – know your accounts and constantly check the health of your business.
› Spend money on research, without it you will be a dead duck.
› If there is a product you want to manufacture make sure, even if you are an absolute wizard in the manufacturing industry, there is someone who is going to buy it.

Sir Gulam Noon, Noon Products

I had to look at the bigger picture and remember that a lot of people had a great experience with us. I had to constantly re-ground myself and remember that it's a give and take relationship with the press. The media was incredibly useful in building the brand; we got acres of free publicity and we couldn't have built our brand without it. I couldn't take that for granted – it worked both ways.

Ultimately, she and Brent Hoberman decided that the only way to deal with the criticism was to use it as a motivating force to encourage lastminute.com's staff to prove their detractors wrong. It proved a turning point.

Telling the story

There will always be clear differences in what the media wants to write about and what the business leader wants to say. This anomaly makes many chief executives, particularly newly promoted ones, cautious of the business press. They instinctively prefer a more low-key, conservative approach. No matter how they feel, however, there are a few definite do's and don'ts when it comes to talking to the media.

'I do bear a grudge. I don't like being lied to and I don't like being treated like an idiot'

Jeff Randall, *Daily Telegraph*

Rule number one is, never lie. Not ever, not even to get yourself out of trouble. The most unforgivable sin in a journalist's book, far worse than inaccessibility, is to lie to them. And if a business leader ever tells an outright lie to a journalist, their name will be indelibly marked in that journalist's little black contact book. Alex Brummer at the *Daily Mail*, for one, has strong views on the subject:

> The worst thing anyone can do is lie, and that actually happens quite a lot. I have one very recent example of an outright lie from a public relations executive inside a company. I had an excellent high-level internal source, very close to the chief executive of the company. I asked the question and they lied to me. I didn't run the story because I thought I couldn't stand it up, but two weeks later it happened. That company has completely messed up because that PR person blotted their copybook. My image of that company is badly damaged by that lie.

Getting things wrong unwittingly can be a media crime, too. Although a speedy response is often vital, particularly if there's a major emergency or disaster, getting the facts right is just as important. *Financial Times* editor Lionel Barber says the most senior person in the organisation has to be in the eye of the storm, facing the press and speaking to those who have been affected. But, he is quick to emphasise, they must speak from a position of authority:

> If there's a gas explosion at a chemical plant, the company will want to find out what happened before they wheel the CEO out. Anything he or she says, especially in America, could end up with them being sued. You would be crazy to react before you

knew the facts. They could present a holding position, saying we intend to find out the facts, but beyond that I would be a bit careful.

The second and related rule to never lying is, always be sincere and straight. The ideological reason for this is that it's an essential quality for any human being, and that includes good business leaders. The more practical reason is that if you're not sincere, you'll get rumbled. This is particularly true when the broadcast media are involved. Robert Peston, the BBC's business editor, is adamant on this point. 'If, at the back of the leader's mind,' he says, 'there is a faint fear that there are parts of the organisation where customers are being ripped off, or they are not 100 per cent confident about what is going on, then the camera finds them out.' There will always be times in every company's life when the odd article is unfair or negative. It's also inevitable that when a chief executive tells it how it is, highlighting a mix of good and bad influences, the journalist will write more about the negative side. But it still pays to be straight with people. Agonising about how a story might look and what spin is needed is a waste of time. Frankly, the interviewee has no idea what other information the journalist has and who else they've spoken to.

In exactly the same way, becoming flustered – a very common mistake made by executives when being questioned by the media

'Credibility is slow to build and quick to evaporate'

Allan Leighton

– is always immediately obvious and definitely to be avoided. Journalists have an alarming habit of being able to smell fear. So if you're not well prepared, and confident of what you're talking about, you will come a cropper. You have to stay focused on the message you want to get across and not be fazed by questions that fall outside your area of expertise. Robert Peston, again, has some useful hints about interviews on radio and television:

> You have got to keep it simple and clear. The BBC's main channels have an audience running into millions, with vastly different knowledge of what is going on, so you have to avoid technical language. The key thing is to have a very clear view of what it is you are trying to say. Business leaders get into a mess and a muddle when they don't really know what their company stands for and what they do. Good communication flows from having a straightforward and coherent strategy. If you are on top of what your company is doing, then you will probably come across pretty well on TV.

My own tips for dealing with TV and radio interviews, based on hard-earned experience, would be as follows:

- Remember who your audience is – usually your customers and your staff. Whether you are nice or not to the TV presenters is irrelevant.
- Be natural and don't waffle. Your interview should be like a conversation – the viewer is someone who is simply listening in on a conversation between two people.
- Be very clear what it is you want to say and don't be fazed by questions outside your area of expertise. Stick to your message.

- Don't spend hours being coached on potential questions by your communications team. A prepared answer always sounds like a prepared answer.
- If a reporter wants to ask you a stupid question live on air, tell them it is a stupid question.
- Recognise you know 5,000 times more about the subject than the interviewer does. Stifle the natural tendency to go into these interviews thinking your interrogator knows 5,000 times more about it than you do.
- Don't be like a politician and dodge the issue – viewers don't like that. Your audience might not agree with you, but they prefer to be told it as it is.
- The most important thing about the interview is the message people come away with.

Some people, when backed into a corner or asked to talk about something they'd rather avoid, adopt a haphazard 'no comment' approach. I don't think this is a good idea. Those two words enable a journalist – and their audience – to infer almost any meaning they wish, usually the one you least want aired. No one has such control over the media that they can stipulate that favourable stories should be run and unfavourable stories sat upon. You can only use the 'no comment' route when you've already been pretty open and have been asked to talk about a very specific topic that you know to be off-limits. For example, if you know you can't talk about something for legal reasons, you can definitely say so, and if you have built a good relationship with the media, the journalist will understand. Patience Wheatcroft, former editor of the *Sunday Telegraph*, points out that, because business journalists have to return to the subjects of their stories again and again, it's not in their interest to do someone down for the sake of it:

> Jeopardising relationships, just in search of a sensational headline, is not as prevalent in business reporting as it is in the media generally. I have some sympathy with a company that thinks that a deal is never done until it is done and dusted. There's no mileage in them saying that, for example, it's on the way. A 'no comment' works. It's a very foolish journalist who reads too much into a 'no comment'. Saying no comment if you really don't want to comment or can't comment seems to me to be the most sensible way to behave. There's a risk that some journalists go away and think no comment means they are definitely doing the deal. I wouldn't take that risk.

Just as throwing 'no comment's around is not a good idea, hiding behind a PR machine, particularly when the going gets tough, is certainly not the answer either, according to Lionel Barber at the *Financial Times*:

> It's regrettable that you can now barely talk to a businessman without their having a PR person in the room. The CEO should feel they can have a relationship with me based on trust. If I'm having lunch with a CEO I don't want anyone else there and if they don't like it, too bad. PRs do have a function, but not when editors meet chief executives. To be honest, they shouldn't need to be there.

He has some useful tips on the etiquette of a conversation with the media:

CEOs have to be in full agreement about the terms of the conversation. I don't have a lot of time for people who come in and say, 'this is off the record' or 'that is off the record'. During the resultant conversation nobody knows where they are. The terms of engagement have to be clear. If somebody comes to lunch at the *FT*, I say that it's on background, meaning that we can't use it. We do take notes, but we won't write a story based on them unless the CEO agrees. If there is a story, then we should be able to use it. Otherwise what is the point of the conversation?

Jeff Randall similarly has some trenchant views on the whole issue of off-the-record and on-the-record briefings:

I understand three things about these briefings. Off the record means not to be quoted; on the record, everything can be quoted; non-attributable means I can quote it, but not name the source – in other words, I'll say, 'A leading figure in the oil industry said to me today . . .'

There is one other key aspect. If I find out that Miss X is having an affair with a very senior businessperson, I own that intellectual property and can do with it whatever I want. If Miss X comes to me and says, 'I am having an affair with a very senior businessman', I believe that she owns that intellectual property because she brought it to me and I didn't know it. I am now prepared to play by Miss X's game. There is a morality there: she brought the story to me stone-cold and I knew nothing about it, so she has a right to control that story.

Quite a lot of businessmen know this and abuse it because they then make journalists insiders. I can think of one who is a master at it. He says, 'Look, Jeff, you can't use this for the time being, but . . .' and then he tells me something really interesting. Of course, then I'm an insider and compromised by it. He knows I won't write it. Now I think very carefully before I say, 'OK tell me.' I sometimes say that I don't want to be told whatever it is because I can find it out for myself. The vast majority of business people are not that scheming. But one or two are.

It all comes down to having good relationships with a few trusted key journalists. If these are in place, then off-the-record briefings definitely have their place. After all, they are the honour system on which the whole world of press and communication relies. Without off-the-record briefings many of the most famous scoops would never have seen the light of day. Journalists love these so-called 'deep throat' contacts and pride themselves on the number of contacts they have who are happy in off-the-record territory. For the business leader it is well worth the investment in time to occasionally invite a trusted journalist for a cup of tea and a chat. You don't have to have a world exclusive at your finger tips to tempt them over – they will be flattered to be asked and the experience can be very rewarding for both parties in the future.

I reckon it's a good idea for anyone who has to talk to the wider media on a reasonably regular basis to get some training.

'Get to know the journalists you think count, who are influential and you can trust. If they understand your story, you are much more likely to get a fair shake'

Jeff Randall, *Daily Telegraph*

As Robert Peston at the BBC says, 'If you are a business leader who expects to go on TV regularly, then it would be foolish not to get some advice on how to look relaxed and dress and what language to use. Good leaders, like the rest of their workforce, should never rest on their laurels and think there is nothing left for them to learn. It is a good idea to acquire the fundamentals of broadcast.' For those business leaders who are not confident about their ability to build close, one-to-one relationships with senior journalists, financial PR is an option. Since the concept of financial PR took off in the 1980s, the industry has been growing at a terrific rate. The agencies have close relationships with the financial press and can talk up the prospects of a particular company, or conversely plant negative stories about competitors. These financial spin-doctors wield enormous influence. Most importantly, the big players have the ear and respect of the key editors, such as John Waples at *The Sunday Times*. He looks at it like this:

> **Financial PR has become immensely powerful and there are some very eminent players in the industry. If the best people are advising, then the press knows that the company will abide by the rules. I've nothing against financial PRs and nothing against spin. Spin makes business journalism more interesting. If two companies are engaged in a takeover, there's always conflict. The only way the conflict becomes interesting is if people are prepared to speak out on either side and feed information to the press. Whether it's questioning the accountant on one side, or the serial cock-ups on the other, if PRs are prepared to spin it's really helpful. It helps to be led to weaknesses on both sides that perhaps the journalists may not have seen themselves.**

Ultimately, though, I still think it's best to get out there and front things yourself. My philosophy is that it pays to be accessible. That is not to say I am at the beck and call of journalists 24/7. The communication process needs to be carefully managed. The handful of journalists with whom I have built relationships know they can call me any time on a story. But, I have to confess, I always keep my mobile phone switched off. That way they have to leave a message and I can control where, when and what I say.

The sort of direct contact with the media I believe in really comes into its own when there's a major problem. Businesses are often very bad at preparing for a crisis, but it's at just such a time that good relationships with the media are invaluable. A crisis managed well not only limits the damage to a company's reputation, but can actually enhance it. By contrast, if it's handled badly, it can destroy a brand completely, or at the very least cause a fall in both sales and the share price. The media is seldom neutral – it is either for you or against you. I firmly believe that if it is truly against you, the best you can ever hope for, even if you handle the crisis in textbook fashion, is a draw. You will never win because you will never change their minds outright.

Of course, it is important to establish whether the problem is a media storm or a customer storm. You can survive a media storm, but if it is a major issue with customers it is unlikely that you will.

A media crisis doesn't have to come about as a result of a major event, such as a train crash. It could be a security breach, a product recall, employee harassment or fraud. Sometimes they begin as a small issues that escalate because they are ignored. If the business leader doesn't get on top of the situation and manage the flow of information, the media will do it for them and a rash of speculation will fill the vacuum. It's not enough for a chief executive to stand up, make a stirring speech and believe they've done their bit. The media, not companies, decide when the crisis is over. Someone once likened it to wrestling a gorilla – you take a break when the gorilla does.

I really admire the way Richard Branson handled the derailment of one of his Virgin trains in Cumbria in February 2007. His swift action in getting to the scene and speaking to the injured and the family of the pensioner killed in the crash sent an extremely powerful message, as well as being the right thing to do. The way he praised the bravery of train driver Iain Black made people feel that this was not just a piece of PR but that Branson was genuinely involved and concerned. He is the master at this and that is why the Virgin brand is so strong.

Sometimes, by going on the offensive, rather than waiting for the skies to fall, you can actually turn things around to your own advantage. I always remember one occasion at the Royal Mail when we were embroiled in a classic row with the postal regulator. We were about to be fined over something or other, and I knew that if I didn't do something quickly I'd spend the next morning looking at endless negative headlines. I decided to grab the initiative, and made a statement in which I described the regulator's ruling as 'Pythonesque'. It worked like a charm. Instead of running stories along the lines of 'Regulator Fines Royal Mail a Big Sum of Money', every paper led with 'Royal Mail Chairman Accuses Regulator of Being Like Monty Python'. All our people were overjoyed.

'Forget keeping bad things out. If there are bad facts out there, they will come out'

Jeff Randall, *Daily Telegraph*

Failing to communicate at all is never, as I've already said, the right answer. Airline Pan Am hid behind a wall of silence when its aircraft crashed at Lockerbie in 1988. The company subsequently lost nearly 15 per cent of its transatlantic business and eventually went bust. By contrast, when a British Midland plane crashed at Kegworth in 1989, chief executive Michael Bishop was on the scene quickly, talking to the press and others, showing he was in control. The airline lost no business as a consequence.

Fat cats on the radar

No examination of the relationship between business and the media would be complete without some discussion of the 'fat cat' issue. It's something that first came to prominence in 1995, when there was much publicity over a pay rise given to Cedric Brown, chief executive of the newly privatised British Gas, as well as the boardroom bonuses at lottery operator Camelot. Patience Wheatcroft, for one, predicts that the emotive issue of high executive compensation is one that will increasingly grip the public's attention and will therefore be relentlessly pursued by the press. 'The greed at the top of business,' she says, 'is becoming a real issue. It's going to become counterproductive and the media will focus on it.'

> A lot of it goes on in the City, where bonuses are huge, and structured so that even the secretaries tend to do quite well. But if you look at our big companies, and the different growth rates between salaries at the top and the bottom, there is an issue and it is a cause for public alarm. Even quite middle-class people,

who normally would be very pro-business, are beginning to remark upon it. The multiples at the top compared with those at the bottom are enormous, probably greater than they ever have been and good leadership would do something about it. The answer has to be a bit of restraint. Turn that ratio around so that those at the bottom do get more, whether it's through bonuses or shares.

The press lap up issues like these and people say they love reading about them, so it's quite understandable that the subject of executive remuneration should become a major story.

I'm going to put my cards on the table and say that, in my view, people should be paid to do a job and if they're running a successful company, such as Tesco or Barclays Bank, then they deserve to reap the rewards. The fact that a particular company does well is not a coincidence. It's because it has good people running it on a day-to-day basis. When I think businesses score an own goal is when they reward someone who's running a company that's clearly a basket case, shedding jobs all along the line and clearly under-performing. It's not surprising that in such cases the media talk about 'snouts in the trough'. Similarly, I think it's very foolish for business leaders to ram their success down other people's throats. In a funny sort of way, I suspect it's often not the money itself that causes the antagonism, but the trappings – the boats, planes etc.

I'll leave the last word here to Sir Christopher Gent. He became a target for media wrath in 2000 when unions and shareholders tried to block a £10 million performance bonus following the takeover by Vodafone of German mobile phone group Mannesmann. He's not embarrassed about the rewards he received

> 'Reputation probably matters now more than ever. If you get things wrong and don't know how to manage it, you can see your share price go through the floor'
>
> Lionel Barber, *Financial Times*

then, and says that if the principles behind compensation are consistent, then they are both sensible and defensible:

> It's a marketplace and will ever be so. It's very important that if people are rewarded well, it is on the basis of performing well. If you don't perform, you don't get rewarded, or you go. There should be alignment between compensation, business performance and shareholder benefit.
>
> If you're a rainmaker and can make things happen for your clients and the people you work for, then you'll command a premium. Those sorts of people really are worth their weight in gold and will be rewarded accordingly. I understand that people and the press find that difficult to cope with. But the real risk takers and wealth creators will create wealth for themselves if they are successful. That is the way the world should be. One needs incentives, motivation and rewards.

Chapter 9
Talking to the Moneymen
How to keep both sides happy

Everyone talks about the private jets and helicopters, the annual seven- or even eight-figure bonuses and the A-list celebrities hired to entertain them at glamorous soirées. Yet no one really knows much about the mysterious world of the small band of top moneymen who buy and sell vast corporations or advise the globe's top companies about mergers and acquisitions and how to fund them. These powerful figures rarely, if ever, give media interviews, partly because of the punishing hours they work, but also partly because what really matters to them is their relationship with perhaps just a handful of key business chiefs and trusted lieutenants. At its simplest, they just don't need to talk to anyone else.

The secrecy, combined with the huge amounts of money involved, make some of the big deals seem the stuff of paperback bestsellers. Here, for example, is Simon Robey, of investment bank Morgan Stanley, on the subject of the turbulent – and very public – bid for Marks & Spencer in 2004.

Firstly, we had to change the chief executive instantly. I got involved [as adviser to M&S] on the Thursday that Philip Green was rumoured to be about to bid. By the weekend we had replaced the then chief executive Roger Holmes with Stuart Rose. There was such urgency that we had to get completely on top of the thing.

Paul Myners was the new chairman, Stuart Rose was the new chief executive, I was the new banker and the other senior banker, Robert Swannell of Citigroup, was also new to M&S because Stuart had brought him in. The top four people, who were running the kitchen cabinet and steering the defence, didn't know each other particularly well, other than Robert and Stuart. I'd never met Paul or Stuart before, so we were all feeling our way and growing together, which is very unusual in a defence. I had to find a way of quickly establishing trust and credibility and a level of personal friendship. It was the most challenging set of circumstances where I had to instantly establish relationships.

It was not a bid played by conventional rules. We were trying, as you always do in these things, to stay a step or two ahead, or at least never fall behind, our opponents. But in this case, Philip and Goldman Sachs were playing by different rules – very few, if any, rules at all, to be honest. We had to be flexible about the way we thought about things. In normal deals you follow a timetable and people like me get involved along the way at particular points. In this case, things changed daily.

The whole thing was extremely challenging and entertaining and these things don't come round too often. It was also gruelling. We worked on it seven days a week, for many hours a day, for many weeks on end. It is very intense, but in some ways like playing sport. You try and win and play very hard, but when it is over you can all be friends.

LEADERSHIP LESSONS

› Always tell the truth. A lie will get found out.
› Never bullshit people. Give them the hard messages as soon as you feel they need to hear them.
› Have a thirst for self-improvement. Step back a couple of times a year and ask how good a job you are doing for your clients, your team and on specific goals. If your colleagues see you placing demands on yourself, it is easier to place demands on them.
› Listen to your team. The advice you give will improve and they need to know that they can influence things.

Simon Robey, Morgan Stanley

It's stirring stuff, but this is only one aspect of what the moneymen do. On a day-to-day basis, they are also the people who help businesses stay on course. Once upon a time, they had the reputation for doing deals regardless of any drawbacks – after all, they only get the big money once a transaction is signed and sealed. Now, though, they're just as likely to advise against doing a particular deal if they think it's not in their client's interest. To someone like Bob Wigley, Merrill Lynch's chairman of Europe, the Middle East and Africa, this is an essential part of what he does: nurturing his client, thinking through the implications of possible strategies. He recalls once getting a call from a company chairman whom he had never met, asking for a meeting. 'I said, "Sure, any clues as to why?" He told me that he'd heard about me from his chief executive, who said that I'd advised him against doing a deal. He said, "I've never heard of a banker telling a company not to do a deal before, so I thought I had better meet you."'

Bob reckons that the relationship between an investment banker and their client these days can be similar to that between a doctor and patient. They want to talk to you about things they can't talk to anyone else about and good bankers help look after the health of the company. They will be confided in because they stand outside the organisation and can play the part of a dispassionate adviser. As Bob says, 'At least half of the conversations I have every day start with the words, "Please keep this to yourself." In fact, I have few conversations that are not at least partly confidential and most of them are confidential to the point of total secrecy. If a client thought for a second they couldn't trust you, then that would be your last conversation.' But in such a hermetically sealed environment it's possible to discuss the most sensitive topics:

How do I fire the finance director? What do I do about this potential profit warning? I've got a problem in my ball-bearing division, how am I going to deal with that? They need someone who isn't part of the management team to unload some of these issues on and work out the right answer. If you're good, they'll call you about anything, no matter how confidential.

David Mayhew, chairman of JP Morgan Cazenove, takes a similar view. In some ways he seems to fulfil the City stereotype that so many people carry in their minds. He has an alarmingly

› Interact with people or you will not get the
best out of them.
› Never forget that clients come first.

illustrious reputation; it has been said that when David walks into
a City dining room, others fall silent, nudge each other and crane
their necks to see who he is with. When we first met he was
stationed in an elegant eighteenth-century brick townhouse tucked
into the corner of Tokenhouse Yard, a cul-de-sac behind the Stock
Exchange and Bank of England. Its entrance was guarded by a
uniformed porter, and its richly panelled rooms, where multi-
million pound bids were hatched, were presided over by a butler
who served drinks on a silver tray. But underneath the strict dress
code of highly polished brogues, cufflinks and expensive pin-stripe
suits, David is a down-to-earth man of impressive common sense.
I got to know him when I was at ASDA, and he always gave me
great advice on a variety of potential strategic moves. His policy
is never to tell a chief executive or chairman what to do; he waits
to be asked and then confines himself to observing what the consequences of a particular course of action might be. 'The role of
chairman or chief executive is quite lonely,' he says. 'Everyone can
ask questions upwards without great concern, but asking down
the way is different and can suggest uncertainty, which a lot of
people find difficult to handle. In that respect the role of a trusted
outsider is that of someone to bounce ideas off.' He goes on to
elaborate on what he sees as his part in running a business:

It is rather important that people don't feel that I know all the answers. None of us do and no one's going to get everything right. They want advisers to converse with them by listening rather than preaching. It's important to listen. I have never pretended to know how to run a retail store, or a technology company, or an insurance company, or a bank; but I may have a view, because I have seen a lot of people trying to do it.

If you spread yourself across a wide range of business, you don't know as much about any particular one. Your view is a product of your own prejudices and perspective. The guy actually running the shop is going to know more. They may, however, miss some of the advantages of being able to stand back from it. In that respect an adviser can sometimes help to unclutter people's thoughts and distil them down to the really important issues.

This 'psychiatrist's couch' approach to giving advice is also the way that Marcus Agius works. He spent thirty-four years at the independent bank Lazards before moving on to become chairman of Barclays Bank in January 2007. He believes that this sort of softly-softly approach can work throughout the upper echelons of a company:

Very often, in my merchant banking life, one of my clients rings up with a fantastic idea they want to talk over with me. So you go around, get the fantastic idea – and it's unworkable. Of course, you can't really say it's unworkable, and no one expects you to. What you do say is that it's interesting, and you need to think about it. Then you ask them if they've thought about this and if they've thought about that. Little by little you absorb the force of the punch. You gradually defuse the idea and help the client realise it.

In many ways it can work the same way with a chief executive. They want to be headstrong and come up with ideas, so the chairman has to absorb the force of their personality. You don't stick your chin out to absorb it, or it leads to pain on both sides – you roll with the punches. It's the same thing around the boardroom table. If someone is trying to be a bit aggressive you absorb the energy of the challenge and then regroup and go forward.

Marcus rightly says that merchant bankers deal in corporate life and death. 'According to the statistics, the average FTSE chief executive has tenure of about four years,' he said. 'He has got there after around thirty years of climbing the greasy pole.' He goes on:

By and by, along comes some smart investment banker saying, 'Here's a good idea', and tables the transformational transaction.

LEADERSHIP LESSONS

› There are few laws in investment banking, but the most important is to think, 'What is going to happen next?' Don't just think about what you are working on, but about what you haven't thought of. The process is always dynamic, never static.
› Spinelessness is weak and wrong. Never duck the difficult questions: they usually get worse.

Marcus Agius, Barclays Bank

If it works out well the guy's a hero. If it craters, he's toast and his career may never recover.

In these circumstances it cannot be surprising that leaders, however hard-bitten they might be, get a bit anxious. They look over the cliff and see the surf pounding on the rocks 300 feet below and realise just how close to the edge they are. When that happens they can find it difficult to think rationally – not impossible, just difficult. What the leader needs then is an adviser who can be trusted and who can be counted on to be objective. There are extraordinary moments when a business leader turns to the banker and asks, 'What should I do?' At that moment you have his corporate life and thirty years of history in the palm of your hand. It's a powerful moment.

It can sometimes be the case that you do build up great relationships with a few trusted financiers, only to find them on the other side in some crucial deal. For example, when I was working with Galen Weston's Wittington Investments to buy Selfridges in early 2003, I found that Bob Wigley, a man with whom I had worked when at ASDA and several times since, was advising on a rival bid by the management. The following year, I found myself working with Bob once again when I did some work with Philip Green on the unsuccessful bid for Marks & Spencer. This time, however, I found Simon Robey and David Mayhew lining up against us on the management side. I don't think, however, that our relationships were harmed by this swapping between teams. We all had the attitude that you win some, you lose some.

The best financiers understand the need to foster personal relationships. I remember, when Archie Norman and I first started at ASDA, that Bob Wigley, who at that time was at Morgan Grenfell,

› Focus on what matters and do it with
   excellence.
› Surround yourself with people who can do the
   things you can't do.
› Be completely intolerant of anything that is
   not a first-class performance.

Bob Wigley, Merrill Lynch

saw a press report that we were considering moving our business to Lazards and he got on the phone to Archie immediately. That in itself was not remarkable. Archie had already received several calls from the Square Mile that morning. But Bob's question to Archie was, 'Can we come up [to ASDA's headquarters in Leeds] to see you?' Every other City institution had asked when Archie would be able to visit London to hear their pitch. Archie was duly impressed, and four days after that initial press report, the Morgan Grenfell team were in Yorkshire making their first pitch. They became our advisers the following day. Bob quickly became part of the team. In 1999, when ASDA was sold to Wal-Mart for £6.7 billion, he was with us every step of the way.

Given the sums of money involved in so many deals these days, it may seem slightly surprising that these sort of personal relationships are so important – but, as I've already said, much of what a good banker will do for their client doesn't involve deals, and, frankly, even when big deals are involved, the fact is that people don't tick differently simply because a lot of cash is at stake. They still need others around them they can talk to and trust. Bob thinks that this personal element is an absolutely essential part of what he does:

> My attitude is to get in front of the person physically. One great weakness in our industry is that everybody thinks you've got to turn up with a book containing a big presentation. Actually, the best meetings are the ones where there's no agenda. You're there to talk about what the client wants to talk about and you go with the client's agenda. You have to be able to react and say something substantive and meaningful to the client without a presentation book. A book is a huge distraction. It just interrupts what the client wants to discuss.
>
> I've seen so many investment bankers walk into a room, say hello, sit down with their presentation, deliver their presentation, shake hands, say goodbye, and leave thinking they've had a great meeting. They've probably told the client nothing that he wants to know and the client may have had three things he wanted to talk about that were not even covered.

Short-termitis

So far I've talked about the positive things that the financial community can do for business leaders. But the experience is by no means always idyllic. The biggest complaint about the Square Mile or Wall Street is that institutions and major shareholders force public companies to be too short term in their approach. Ken Morrison of Morrisons is one among many who has found the demand for instant and ever better results unrealistic and debilitating. 'There's a great deal of short-termism now,' he complains, 'but I've always thought that we'll be here next year and the year after and so on. In some ways I'm a little grateful that my career is drawing to a close; I won't have to contend with that short-termism.'

James Dyson feels a similar sense of irritation and frustration. He encountered appalling apathy and lack of imagination when trying to raise private equity for his innovative Dual Cyclone vacuum cleaner. Ultimately, he had to sell licences to America and Japan in order to raise money. Although he has often spoken out against British industry for not doing enough to look after its own and stifling the potential regeneration of the country through engineering and design, he is also enormously critical of the financial community for being too inwardly focused and reliant on short-term deals. He reckons that when he went around the City, they simply weren't interested in putting money into a manufacturing venture. They were far more interested in endeavours that would give a quick return, and that they could get out of quickly if problems arose – retail and service industries, for example. 'There was a lot of head-scratching in the City,' he recalls, 'and comments like, "Oh, it doesn't have a bag." One or two of them were reasonably honest and just said they weren't going to back an engineer.'

I'm used to the fact that an engineer is considered a crank. But I was disappointed. I had proved the technology worked, proved the punters were interested in it and buying it, but they still weren't interested.

They had to make a judgement about me and whether the product would be successful or not. Manufacturing and R&D is a long-term thing. We spend up to £60 million a year on R&D, an enormous amount, but the new motor we've got in our

Japanese machine took ten years to develop. It is a long, long payback. I can't imagine a City banker wanting to wait ten or twelve years. But my counterargument is, I started with £2,000 and now have a £1.5 billion business because I was prepared to think very long term.

This is not an uncommon view. Sir Philip Green, for example, has refused to have anything to do with public companies since his experience in the early 1990s at Amber Day, a quoted menswear retailer where he had been chairman and chief executive since 1988. When the company suffered a series of profit downgrades, investors demanded his head. He left in 1992, and although he received £1.1 million in compensation, the whole experience rankles, even now. As he says:

I worked no less hard at Amber Day owning 10 per cent than if I owned 20, 30 or 100 per cent. It was a horrible, thankless task of being accountable to people who have no concept of how, what or where. It was a miserable experience. The irony is, if the City had left me alone, they might have made several billion with me. A lot of the deals I have done since might have been in that public company. The very first time I looked at Storehouse or Bhs was in 1990, planning a deal using Amber Day paper. I also employed a consultancy group at the same time and did a report on the potential for a break-up of Sears. Then the world changed.

I have not owned a public company share since the day I sold that stock. That was a lesson for life. I don't buy shares, because then I would not be in control of my own destiny. Over the last five years lots of deals have been done in which I have been offered an interest, but I am not a good minority shareholder.

Running a public company is fundamentally different from being an owner. I don't want to own 10 per cent and do 100 per cent of the work. It engulfs your whole life and you end up spending a huge amount of time selling yourself to people who have probably never been in your shop.

What is fundamentally different now is I go to a bank and I have only got to sell myself or my concept once. They either lend me the money or they don't. It is me and them. They leave you to get on with it and you sink or swim. Whereas, in that public arena, you are continuously working out how to sell your story. It is like needing a new investor every day. What sort of life is that?

Some very senior financial figures would go along with this analysis. Peter Peterson, for example. A legendary US banker and author, who served as Secretary of Commerce in Richard Nixon's cabinet as well as chairman of the Federal Reserve Bank of New York and his own investment firm, The Blackstone Group, he feels that 'short-termitis' can have a debilitating effect:

Executives are under immense pressure to provide earnings guidance and, if they miss the quarterly target by just a penny or two a share, they end up getting severely punished in the market price. The theory is that business leaders should be concerned about the future, but short-termitis puts immense pressure on short-term results. There may be some highly desirable restructuring steps or long-term investments that get avoided because of the impact on short-term earnings. There's an inevitable lumpiness to earnings in business: it's unnatural that every quarter you have to go up. The market doesn't seem to understand that notion, and what it's doing is offering a huge incentive to avoid some fundamental steps – restructuring or investment, for example – for the sake of anything which impacts short-term earnings.

This sort of attitude is a real problem for start-up companies of the Dyson variety, and also for established players who face the real headache of having to deliver consistently on a quarterly basis. The only comfort I can offer to start-ups is that people with good ideas and absolute determination – like James Dyson – do make it, and, as I said in Chapter 1, to an extent they thrive on the challenge and the determination to prove the nay-sayers wrong. So far as established companies are concerned, I think part of the way to deal with what may seem unfair short-termism is to manage people's expectations. In other words, don't promise what you can't deliver, and don't let people get carried away on misplaced waves of optimism. lastminute.com's Brent Hoberman knows the dangers of this to his cost:

The short-term nature of the stock market means that there's a game people must play about managing expectations. Many

LEADERSHIP LESSONS
› To run a business, a leader needs convictions and the courage of those convictions.
› Leaders take civic responsibility.

Peter Peterson, The Blackstone Group

parts of our business were growing at 100 per cent in the beginning. If it only grew at 80 per cent in one quarter, that was terrible. That's when we really suffered. I was like, sorry guys, it's kind of hard to forecast between 80 and 100. It could have been 120, I wish it was, but it ended up being 80 per cent.

Carphone Warehouse's Charles Dunstone takes a more phlegmatic view, and ultimately, I think, the route he outlines is the one to take:

People in the City are doing their job and making money, irrespective of how we get on. They're doing their business; you're doing yours, so you mustn't let it get personal. The two things that I've learned are that you have to manage expectations, so try hard not to disappoint and, second, have a plan. If you have a plan that you can articulate, everyone will know why they do or don't own your stock. If you don't have a plan and people own your stock but don't know why, then life gets very uncomfortable.

The punishment for poor performance is your stock price will be lower. If what you are doing is right in the long term, your stock price will be higher. If you've got a long-term plan and say, 'Look, we won't make so much money today, but we will in two or three years' time', your stock price will be higher in two or three years' time. You shouldn't expect it to be higher today. There will be some people who believe it and some people who don't – that's their choice. I think anybody who says our company is misunderstood or our stock price is too low is wrong. The market can't be wrong. The market is the market and reflects what people think. I don't like to try and hide behind things and say, it's not my fault, the City doesn't understand us. It's your job and you have got to carry the can.

Public or private?

The alternative, of course, is to look to private equity. In the private environment you may well be able to take on the costs of change and pursue strategies that might not offer immediate returns but are nevertheless right for the business. Long-term decisions can be taken without one eye on the reaction from the City and quarterly earnings targets, two things which plague many publicly-listed companies. You can also take on higher debt levels than analysts would be happy with in the public arena. Put simply, the advantage of taking a company private boils down to control. I can see no downside.

Brent Hoberman says he often wishes he'd taken last-minute.com private again:

If you are an entrepreneur, you love doing business and you love doing deals. Instead you have to spend a lot of time painting a picture and perfecting it for investors. I would rather we had gone back to being private at some stage, which would have been far more manageable.

In the past few years there has been a massive shift in the financial world. Today it's no longer investment banks that wield the power in the City. In my career I have seen an amazing transition away from the dominance of banks and the emergence of a small group of venture capitalists (VCs) controlling tens of billions

of pounds, dollars and yen. This new generation of financial buc-
caneers seem to swoop out of nowhere, snap up unsuccessful
businesses, revamp them and sell them on at vast profit. They
wield enormous power and now employ nearly a fifth of private
sector workers. That's quite a change in a few short years.

One of the earliest signs of the shift in power took place in
1999, when private equity firms Cinven and CVC Capital Partners
bought William Hill from Nomura for £825 million. What unset-
tled investors was that the deal aborted the flotation of the
company by Warburg Dillon Read, one of the City's grandest corporate finance houses, just days before trading was scheduled to start.
Lukewarm institutional appetite for the offer, which had already
seen the price reduced, saw Nomura's star corporate financier, Guy
Hands, looking elsewhere. Commentators at the time said that the
move had created more ill feeling in the City than any other
takeover bid in recent history.

Guy Davison, a partner at Cinven, says that the William Hill
story is a prime example of a business that was actually better off
being groomed in private equity hands:

**William Hill was a bookmaker without the best of reputations
and it was not seen necessarily as a public company. We bought
it at the eleventh hour, when Nomura had tried to float it, but
the investors were a bit iffy about whether its prospects were
quite good enough.**

**We had a very effective few years with the business, moving
it on from being a successful high street bookmaker with new
routes to market such as an internet and telephone business.
After three years of development, we decided to see if the stock
market would take to it this time, and it did. The offer was ten**

times over-subscribed and it has been a very successful business on the stock market since. Under private equity ownership William Hill was able to develop and become something the stock market was very comfortable with.

Taking a business private certainly answers the problem of the short-term nature of the City. A business run without the scrutiny of shareholders can really look at creating long-term value. Although VCs are often – falsely in my view – accused of asset-stripping, I reckon that a good team actually runs a company for the long term to create value. It's not asset-stripping to rip out a lot of costs, such as a hugely over-manned head office or complicated, multi-layered supply chains. Public companies carry too much cost. If it's possible to take the cost out without affecting sales, then it's clearly the right thing to do.

Of course, there will be good and bad transactions, but in the main they are hugely positive for the companies involved. However, it is now time for the industry to put its own case forward more strongly in the face of increasingly bitter attacks by unions and politicians which mainly focus on rewards for top executives while jobs are slashed. Gone are the days when this industry can just put its head down and get on with it – private equity has become so dominant, and so many big name companies are involved, that they have to put their heads above the parapet and explain their case. And, as I've said, I do think they've got a strong case. All the private equity-run businesses I know look after their people well. Yes, the management are heavily incentivised on performance, but that is a good thing for the companies involved and everyone who works in them.

The private equity groups are in business to make a return on their money, but there are a number of hugely positive aspects to private equity ownership. One of the most significant benefits is that private equity firms stay in the deal. Everyone thinks private equity is in it for the short term, but they actually take a longer-term view. They appoint a strong management team and stay closely involved in the day-to-day running of the company. Historically, banks and advisers would do a deal and that was that – providing the money was paid back, of course. In a private equity deal it's their own money, so they stay in.

Henry Kravis, a founder of US private equity giant Kohlberg, Kravis, Roberts & Co (KKR), says private equity firms are much more concerned with driving cashflow than their public company counterparts. The list of companies Henry has bought and sold over the years includes many of the great American brands, such as Autozone, Gillette, RJR Nabisco, Beatrice, Safeway, Borden and Legrand. He summarises his priorities:

> Number one, we're looking for results over a long period of time. We like to ask a CEO running one of our companies where they want to be in five years, and how are they going to get there. Our average holding period is seven and a half years.
>
> The question from the hedge fund guy is, 'Where are you going to be 10 minutes from now and what are you going to do to get there?' And if you don't get there, they'll sell your stock.
>
> We encourage people to take the long view and not to think about next quarter's earnings; it's not important. We think longer term about building value over many years. That's the way to really create value for management, our investors and us.
>
> Secondly, we encourage managers to take risks, whether it's starting a new business within their company, starting a new line or starting a new market. In a public company they'd say

that they couldn't really afford to do that. They don't want to lose money for the next twenty-four months, even in a good long-term investment. As a private company, we encourage our managers to think differently and foster a different risk profile.

The management of every private equity business is an owner, as opposed to what I call a 'renter'. Renters are certain public company CEOs who don't own the business, but have some options and don't act or think like an owner. The private equity group is a real watchdog, very close to the management and very close to the company, speaking to them on a daily or weekly basis. They see the abnormal things. People are not watching the store as much in a public company. The share register in most public companies turns over every couple of years on average. Institutions and hedge funds are in and out constantly. Our average holding at KKR is seven and a half years. We're in it for the long term. We can make those long-term decisions and work well in partnering with the management. There is a big difference between being the owner and the protectorate.

LEADERSHIP LESSONS
› Keep the organisation flat. That way you will get to know everyone and decisions can be made quickly.
› Encourage everyone to speak up. Nobody ever has a dumb idea, it is just some ideas are better than others.
› Leading by fear is a disaster.

Henry Kravis, KKR

Stephen A. Schwarzman, chief executive of The Blackstone Group, is similarly forthright. He lays the blame for what he calls 'a systemic anomaly', which allows such profitable public to private activity, at the feet of the City and Wall Street:

> The fact that businesses seem to perform better as private companies is simply because they do. It's not because the previous management were hiding value from the shareholders. There is a variety of complex reasons why management typically doesn't do all the right things when they are running public companies. The first is a changed relationship between management and their board of directors, where boards are spending more time on compliance than previously and are much more concerned with legal issues. As a result, the chief executive is much more on trial. This creates a less risk-prone senior management.
>
> The second thing is institutional investors and hedge funds demanding quarterly earnings performance. That creates enormous difficulties for managers. Specifically, they fail to restructure or do the right thing for their business because it will result in their missing earnings projections. If they miss those earning projections, their stock goes down significantly, their shareholders are angry and their boards are unhappy. That message is understood quite clearly by CEOs and management. They will do almost nothing, regardless of its good for the company, that will interfere with the expected earnings progression of a company in the short term. Corporate managers think much more in the short term, as opposed to the longer view they took ten years ago.
>
> When a company is taken private, there's a whole series of

steps that managers can take almost immediately. They are the right things to do, but would never be done in a public company. The people who complain that the managers are 'stealing the business' are the same people who destroy stocks when the company misses their earnings by a penny. They can't have it both ways. Their criteria lead to companies not optimising their long-term potential. Unfortunately for the system, it is to our benefit.

Lessons learned all round

Even if sometimes it is not an easy relationship, the various sides are joined together by a common bond. Everyone needs each other. Just as the rainmakers – the City grandees at the top of their profession – are sought out by chief executives when they embark on an important deal, the moneymen are constantly on the look out for exceptional business brains.

These days the City movers and shakers are not just confined to advisory roles: given that bankers and the barons of private equity play an increasingly important role in major mergers and acquisitions, Wall Street and the Square Mile have both become careful observers of blue-chip leadership skills. They do, after all, need safe, and dynamic, pairs of hands to lead their big purchases. Indeed, there is now even a notable trend among public equity groups for 'collecting' an exclusive group of trusted leaders with whom the VCs have worked on previous transactions and who understand the process.

John Lovering is a classic example. Dubbed a 'serial dealmaker' by the media, John has been involved in no fewer than ten private

> 'There are a lot of people around who accept what happens to them, and the day drives them rather than them driving the day. They are people I call "satisfisers" as opposed to "optimisers". What separates the best from the rest is they are optimisers not satifisers'
>
> Bob Wigley, Merrill Lynch

equity deals in the last decade. Within that figure are four of Cinven's acquisitions. The first was shoe and sport retailer Hoogenbosch in 1996, followed by discount fashion chain Peacock in 1997, Odeon Cinemas in 2000 and Fitness First in 2003. John's finest hour was the rapid improvement of Debenhams, where he was appointed chairman by the consortium of buyout firms, CVC and Texas Pacific, in 2004.

CVC's Jonathan Feuer says this so-called 'serial manager' approach works well for all sides. As he told me, 'You know what they are like, you know their track record and there are always fewer problems with people that you know. They like it, too, because, if they are good, they are given flexibility and authority. You do have to be careful that they are the right people for the right moment, though. Every company is different; the cookie cutter is not the same.'

Interestingly, in spotting leadership talent, despite all the statistics and financial variables which they have at their fingertips, the key factors that the City looks for in a leader are those very human qualities of trust, authenticity and imagination. As

Morgan Stanley's Simon Robey said to me, 'There is no chance of anyone leading me, or anyone else, if I don't trust them. I'll go to the wall for somebody if I think they are doing the right thing and dealing with me in a way that is straightforward. That is what I look for.' He went on to say:

Even if people don't like what they hear, or don't even necessarily agree with what they hear, the leaders I admire are those who can persuade them that they are more right than wrong and really do have the team's best interests at heart.

Simon is also inspired by leaders who clearly have their own views and ideas:

I was lucky enough to work on a few deals with John Browne at BP. I learned from him that it is not good enough to have wonderful people working for you and coming up with good ideas. You have to have a lot of good ideas yourself. John didn't

have all the good ideas, but he had a lot of them. It added to the sense that he was leading by example, not just presiding over the company.

Business leaders and the City can learn a lot from each other, as can public companies from private ones. Ultimately, they're looking for the same qualities in people, and these are the qualities that ensure success.

Chapter 10
Business versus Politics
Never the twain shall meet?

It's like a classic, doomed romance. The early heady days in the courtship between business and politics start swimmingly. In the run-up to an election, the dominant political parties make all sorts of promises about how happily they will live and work side by side with business in the years to come. Warm words and smiles are exchanged and, despite having been let down in the past by similar passionate declarations, businesses relent and try to hide their cynicism. The election takes place and the new relationship starts off enticingly well, as a number of promises are immediately fulfilled with due public fanfare. Then the government gradually realises that it can't actually keep all of its pledges and that there are other, more compelling suitors. It slowly has to let down its new beau or, worse still, ignore it altogether in favour of what it sees as other more pressing claims on its attentions. By the end of the first term of government, the relationship, the subject of such high hopes, either descends into mutual loathing or apathy about each other's existence.

This is not a syndrome specific to any political party; it's specific to politics. The courtship is great, the engagement good, the wedding never quite takes place, and it all deteriorates rapidly after that. But politicians and business people need each other, so a divorce, amicable or otherwise, can never be on the cards. Instead what is required is a bit of marriage guidance. And, as always with these things, the road to reconciliation starts with understanding where the other partner is coming from.

Politicians vs business people

Tempting though it is to start by setting out my own views and grievances, I think, in the interests of making this marriage work, I should let the politicians speak first. And they all say the same thing: what may seem easy or logical for a business may well not prove to be so once there's a political dimension. Lord Wilson of Dinton, head of the Civil Service between 1998 and 2002, tells a story that perfectly sums up the problem:

> When I was at the Home Office, there was a new system allowing prison governors to manage their own budgets to encourage them to be more innovative and entrepreneurial in what they delivered. One governor had a control problem in his prison. He knew his inmates were keen on football, so he invested in a contract to provide an all-year football pitch. The idea behind it was they would go out, play football, tire themselves out and reduce the control problem. In a matter of weeks, a newspaper got hold of it and wrote a terrific story saying the inmates were being mollycoddled with an all-year football pitch, while the

village school was selling its playing fields. There was a terrific hullabaloo and demands for an emergency statement in the House [of Commons]. Politically, there were demands for this governor to be sacked. It seemed to me that he'd done what he was told to do. He'd taken a small risk and achieved something, but, in political terms, it was unforgivable.

'Time and again,' Lord Wilson concludes, 'there are things that in management/leadership terms lead an organisation forward, but the politics of it are wrong.' Take, for example, the issue of airport expansion in the UK, and the experience of the British Airports Authority. The business case seems pretty straight-forward: air travel has grown exponentially in the past few years, thanks to low-cost airlines, and there's no doubt that consumers want to make use of this new freedom without restrictions. More-over, if we don't do something to create extra capacity, commer-cial customers will start moving elsewhere. Most politicians would go along with this, but they would also say that they have to take account of the huge number of other people involved – passen-gers, politicians, airline employees, media, environmentalists and local residents. It's not just that you can't ignore the fact that airports and the construction of new terminals or runways are hugely emotive subjects, but you also have a duty of care to the community that elected you.

In some cases, the business community has failed to keep its own house in order, and politicians would argue that, in these instances, they have to intervene. For example, there has been criticism of corporate involvement in new hospital builds and the influence of major property developers over local council plan-ning decisions. The corporate lobbying power of large biotech and

› Set up values and live by them.
› Create confidence in the people you are
    leading.
› Show you can be trusted, are competent and
    can do what you say.
› Commitment is essential.

Lord Wilson of Dinton

pharmaceutical groups has also come under fire, and big business sponsorship of university research departments is seen as reducing the quality and availability of independent scientific research.

Most politicians would also say that few business people actually bother to try to understand or appreciate these complexities. Baroness Prosser, for example, who as a trade unionist, non-executive director at the Royal Mail and a member of the House of Lords has worked on both sides of the business/politics divide, is critical of the failure of the business community properly to accept the reality of the political process:

Their experience has been founded on the need to make decisions on the business case, based on logic and finance. They've got a product they're going to sell and a market to sell it in. But there are a lot of businesses over which government and the world of politics has some control or influence, either in planning or regulation or as a stakeholder. Then there are other things that have to be dealt with, like making sure that the political players understand what the company is doing so that

they in turn can sell it to their stakeholders. It's not the normal business experience.

Bill Morris [General Secretary of the T&G union, 1991–2003] used always to say that these are the 'extra democratic hurdles' we had to jump over. It meant decisions couldn't just be based on the business case; they had to be got through a committee with other interests at heart. There are a lot of other issues that have to be brought into play.

It's true that people outside the political arena often have little understanding of the complexities of politics. One of the real joys of business is the freedom you have to take decisions. There's a relatively short chain of command and no need to have a paper trail for everything. People outside government don't really appreciate the pressure the Public Accounts Committee and parliamentary questions put on the way you do business. An AGM is nothing like as demanding as an appearance before the Public Accounts Committee. Once they engage with the political world,

LEADERSHIP LESSONS
› Be determined to deliver what you say you are going to deliver.
› Give good leadership to people who don't have the time, inclination or opportunity to do it for themselves.
› Accept that things are not always going to be nice. Politics is a bit of a dirty game, but you've just got to get on with it.

Baroness Prosser

business people can be guilty of being naive or, at the very least, blinkered.

Business people vs politicians

The business view, inevitably, tends to be rather different. One frustration many of us have is that the political world of Westminster seems like an island, cut off from anything else happening in Britain. After all, nobody else works in a building like the House of Commons or engages in lengthy daily debates seated on green baize while following the most unusual and anti-quated protocol. Moreover, for most career politicians, this is the only world they know or will ever know. They have actually done very little in the outside world, and their instincts are narrowly political and presentational. For a really caustic view of the average minister, you can't do much better than turn to the views of the former political grandee and millionaire businessman Lord Michael Heseltine. Years in the political limelight, including a spell as Defence Secretary under Margaret Thatcher, have not exactly left him with the most favourable opinion of those in charge:

> Not many people actually stand back and think about the meagre range of choice a prime minister has in forming a government. The chances are he will have something like 350–400 people of his own party. A hundred of them have probably had some sort of past experience, but are too old, or have failed in the opportunities they've had. Another hundred have probably just come into Parliament and no one knows much about them. They certainly have relatively little experience, and may lack the right

qualities. So, you've got a swathe in the middle of about 150 to 200 people from whom you have to choose a hundred.

He goes on to apply these damning ratios to a business context:

Imagine trying to run a major corporation and the whole constituency from which you can choose to do that is of that tiny scale. Then, when you look at the cvs of that group, the vast majority have had no senior management experience at all. It is no surprise that, if you are that constrained, you don't end up with a very dynamic team. You may have one or two good people, but the ordinary run-of-the-mill minister is going to be pretty inexperienced and, being as fair as you can, quite unsuited to senior management. Management is a very specific skill. It is not a natural skill that is necessary in political success.

Everyone has strong views about the natural abilities or otherwise of the average politician. But what I do think is a huge problem

LEADERSHIP LESSONS
› Choose the right team and delegate.
› Those with power and privilege have responsibilities.
› Speak the truth. The world is full of people who kept a little quiet.

Lord Michael Heseltine

– perhaps the biggest – is that, because of the very nature of the political system, politicians invariably take a short-term view of just about everything. Governments expect to be in power for only four or five years. They know that people have high expectations of them and that they need to tell a good story. So they'll do the easy stuff, put off the difficult stuff and dither about the controversial stuff. And even on the easy stuff they'll tend to chop and change their minds – an even less pardonable sin in my book. Or they'll follow one idea with another one, before they know whether the first idea has worked or not. Lord Wilson of Dinton recalls meeting a group of business people a few years back who expressed themselves bewildered by the way the government of the day was launching new initiatives before it had completed the old ones. He recalls, 'They said that no one in the private sector would launch a new product before they had finished introducing the old one. It simply didn't make sense.'

I do also sometimes get the impression from some career politicians that business is not to be trusted: that we're all out to make a quick buck, pollute the planet and do dodgy deals – in other words, that we need constant watching and regulation. Not enough recognition is given to the positive aspects of business, and to the good work that many business people do well outside their immediate ambit.

There are too many rules and regulations, when the best way to regulate is to self-regulate. Indeed, the best form of regulation is consumerism – that is what really counts because it hits you in the pocket.

Take corporate social responsibility (CSR), for example. There are thousands of political initiatives to do with social responsibility and the environment that all end in nothing, whereas where

'To enjoy good relations with the regulators and the government you have to work at it very hard. Some industries think of them as the enemy, but you have to engage with them constructively. It is all about fighting intelligently to protect your market for as long as you possibly can'

Marcus Agius, Barclays Bank

businesses take a stand on CSR it has a real impact. Just as businesses can have more of an impact on the economy than the government, so they can have more impact on environmental and social change. Winning consumer hearts is now as big a deal as winning their cash. The environment has become a big issue – particularly among young people who are the customers of tomorrow – so it cannot be ignored by business. Companies that do ignore it are going to have a big problem, because it will hit them where it counts, on the bottom line. They should do something about CSR because it is the right thing to do – not because there are 57,000 rules telling them to.

Business has had to take the lead in education too. Many companies, exasperated by the lack of progress or attainment in the state system, are now looking at funding schemes for their next generation of colleagues. Philip Green has put £10 million of his own money into the UK Fashion Retail Academy after repeatedly being unable to fill vacancies at his Arcadia clothing empire. James Dyson, meanwhile, has invested £12 million in the

Dyson School for Design and Innovation in Bath. It's a new kind of school to encourage Britain's next generation of entrepreneurs, designers and inventors, and he thinks it will help address a very serious problem:

> **Britain's balance of trade is sinking into the red. We will be in big trouble if we don't change. There's a feeling that manufacturing is somehow a thing of the past, a dinosaur, and that the future lies in software and service industries. But do we want Britain to be a theme park or a hub of business activity? We produce only 24,000 engineering graduates a year, as opposed to 350,000 in China and 2,000,000 in India.**
>
> **The scale of this problem is enormous, yet people are culturally interested in engineering and invention. It's a natural thing to want to make things and make better things. We did a survey among fourteen-year-olds and found two-thirds of them would take engineering GCSE if it was offered to them. It isn't at the moment, but we have potential there. I think if we can catch people in the fourteen- to sixteen-year-old age group and get them interested in engineering, then there's a chance we can get them doing engineering as a career.**

Bob Wigley at Merrill Lynch is yet another example of how cooperation between business and education can be to everyone's advantage. Bob began developing his own leadership skills early, thanks to a farsighted scheme led by Young Enterprise when he was still at school. He believes, as I do, that concentrating on studying and passing examinations in schools is very important, but that it's equally important to prepare young people for the world of work:

In my O Level year I set up a company with a group of class-mates, spending two hours a week on it. It wasn't a game; it was a real company. The idea was to sell shares totalling £500 to a group of people, mainly parents, and with the capital go off and manufacture something. There was a finance director, an HR director, a managing director and others who actually made the products. We produced notelets and lampshades – obviously, due to the skills of somebody in the group. At the end of the year, we liquidated the company and made a return of 100 per cent.

The great thing was that we really got to understand what a company does and what the roles in the company are. It excited me. Everybody at school said I was bright and should go to Oxford or Cambridge, but I said I wanted to go into business. So I went to Bath University and did a business degree. Having my eyes opened to the business world did a lot for me and I wanted to put something back. When I got my first job at British Gas, I persuaded them to sponsor a Young Enterprise company. I was a mentor to one company that went on to win the national competition. The publicity around Young Enterprise was so weak that I wrote to Margaret Thatcher who was then prime minister. I said, 'This is a fantastic scheme, you need to get behind this.' She replied by return inviting the sixteen-year-old winners and me to give a presentation at 10 Downing Street. She also invited the chairman of the Stock Exchange, the Governor of the Bank of England and various other City luminaries. It was a fantastic experience for me as an eighteen-year-old and I am absolutely convinced this is why I am chairman of a bank and on the Court of the Bank of England today.

Working together

So does the mutual incomprehension between politicians and business people matter? After all, most of us are so busy doing our jobs that we don't have time to worry about outside concerns, let alone what's going on in the political sphere. Well, yes, I believe it does matter. After all, politicians and business leaders world-wide share many of the same goals. We all want faster economic growth and we want to create and protect jobs. Ministers can be fantastically useful in promoting the interests of British business abroad. And what politicians do in the legislative sphere directly affects business – recent examples include the introduction of the minimum wage, the 2002 budget announcement that National Insurance Contributions (NICs) would rise by 1 per cent, and the increase in the tax burden on businesses (the CBI calculated in 2006 that during the time Labour have been in power business has coughed up £54 billion in tax revenue over and above what it would have expected to contribute). If the business community stands apart from the political process, or fails to make its case adequately, then it can't hope to influence decisions.

I accept that many people are frustrated by the overkill of spin, cynical about policies that appear to have no real substance, and antagonised by the endless succession of new initiatives that have no follow through. Yet although it can take some grubbing around to find an instance of good political decision-making, it can happen, and, as I've already said, it generally happens when business and politics engage in dialogue.

An example of regulation of business that will, I believe, on balance prove beneficial is the Higgs report. After a lot of to-ing and fro-ing between Whitehall and the wider business community, the corporate governance proposals, by former investment banker Derek Higgs, were devised to kick-start the overhaul of company boardrooms. The report called for non-executive directors to have regular meetings with shareholders and report back to other non-executives. It called for a ban on the company chairman heading the nominations committee as a means of stopping the back-scratching that turned some non-executive appointments into jobs for the boys. The review was prompted by a series of financial scandals in the UK and US (the collapse of Enron, for example) that had exposed weaknesses in the boardroom. Higgs began from the premise that a company has far wider responsibilities than just making money. It's up to the board to make sure everyone is playing by the rules.

On its launch in January 2003, it was immediately met with howls of derision and business leaders said it 'damaged relations' with government. A CBI survey showed more than 80 per cent of major companies were opposed to a number of its proposals. There was considerable lobbying and protest, but eventually most of the recommendations were adopted by the Financial Reporting Council.

As with all these things, it's possible to take exception to some of the provisions of the report. Some would argue, for example, that in some areas it's too prescriptive and doesn't allow the flexibility that all companies need as they meet new challenges. Nevertheless, I believe the principles are right and that they can be executed in different ways. The report offers a template, and I think the dialogue between politicians and business people that preceded its inception was a fruitful one.

Even really thorny issues, like the expansion of Britain's airport capacity that I mentioned earlier, can be moved on when proper dialogue takes place. It's hardly surprising that, with a political hot potato like this, no new runway has been built in the southeast of England since the Second World War. Indeed, the new £4.5 billion Terminal 5 building at Heathrow Airport will have taken twenty-three years from the moment of the first decision to build it to the day the first passenger checks in. It was the longest planning enquiry in British history.

Former BAA non-executive chairman Marcus Agius spent four years at the airport group before he sold it to a consortium led by Ferrovial of Spain in June 2006 for £10 billion. He said that managing the Terminal 5 process was a constant trade-off, knowing you couldn't please all of the people all of the time. Even pleasing some of the people some of the time was something of an achievement. But progress has definitely been made:

> Politicians have always had difficulties with transport. Until Alistair Darling became Secretary of State for Transport [in 2002], it was the ministry with the fastest revolving door ever. Everyone saw it as an awful place to be and ministers got out of there as fast as they could. Clearly there could be no continuity of policy and the people in the job had their minds only on the next job. The simplest thing for any Transport Secretary to do was to defer a decision on a controversial subject such as where the next runway is going to be built.
>
> It's certain that if a minister said it's going to be at Heathrow, Gatwick or wherever they're going to upset people around the site and lose a lot of votes in that constituency. Yet they wouldn't get any additional votes out of the people they pleased by staying out of their backyard – it doesn't work out that way. The real

benefit would happen when the runway was eventually constructed and that was way beyond their tenure.

Alistair Darling, however, decided that doing nothing wasn't an option and that the government had to produce a transport white paper allowing for the construction of a second runway at Stansted. That's the mark of a great politician: he recognised a problem and tried to do something about it. Airports, roads and the rail network are national assets, everybody uses them and they make the country work. The economic development of the country depends on transport infrastructure.

So how does one go about trying to make things work better? Key, I think, is building relationships – a recurrent, if not obsessive, theme throughout this book. Business people have to engage with ministers. They also need to engage with senior civil servants who provide continuity in government and have an excellent knowledge of the background of every issue. As Lord Wilson says:

> It's frustrating for people in the outside world to have built up a relationship with a minister, nurtured it and invested time in it when suddenly the minister moves on. There's good sense in getting to know the civil servant who will be briefing the minister for the sake of continuity. That doesn't mean that the policy goes on regardless of the minister, because the job of the civil servant is to serve their minister and reflect their views. But the department is also in the business of trying to get things done.
>
> Deal with the civil servants. It is well worth investing the time and trouble in getting to know the advisers.

In the view of BUPA's Val Gooding, business leaders should never, ever pass up an opportunity to meet a minister, no matter how uninspiring the invitation:

> Health in the UK is far more politicised than it is in the other countries where we operate. Each party seizes on health and tries to get a political advantage out of it because the government runs the NHS. Generally speaking, what we do at BUPA is to try to be quite humble. Government ministers are always busy, so I take any chance we get to meet a minister; it's sometimes inconvenient, but you go anyway. We are trying to provide better health care for the people we look after, so if we can make a contribution to that through better relationships with government we have to seize every opportunity.

Val rightly believes that these sort of conversations play a major part in helping her get her message across, and she illustrates her point by reminiscing about an exchange she once had with the man at the top – the prime minister:

> When I first met Tony Blair, he suggested that the science of genetics was going to kill off private medical insurance. This was a rather uninformed statement voiced in front of a number of my corporate customers. I couldn't have the prime minister making a statement like that, so I said, 'Prime Minister, your people [I didn't say he was] are completely wrong about that.' When I got back to the office, I sent him a note about it too.
>
> I didn't expect him to remember the conversation, but he did. A year later, when I met him again, he said in front of everybody else in the room that I'd taken him up on something and

that I was right. I know professionals in his office, who pass him little notes, probably prompted him, but at least he was brave enough to admit in front of everyone that he was wrong. Not a lot of people would do that in business or politics. But you have so much power as a leader that you lose nothing by doing it. In fact, you go up in people's estimation if you are prepared to be humble.

There's room for optimism when the two constituencies can work together. The secrets to the process, I think, are to accept the different priorities that each side is likely to have and to learn from each other. The public sector is not better than the private sector, and vice versa. They're both good at completely different things. The private sector is fantastic at being results orientated, even if, from time to time, the process leaves a bit to be desired. The public sector is fantastic at process, but doesn't always seem to be too bothered about whether there's a good result at the end of it, as long as they can point to the fact they did it in the right way. Mutual respect has to be the way forward.

Learning from politicians

So can business learn anything from the way that things are done in the political arena? Yes, I believe it can. Admittedly, sometimes the lessons are negative ones – you see a politician mishandle a situation and you pray that you never make the same mistake yourself.

Having said that, I think there are positive lessons to be

learned from the political field. First, many of the communication skills that the best politicians clearly have are as applicable in a commercial environment as they are in Westminster or Washington. The most inspiring political figures often have an ability to preserve an impressively 'human' voice, even when addressing thousands of people. They emphasise logic, reasoning and evidence, but they never forget that both they and their audience are emotional beings.

Take someone like former US president Bill Clinton. He is without doubt one of the most gifted communicators I have ever seen. He comes across as being articulate and intelligent and avoids the terrible pitfalls of appearing aloof or pedantic. The issues he engages with may be global topics that lie outside the experience of his audience, but through a combination of storytelling skills and a down-to-earth style, he carries his listeners along with him. This ability to come across in a very human light is an impressive one, and something worth trying to emulate.

'The ability to keep the ball in play is a much more sophisticated one in public life. In business it is very difficult to escape the discipline of the bottom line. But there isn't a bottom line in that narrow sense in politics. It is a much more loosely defined feeling of being on top, succeeding and appealing to the public'

Lord Michael Heseltine

Great politicians also have the ability to cut through the numerous issues that lurk at every turn, and focus on the handful that people want to hear about. Going hand in hand with that, they can be astonishingly intuitive, able to read the mood of the day both inside their party and in the world at large. And while this ability to sense what people are really thinking may be lost as the pressures grow, it's still definitely there at the start among people in high office. Tony Blair, for example, throughout his early years in power, showed a strong intuitive grasp of events. Similarly, the former Conservative prime minister, John Major, was very canny, according to Michael Heseltine, when it came to interpreting people's behaviour and at sensing what was really going on: 'John Major was always very acute on body language. He often said to me after cabinet meetings where contentious issues had come up, "Did you feel the body language?" Not everyone has that ability.'

Another key political quality that has direct relevance in the business arena is the ability to hit the ground running, not stumbling. Quick wins are as essential in business as they are in politics. A strong start shapes the public's perception of a new leader as a winner and establishes the idea that this is someone who can get things done. The media and opponents take note and might even give them some breathing space. In the business sphere, it happened for me at the Royal Mail when I very publicly changed its name back from Consignia. In the political realm it happened for Gordon Brown when he granted operational independence to the Bank of England just after becoming chancellor in 1997. It was a clever move that took the politics out of interest rates and so very quickly got businesses on his side.

Then there's moral courage, often in the face of relentless

pressure. Whether or not you agree with a particular politician over a particular policy is not really the issue here. You have to have admiration – however sneaking – for people who stand fast to what they believe in. Take, for example, Tony Blair's speech at the 2003 Labour Party conference when, in the face of mounting fury about the war in Iraq, he said, 'I can only go one way, I've not got a reverse gear.' It struck many at the time as a nod to Margaret Thatcher's famous 'No turning back' speech of October 1980, which she made at a time of comparable mid-term difficulty. 'It is the only type of leadership I can offer,' he went on, 'and it's the only type of leadership worth having.' Moral courage is not something to be sneezed at; it's something any business leader worth their salt should aspire to.

And finally, the best politicians are not afraid to surround themselves with talented people. Indeed, they often actively seek alliances with rivals. Michael Heseltine's rule of thumb for valuable colleagues is as applicable to the business world as it is to the realm of politics:

> I always look for people who can think. If people can think they are progressively valuable. They don't accept the status quo, they actually look ahead, analyse the facts, ask difficult questions, and have a sense of history and perspective. These are hugely valuable qualities.

Chapter 11
Looking to the Future
How to create enduring success

The financials are fantastic, customers congratulate you in the street, the City applauds you and even the media gives a grudging nod in your direction. Job done. Or is it? How should a leader quantify success? Perhaps your real value is only understood some years after you've moved on. After all, only time will tell if what you did provided a lasting and sustainable legacy. If it all falls apart in months, everything you thought you had achieved is wasted.

Of course, a lot depends on who takes over the company, and it's every leader's responsibility to make sure that they not only run their business well but that they plan properly for the future. At ASDA Archie Norman and I began planning the succession almost as soon as we arrived. Everything we did, we did with one eye on spotting and nurturing rising stars. We put in place a range of initiatives to challenge the next generation of prospective leaders constantly. Those who rose to the challenge flourished and learned valuable lessons. Indeed, many ASDA

'I always hire people who absolutely want my job. Not just in a "that would be nice to have her job" way but with an absolute "I can do it better than her" attitude. It doesn't make for a comfortable life, but appointing really clever people, who challenge you all the time, makes a successful career'

Rebekah Wade, *Sun*

directors became targets for headhunters, and the senior team, which was instrumental in the recovery story of ASDA in the early 1990s, has graduated to become another generation of hugely capable business leaders, heading a number of blue chip companies.

Justin King is just one example. An alumnus of ASDA, he is now chief executive of Sainsbury. Looking back on his days at ASDA he says:

> If you take the management board of ASDA in 1999, there are probably ten or so chief executives in the world today from there. That's quite an achievement. The biggest test of my success at Sainsbury is whether, when I do move on, the business continues to be successful for many years. That will tell the world two things. The first is that I left behind a business running well with good momentum. The second is that I had in place a management team directly below me and below that layer, too, that can take the business forward.

Recruiting the right men and women is certainly not an exact science, and a lot of chief executives say that they have to rely on gut feeling. I'd go along with that, and I'd also agree with Archie Norman that, as a rule of thumb, if you recruit five people, one will be outstanding, one will be a terrible mistake and the rest will be somewhere in between. Finding that big talent, the person who will develop and go on to lead a blue chip company, is the target – and the reward.

When looking for the next generation of leaders, some people tend automatically to look outside the company, perhaps assuming that what is home grown somehow can't be as good. I think it's certainly important to be prepared to look further afield and to find external people who will look at your business with fresh eyes, but I also believe that the first and most obvious place to search for the next generation of leaders is within your own organisation. There has to be a rich vein of internal talent. I also believe in the virtues of promoting early. People took chances on me when I was very young and taught me that ability is more important than experience. It's essential to remember that what one is looking for in the next generation are abilities such

'Mistakes are made in recruitment when you allow things like technical competence or a good cv to override an abiding sense of whether or not a candidate is actually the right person for the job'

Justin King, J Sainsbury

as intellectual capacity, precision, supreme focus, interpersonal skills and the capability to handle stress. These qualities are much harder to find in a candidate than simple experience of the various requirements of a senior position. If there is a candidate who has those essential capabilities, they can get the relevant experience; if they've got experience, but don't have these key characteristics, they're not something you can teach them.

Many organisations introduce a complex array of psychometric tests when selecting a candidate for an executive post. It's a process that can take months, but is frankly absurd when assessing an internal candidate. If the person already works for you, it's easy to observe how they do their job, how they react when things go wrong and how they deal with people. Why create a false climate when they're already in the real situation? Good leaders are good watchers. They continually see how people work and how they develop. Lord Browne, for example, who retired from BP in May 2007 after a lifetime at the oil giant, kept a constant and vigilant eye on his deputies – or Teenage Mutant Ninja Turtles, as he once affectionately referred to them – to see which of them might follow on after him:

> Even before I became chief executive in 1995 I started by taking the best and the brightest to work with me in my office. I told them to just do everything, watch and learn. It is a great way to coach people.
>
> In doing that I have seen twenty-five people who have all been terribly successful and some very successful indeed. Of course, some people cannot convert their very good analytical

business skills. They are fabulous general managers, but they can't make it to the next level. You have to have aptitude, but it can be honed and moved to a new order of quality by coaching and experience.

PAGs and planks

A great way to spot potential and keep your rising stars motivated is to introduce positive action groups, or PAGs. There are always things in an organisation that need to be fixed, so, if there's an issue, I put a PAG on it. They're not permanent groups: they take action quickly and then disband themselves. I choose seven or eight people with real potential from across the business. I'll pick one as leader to report directly to me, and that person may well not be the most senior man or woman in the team. However, that's part of the development process: you develop people by giving them challenging things to do.

PAGs were first introduced early on in the recovery process at ASDA. Apart from their immediate function of devising solutions to some major problems, they were a way to motivate and retain the interest of the highly competent senior managers who might otherwise jump ship if they saw no clear route to the top. I knew that I needed someone or, better still, two or three people who could take over from me, so I lined up Paul Mason and Tony De Nunzio, both of whom could do the job, and indeed went on to do so. Under them were Richard Baker, Andy Hornby and Justin King – all more than capable of doing the job in the future. There was even a layer under them being groomed for the top job, including Andy Bond, who also went on to become chief executive at ASDA. In many ways we were spoilt for choice, and inevitably in this situation you know you're going to lose some of your talent to other companies. There are, however, worse problems you could have.

Richard Baker, Justin King and Andy Hornby all ran PAGs at ASDA. This gave them early responsibility and me the opportunity to spend more time with them. I was also able to put them under more pressure and see how they would react.

Justin for one reckons that PAGs are invaluable. He reckons they gave him a broader view of the business, taking the focus away from the nitty-gritty issues of the day and opening up a broader horizon. And, as he points out, they help companies prepare for whatever the future throws at them:

There's a time in a recovery story when a business leader has to think about leaving a great legacy and creating the calibre of

management to take the business on when the chief executive chooses to move on. The reality is that most chief executives don't go at a time of their own choosing. Generally, chief executives who bow out according to their plan leave a lasting and worthwhile legacy.

The other method of continuous improvement put in place at ASDA to test the team consisted of the stores head office interactive trading meetings, also known by the more memorable acronym SHITMs. As with so many things I've done in my career, this was a concept I 'borrowed' from Wal-Mart. The idea behind it was to set up hard-hitting meetings to discuss difficult issues that might otherwise be continually pushed to the back burner. Not surprisingly, the meetings could be pretty confrontational, but it was a fantastic test of the senior team.

'Great leaders have a vision, a strategy and a long-term plan. They invest time growing potential successors and are extremely focused on professional development in their organisations. They try to make clear to their people what their goals are, so that people know what they are supposed to do and whether or not they are accomplishing their goals'

Josh Bekenstein, Bain Capital

Every month, anyone from regional managers and store managers to traders and suppliers were invited to ASDA House to air their grievances. We put all the issues on the table and sat down for a gruelling three hours at a time to thrash things out. It was all very tense. In this no-holds-barred atmosphere, regional managers would accuse head office of dumping things in stores with little thought to sales, while the buyers would come right back at them, accusing them of messing up their carefully thought through strategies. I usually let the meeting get pretty close to boiling point, before stepping in to calm things down.

To inject some degree of levity into this hothouse of confrontation, we put a plank on the meeting room table, designed to resemble the plank that pirates are supposed to have asked their victims to walk along in days gone by. I'd then ask, say, the traders who they would like on the plank and they would pick, say, a regional manager. The manager would get on the plank and the process would begin. Questions would be fired at the victim from the traders, and every time he or she was stuck for an answer he or she would have to shuffle further along the plank. I think this was a good way of defusing an otherwise tense situation and it became something of a legend in the company. In my travels around the corridors I would often overhear people muttering that so and so had to be 'got on to the plank'.

PAGs and SHITMs, then, are a powerful way to get the senior team involved in the day-to-day running of a business and offer the person in charge an excellent opportunity to observe how they react. They also introduce a little humour into the job of dealing with what can be tough problems.

Young minds, new approaches

In the past few years, a new generation of young, hugely capable chief executives has emerged who have blown away the perception that getting to the top is all about age. Certainly, few people now have much truck with the once widely held view that would-be major company chief executives had to be well into their fifties if they were to have sufficient experience to run a company. Why the change? Much of the reason, I suspect, is that it's easier now than it's ever been to build up relevant experience. People today can travel more frequently, communicate more easily and have access to innumerable sources of information via the internet. Everything is now so much more available for so much more of the time.

Business is moving at the speed of the twenty-first century, not the twentieth. Younger chief executives can be more in touch with their customers and have a better understanding of the world they live in. By contrast, a fifty-five-year-old leader is almost a whole generation away from what is happening on the street.

Justin King certainly feels this. He became chief executive of Sainsbury in 2004 at the age of forty-three, having begun his career at Mars, as I did, and finding himself, within two weeks of joining the confectionery giant, running the production line for

> 'Young people can teach you as much as you can teach them. Their minds are not cluttered by past experiences'
>
> David Mayhew, JP Morgan Cazenove

Galaxy chocolate – career progress at a speed unheard of in other companies. He says that companies are now more open-minded about the experience they give to people in their early twenties and have produced the phenomenon of younger chief executives. Timelines to master a job have been shortened to a matter of months:

> On my second Monday at Mars I started running a production line. That's the equivalent of running a small shop at Sainsbury. We're trying to change at Sainsbury, but you still can't imagine running a small shop within your first three years at the company. Even three years is a short time.
>
> The timelines people spend in their jobs in their twenties have shortened. In the past, managers would say that you can't be in that job unless you've done this one for two years; then you have to work in that department for two years; and then do something else. Many organisations have short-circuited, thanks to that process.
>
> Organisations now are also flatter; that goes hand in hand with this process. If a person is shining at one level, someone has got to take a punt to move them on to the next level. The flat structure means giving a person exposure and stepping them up very quickly if they display the talent. They learn the breadth of the business a lot more quickly than they would on a functional line. It's very rare these days for people to go straight up a functional line and become a chief executive.

Andy Hornby, who took his first chief executive role at HBOS aged thirty-nine, is another who believes that experience is more important than age:

The age you get the job doesn't matter. What does matter is whether you've got the drive and whether you have the experience. I was amazingly lucky to be on the main HBOS board for six years before I became chief executive. So I had years of experience, even though I was very young.

The world is becoming increasingly a meritocracy, pushing people through quickly if they're different.

People complain that Plcs are under too much short-term pressure from shareholders. I see the reverse. I see that pressure as very positive, because, rather ironically, it makes it easier for young people to come through very quickly – the urgency for delivery gets higher and higher. Providing that you're performing, you can break through quicker.

I was definitely a beneficiary of this at ASDA, where they wanted to rebuild the business really quickly. They were able to take some risks on people and push them through very fast, provided they were delivering. It all came from the shareholder pressure to sort things out very quickly.

I don't subscribe to the view that it's all about energy. Energy is hugely important when you're a business leader, but you can have a lot of energy when you are fifty years old and a lot when you are thirty. I've seen a lot of hugely charismatic and energetic leaders in their fifties. The important thing is a combination of experience, drive, being brave, taking key decisions and genuinely rewarding people who have delivered, regardless if they have been doing that job for ten years or thirty years.

The virtues of younger leaders can be particularly noticeable when they're brought in to deal with problem companies. Leaving aside the consideration that desperate corporate circumstances

> 'Good leaders bring up people who can replace them. They stand back and give them the reins. There comes a time when everyone needs to be replaced, and if there has been no preparation, the business will suffer'
>
> Jonathan Feuer, CVC

can mean that the boards of stricken companies are more prepared to take a risk as to who they put in, the fact is that the best person to shake up a business is likely to be someone who is young and eager, not someone who is contaminated with the sort of pessimism that you can find among older people.

Richard Baker is a good example of what I mean. When he was brought into Boots at the age of forty, Boots had suffered for many years from archaic supply systems, an over-staffed head office and over-priced goods. Similarly, when Justin King joined Sainsbury, he came in at a time when the company was in real trouble, facing an investor revolt, the prospect of an unwelcome bid, disaffected customers and a rapidly slipping market share. Both turned things around.

Adam Crozier faced the same sort of problems when he joined the Royal Mail. As I've already said, it was close to insolvency and suffering from decades of inefficiencies, industrial unrest and staff absence. Adam, however, had already gone through a previous baptism of fire in 1995 when he was made chief executive of advertising giant Saatchi & Saatchi on the day after Charles and Maurice walked out, taking a third of the staff and half the business with them. 'I was twenty-nine years old,' he recalls, 'and vividly remember appearing on *News at Ten*, blinking like a rabbit caught in car headlights.' And what Saatchi & Saatchi did for him was to provide a vast amount of essential experience in a very short space of time. As Adam says:

> Giving people the opportunity to shine usually means taking a chance and giving them a problem to solve. The reason I've done what I've done is that I've always wanted to work with the clients or companies that no one else wanted to work with. So what if you do another great advert for an advertiser who always does great advertisements? If you turn the difficult one around, you have really achieved something.

Some of the experience he gleaned turned out to be very practical:

> In periods like that you learn so much more about people than when things are going well. In advertising there are a lot of showy people and in a real crisis they aren't people you can rely on. There were some really stable people doing a steady job who actually made the difference. Everyone looks for stars in the top three levels, but what I discovered was that the stars were often in the strangest places. There was the amazing tea lady who made everybody feel good and the great girl in production who made everyone laugh and who the clients absolutely loved. It's a question of finding the stars wherever they sit. The only way you can really tell who the stars are is to give them a chance to shine.

Some of the experience Adam gained was more to do with learning to develop the right attitude to things. 'One of the reasons Saatchi was so successful,' he says, 'was that it had just had one simple thought – "nothing is impossible".'

That incredibly positive attitude drove through everything everyone did. When I started at the Royal Mail it was all very negative. I often heard, 'Well we tried that and it didn't work' or 'The union/regulator/government won't let us do that'. There were lots of barriers and reasons why they couldn't do what we wanted to do.

The net result at Saatchi & Saatchi was that 'within a year, we were bigger than we were before all the upheaval took place'.

At the Royal Mail, Adam wants to get the next generation to step up to the mark in the way he has done in the course of his career:

We try to give some of the really difficult issues and problems to upcoming people. We say, right, have a go at that; it's broken anyway; see what you can do to fix it. That's how you learn a hell of a lot about people. Not just in the solution, but also in their approach to the whole thing and how they take people with them. Can they persuade people to do something they don't want to do for the good of the company? The trick is to make sure you're there for them as they go through it. They'll learn a lot and so will you.

A leader has to get rid of those barriers and say that it's about everybody being the best they can be – here we go, let's do it. In a situation like this you have to have the energy and

ability to roll with the punches and take the blows, including the very public ones. That means always doing the right thing, however difficult it is.

Making women welcome

The shift towards a younger generation of chief executives doesn't, sadly, appear to have ushered in a new era of opportunity for female leaders. At the time of writing, there is just one woman heading a company in the FTSE 100 and just eight at the helm in a Fortune 500 company in the United States. Women hold only 10 per cent of executive and non-executive directorships in the FTSE 100, and there are also only a handful of female chief executives among the rest of the quoted companies. Moreover, according to the Equal Opportunities Commission, the UK is in twelfth place out of thirty European countries, behind Latvia, Poland and Bulgaria, when it comes to women serving in the highest level of the civil service. Despite the fact that girls consistently out-perform boys at school, more than 60 per cent of female graduates still believe it's easier for men to get ahead after leaving university. According to a recent *Guardian* survey, only 38 per cent of female graduates expect an early promotion in their careers compared with 50 per cent of men. Women also have lower salary expectations, by 8 per cent, than men.

These are depressing statistics. Great leadership talent is in short supply and women represent a mainly untapped resource. So why are there not more of them in senior positions?

Part of the problem, I think, is that there is still a prevalent view that somehow women's 'inherent qualities' rule them out when it comes to certain roles. Carolyn McCall, who is the chief executive of Guardian Media Group and the chair of Opportunity Now, which works for gender equality and diversity in the workplace, has strong views on the subject:

> The danger for women is that they're often seen as the ones who take care of the organisation. They're perceived to have the caring skills of empathy, or being good with people, or being good listeners. Male leaders are seen as very incisive people who take charge and take decisions. This whole 'taking care' versus 'taking charge' thing is very stereotypical and can disadvantage women when it comes to talking about leadership. Actually, I think a leader has to have both traits. You have to be caring as a leader and humane: you have to demonstrate trust and authenticity. But you have to take charge, pull teams together and unify them behind a common purpose. Nothing is as simple and black and white as the stereotype. Everything is more complex.
>
> Research has shown that when ranking leadership attributes, the 'taking charge' style always come higher than the 'taking care' attributes. Clearly this means the stereotype is not good for women.

LEADERSHIP LESSONS
› Be honest, upfront and consult.
› Make sure the organisation understands what we want to do and why.
› If something is not working, change.

Carolyn McCall, Guardian Media Group

Women can be worse at reinforcing those stereotypes. I hear a lot of women say, 'I don't know how I got this job; I'm going to be found out one day.' That's not leadership behaviour, that's rubbish. They project stereotypes on other women and when it comes from another woman it is even more powerful.

Of course, there are practical considerations too. A high proportion of the population lives in a traditional family unit, which means that somebody has to look after the children, and that somebody is usually the woman. Even if women choose to be working mums, they still tend to end up taking responsibility for arranging and managing childcare. A would-be female chief executive, then, often has to weigh up the sheer intensity of the job versus the commitments of a possibly young family. Men, by contrast, have it pretty easy.

Jenny Watson, the former chair of the Equal Opportunities Commission (EOC), says that the long hours culture we now have makes it almost impossible for women – and an increasing number of men – to balance their work and home life. Many don't see why they should have to sacrifice their home lives to make it to the top. There's a groundswell of concern that both women and men are not spending enough time with their families. As she points out:

There are still incalculable differences between work and life balance for women with young children and increasingly for men. If women step back from the workplace to have children it's very hard for them to get back at the same level; if they want to return straightaway they often can't get the flexibility they need. If they do get flexibility at work, often they have to put

› Know what you want to achieve. State what the strategy is and what the problems are that stand in the way – clearly.
› Be clear about what is going to be done next, who is going to do it and how they will do it.
› Be persistent. You need to make it happen in and out of the organisation.

Jenny Watson, former chair, Equal Opportunities Commission

up with watching their peers soaring, as working long hours comes before talent in the promotion stakes. Many women are lost to corporate life because they can't put up with that, or can't resolve the work/home clash. There's also an increasing trend for women to start their own businesses when they decide to return to work. They're a huge loss to big businesses.

Having said all that, there are practical reasons why things ought to be getting easier. Thanks to improvements in technology, you don't have to be in the office all the time and business doesn't always have to be conducted in a face-to-face manner. Carolyn McCall, for example, believes that technology has changed her life:

I can be mobile and in communication at all times. I prefer to be on call 24 hours a day seven days a week, but to my schedule. People say that they couldn't bear that, that they couldn't bear to check the Blackberry on a Saturday and Sunday, but that is

my quid pro quo. I feel I'm far more effective because I am in communication all the time and know exactly what is happening. I wouldn't feel happy if that were not the case.

What now needs to done is for companies to demonstrate unequivocally that women are welcome. It shouldn't be used as a piece of PR because it *sounds* like a good thing to do. It should be done because it is the *right* thing to do. Proportionate representation isn't about numbers; it's about having the best people to deliver results. Staff, male and female, have to see that it's a real commitment based on sound commercial logic. Let everyone see that there's a business case for advancing women: there aren't, after all, an infinite number of talented people out there, so we need to draw from the biggest pool we can.

One thing that's vital is not to assume that most women leave the workforce when they have children and stay at home. The fact is, increasing numbers do go back to work, but only to firms that understand their needs and make them welcome. A business that wants more women coming up through the ranks needs to be more flexible over the life span of a career. The way to avoid resentment elsewhere in the business is to be completely upfront and straightforward. Making family-friendly practices work requires long-term commitment from the whole company.

In addition, it should always be borne in mind that not everyone needs to be constantly on the fast-track to grow and excel. Indeed, there are times when a more moderate pace is essential, such as the early years of child-rearing. But this can be used to advantage. By taking a lot of sideways moves women get the flexibility they need in different disciplines. This will prove invaluable in senior roles later on.

The companies that make this a priority will create a virtuous circle, and benefit from it. As Jenny Watson rightly says:

> When women, particularly women from ethnic minority groups, go into companies, they look for the most senior figure that looks like them. If they don't see anyone they go elsewhere. Research has consistently shown that if companies can't prove that they promote women, women vote with their feet.
>
> It makes a lot of sense for a business to do something about the lack of women in the boardroom – if you don't do it, your competition will and you'll lose these talented women forever.

Keeping it in the family

Finding the next generation for family-run firms is a challenge too. Very few dynasties manage to maintain momentum and success generation after generation. The telling statistic from the Family Firm Institute is that only about 12 per cent of family businesses make it to the third generation and just 3 per cent make it to the fourth. It's not that surprising. The work ethic that drove the founder may not be passed down to his or her descendants. They've witnessed at first hand during childhood just how much was involved getting the company going and may not have the stomach to carry on the battle. And, of course, they may not have the incentive to do so if the business has been successful and the family has become wealthy.

Yet there is something very striking about the dynasties that have been successful. I suppose if you sat down with your family and asked them where they wanted to be and how they wanted to get there, there's a strong chance that everyone would come to roughly the same conclusions. In the same way, what you find among the dynasties that have kept things going is that they have understood and continued the vision. It's almost as though it was in their genes.

Of the various family businesses I have seen at first hand, the Weston family concern has to be one of the most impressive. They've worked hard to pass the addiction to retail down each successive generation and have succeeded in keeping four generations of the dynasty closely tied to the business. Galen Weston and his children, Galen (known as G2) and Alannah, are the third and fourth generations running the conglomerate, since Galen's father, Garfield, and grandfather, George, ran the business before them.

In 1935 Garfield moved to the UK and built the business from scratch under the name of Associated British Foods. He expanded into the United States, Australia, South Africa and Ireland. When he died in 1978, his son Garry received the lion's share of the business, including the prestigious Fortnum & Mason store in London's Piccadilly. Galen, thirteen years younger than Garry, having established the number one supermarket business in Ireland and the most successful discount clothing business – known in the UK today as Primark – was dispatched to Canada to take charge of George Weston Limited.

The rambling company he found on arrival covered everything from paper and pulp factories to salmon farms. It was an ugly mess. Galen had to dump $300 million of unproductive assets to reinvent the company. It was a challenge he relished, however. Retail is his lifeblood: every day as a boy he would hear what his father had been doing and listen to him discuss problems and successes at the dinner table.

As an adult, every Saturday morning, Galen and his wife Hilary would bundle Alannah and G2 into their car and visit two or three stores to talk to associates. As Galen recalls:

> When the children were young we used to give them sweets to keep them comfortable. Then, as they got older, they started tasting the products. They tasted them all. It was super-cool. They were encouraged to pick friends in their class at school to come over and taste the products, too. It was all about earning the privilege of participating in and absorbing the culture of the family.
>
> When I was still at school in London, I used to say to my friends, 'Why don't you meet me at the Fortnum & Mason store? My mum and dad won't mind and I'll be able to make us all an ice cream sundae at the soda fountain' (which still exists today). Being part of the business was made fun and rewarding and it became a way of life.
>
> There's a joy in being able to work and play with your kids, your wife, your sisters and your cousins and have three or four generations of a family in the same business.

Alannah and G2 now hold senior positions in different parts of the Weston empire, Selfridges and Loblaws respectively. Alannah, whose earliest memory is being lost in the china department of Brown Thomas in Ireland, relishes the great name and the great history. It's hardly surprising that her strategy at Selfridges has been to go back to the DNA of the brand created by Gordon Selfridge in the early part of the last century:

The family background is bred in the bone: you either have the gene or you haven't, and the family can see whether you have it or you haven't. That part is unequivocal. Although I have less experience of the retail sector than anything else in my career, it's in my blood. I grew up with it and had it dangled in front of me. Then, even when you love so many other things, you just can't resist. Especially when it's a businesses like ours, which is so dynamic, so exciting, with so much potential to change.

The second, third and fourth generation that chose to stay have done so, as Alannah says, because it's in their genes. There's a heart and soul to these family companies that you cannot replicate. They want to work hard, compete and be winners. It's as simple as that. Employees like to work at stable businesses that are not pushed and pulled by the short-term vagaries of the markets. When there's a family as a major shareholder it's highly likely they are there for the long haul.

Of course, handing on the baton in a family-run business can be fraught with problems. The succession issue can highlight a dual responsibility for the founder of a family firm. Clearly, a company leader wants to do what is best for their business, but they have to do what is right for the family too. They can't put their son or daughter in a position where they might fail. The choice of one heir over another can also cause unpleasant family rifts with a negative impact on the company.

If the head of a family business can't find an obvious heir within their immediate circle, they have to consider very carefully how they groom outsiders to take it over. While it's not always true that subsequent generations can hold on to the success of the first, it's more common for a highly visionary company to lose its way once the family hires managers from outside the organisation.

In the UK, for example, both Sainsbury and Marks & Spencer were at the top of their sector for many years, but when they changed from family control they rapidly lost their way. In the USA Walt Disney famously didn't develop a capable successor and the Disney organisation floundered in the 1970s as executives tried to second-guess what the founder would have done in their position. In all these cases there were some years of struggle before outsiders managed to get the companies back on track.

Even when there is a family member who is just the right person to take over, it's not all smooth sailing. Alannah Weston, for example, has had to cope with endless charges of nepotism. So, too, has the son of one of the world's biggest media tycoons, James Murdoch. According to one former editor in Rupert Murdoch's vast News Corporation media empire, Rupert has a 'dynastic obsession' fuelling his eagerness to leave a substantial worldwide business. He inherited his love of business and, in particular, the newspaper business, from his father, the journalistic legend Sir Keith Murdoch. His fiery determination and love of risk-taking, though, are said to come from his mother, Dame Elizabeth. Consequently, in 2003, when BSkyB wanted to appoint a chief executive, Rupert turned to his own family to produce a candidate.

The succession process had actually started a few years earlier. In 1999 Rupert had declared his eldest son, Lachlan, one of four children of his first and second marriages, as 'first among equals'. However, in July 2005 Lachlan abruptly resigned as News Corp's deputy chief operating officer amid a flurry of speculation about a row with his father.

When James was appointed chief executive at BSkyB in November 2003 Rupert learned a very public lesson about the problems attendant on appointing a family successor in a public company. News Corp owns 39 per cent of BSkyB, and the row over the appointment reverberated for months. What the detractors chose to forget was that there was a rigorous selection process led by a committee of non-executive directors. Indeed, as one of the nomination committee myself I would stake my reputation on the fact James was the best candidate by far. It's human nature to assume that the child of the founder can't possibly have got the job because they are any good. Ironically, just to remain even with their peers, the second and third generations need to be twice as good as the next person, because people expect them to be half as good. Consequently, Rupert's move prompted rumours of a shareholder revolt and even veiled threats of a 'nuclear option' vote at the Annual General Meeting against the entire board, including its chairman. This did not materialise, but the sniping didn't disappear either.

The debate was never really about whether he was the best candidate or not. Rupert quite rightly ignored the hoots of derision and stuck to praising James's quality of leadership. He insisted James was the strongest candidate and even declared he would be prepared to sack his own son if he didn't make the grade.

But still the detractors weren't happy. Some even came up with the ludicrous notion that James would have to address Rupert as 'Chairman' while on company business, otherwise everyone would realise they were related. Great plan – except Rupert is his dad and everybody knows that he's his dad. James has learned to handle the situation in a very natural way. Sometimes in board meetings he calls Rupert 'Pop' and other times 'Chairman'. Because he does this and can clearly delineate between the two, it works. James says his strategy is to ignore the hype, but he does worry about the effects on his team:

> It is inevitable that my last name is going to be relevant. It's a fact of life. I don't complain about it because it has also given me great opportunities in the past growing up around this business. I just had to take it into account and be very, very focused on getting the job done.
>
> It does, however, distract a lot of other people from really thinking about what is going on inside the business, which is a shame. It is all very well for me to ignore it, but the general population of Sky reads the newspapers. They look at the share price and ask what's going on if the share price is down or up.
>
> I've had to change a lot of things in the business to get away from that – from remuneration policies to internal communications strategy. We wanted people to focus on a longer term investment horizon and give them the flexibility to go out and make big decisions.
>
> You just have to be relentless to lead through all that. No matter what the outside throws at you, you have to know you are getting paid to show up for work and do the job; showing people that you're not rattled is crucial too.

The bad news for James, despite the fact he has proved to be a tough, engaging and visionary chief executive, is that he'll never get rid of the accusation of nepotism. He shouldn't, and indeed doesn't, let this affect him. His vindication is simply the performance of BSkyB and now News Corp Europe and Asia, where he became chairman and chief executive in December 2007 following a similar furore.

Selling the idea

All leaders experience an overwhelming love of their business, and pride in what they've achieved makes leaving a company an enormous wrench. If the business is sold, however, it can hit hard, irrespective of whether it is the right thing for the company's future and the good of the team and investors.

Many entrepreneurs, who may have given up everything and withstood years of struggle to get the company off the ground, find the experience particularly devastating. Commentators often ask how an entrepreneur can work for a new owner. The answer is they can't. At lastminute.com, for example, the director of every business they bought left within twelve months. Entrepreneurs like starting things and running their own show. If a company buys an entrepreneur-led business and believes the founder will still be there in a year they're living in cloud cuckoo land.

I had a taste of this when ASDA was sold to Wal-Mart in 1999. After years of hard slog rebuilding the company I stayed on. The sale was absolutely the right thing for all parties, but on a personal level I was left questioning my position. Once you have run something it's very difficult to go and work for another business. Wal-Mart made me feel very welcome, and I had quite a lot of influence over what was happening in the US, but I was always cognisant that I was working for somebody else. My concerns didn't really hit home until they asked me to sign a five-year contract with the potential to work in the US. It would have been a fantastic opportunity, because it's a great, world-leading company, but it just didn't appeal to me.

It was not a surprise when Brent Hoberman relinquished his

role as chief executive of lastminute.com in April 2006, eleven months after the company was bought by Sabre, the owner of US online travel rival Travelocity. Brent put the decision down to lack of control:

> If you take away the control, in our case of technology, and make an entrepreneur go through some bureaucratic process, it doesn't work. You have to justify everything you do and you can't just do something by instinct.
>
> As soon as I became sure that this is the way lastminute.com was going to go, I said that I wasn't the right person to run it because I'm going to let my instinct rule. I can't run a subsidiary; it's just not my thing.
>
> It's all about an overarching ambition, a dream, and believing that you haven't arrived at the end of a journey. We were always at pains to say that you can join lastminute.com now and still be at the beginning of the journey, not the end. It's still going to change, evolve and be exciting.

Clive Jacobs's holiday autos was one of the fourteen businesses bought by lastminute.com. He says he found out quickly that he simply couldn't work for someone else:

> It comes down to a combination of independence, leadership, self-confidence and a load of other factors. One of the reasons I started a business in the first place was because I can't work for someone else: I'm just not good at taking instructions.
>
> Entrepreneurs are not used to playing the corporate game to get up the ladder. They're better at creating the ladder. There's a difference between being at the top of your own ladder and

**trying to climb up someone else's. You are what you are. That is
one of the great things about life; if we were all the same,
wouldn't it be boring?**

End of an era

Perhaps the most frightening move for any leader is retirement.
After having built a company over many years and contributed
so much to its culture, there is always a question mark over what
happens when a key character retires. In some businesses, the
mere mention that a strong figure may one day step aside can
throw those around them into a panic.

Some, of course, will not countenance reaching this stage.
Gulam Noon, for example, is now over seventy but has no inten-
tion of slowing down:

**I'm not a carpenter, I'm not a gardener and I'm not a handyman.
I love my business. Monday to Friday I'm out of the house by
8.30 am and on Saturday I leave at 11. That is my enjoyment.**

Others, such as legendary banker David Mayhew, accept that they will inevitably step down, but want their retirement to be viewed as an opportunity. David said at the time of the 2004 alliance of JP Morgan with Cazenove that he planned to stay with the new venture to ensure its success over 'two or three years'.

Retirement is always a risk to your business because you can never clone yourself. However, looking at it the other way around it's a good moment to get new momentum, new leadership. I'm guilty of having been around rather a long time and shouldn't pretend that my absence wouldn't change things. But I see it as an opportunity for the business to be led in a different way. I can't pretend I am not governed by the history of the last twenty-five years. A younger person could take the view that some of the things that I did or didn't do were actually disadvantageous. The most important thing is that the business doesn't stall while that process takes place.

The JP Morgan joint venture has meant we became a much broader organisation, much less dependent on me from a day-to-day point of view than people suppose. There are people above me, like the chairman of JP Morgan, who can deal with the really serious issues. The reality is that there will be a change, but I expect it to be an opportunity, rather than a handicap. Will there be a change of gear? Yes, probably. If I thought it was the right thing to do for the business I'd retire tomorrow.

The precise time to bow out is never clear cut, as Lord Browne told me, shortly after announcing his decision to retire from BP.

'Leadership is getting results through other people'

Feargal Quinn, founder Superquinn

You just have to look at the circumstances, and to me it was clear that the succession was pretty ripe. To stick around when the succession is ripe is actually pretty destructive. When you are ready to go, the team is ready to reform, so you bow out gracefully. Leave and do something else.

The way I will measure the success of my time there is the quality of BP as it goes forward. Have I put in place the right people? Is the company in good shape to withstand the inevitable changes of the world? Are we doing business in a responsible way? I feel proud of what we have done in these areas.

I fully agree with Lord Browne. The test of his leadership, and indeed any leader, is how good the company is when he goes, not how good it was when he was there. The most important thing that a leader does is to leave a legacy. That legacy should be judged on whether the values of the company continue and whether it is as successful when you have gone as it was when you were there.

Chapter 12
The Anatomy of a Leader
Doing the right thing

Fly across the United States and you'll see it everywhere you go. Giant white letters spelling out the name of global grocery giant Wal-Mart on the roof of every superstore, town after anonymous town.

Bored with flicking through uninspiring in-flight magazines profiling business gurus you've never heard of, you might take a moment to consider which corporate chief decided to display the name of his company where 99 per cent of customers would never see it.

The answer is Sam Walton, the founder of Wal-Mart, and for once the idea has nothing to do with his number one preoccupation – the customer. These giant logos are a legacy of a unique and terrifying trial of leadership – the 'Sam Test'. Sam, who was a keen amateur pilot, used regularly to tour his grocery empire, flying his own six-seater Piper Cherokee. Fortunately for Sam, who was better at running shops than navigating or indeed flying, many US towns identify themselves by picking out their names in giant letters on their water towers. Inspired by this, Sam had

had the Wal-Mart logo painted in a deliberate, large script on the roof of every store to guide him when he flew prospective senior executives to survey the burgeoning empire. If Sam liked his new associate he would suddenly abandon the controls on the pretext of doing something at the back of the plane and would ask the surprised passenger to take over.

In fact, the tiny aircraft was on autopilot, but it is easy to imagine the jolt of fear experienced by a man who has never flown a plane before as the mass of controls swam before his eyes. Indeed, according to Sam, many would-be emergency pilots crumbled. Those who passed it dubbed it the 'Sam Test', and even for them it was discussed with the shrugged shoulder nonchalance of someone who felt that they had come within an inch of the end of their lives. It was worse for those who failed, of course, because they quickly realised that in a single moment they had missed out on the chance of a lifetime.

I chose to open my final chapter with this story because I suspect that, despite everything I've said in this book to the contrary, many readers still believe that all good leaders are a bit like Sam: eccentric, flamboyant, larger than life. They do crazy things, but because they're 'geniuses' it all comes right.

'You can't push a bit of string, you have to pull it. In leadership you have to be at the front where the action is, you have to set the pace. Knowing where the action is is your job'

Sir Ken Morrison, Wm Morrison

Well, no. Every leader is different, with different personalities, skills and values. There's no 'one size fits all' solution. In fact, I would argue the opposite: being true to your own inherent nature is far more important than trying to live up to some preconceived ideal. In the words of Carolyn McCall, chief executive of the Guardian Media Group, 'One of the characteristics of a really strong leader is that they don't try to be someone else. They don't emulate others' behaviour. They are themselves and they have their own conviction. That authenticity counts for a lot when people are working with you and observing you.'

Being true to yourself demands real self-knowledge, and this is a quality that is often in scarce supply. You need the honesty to understand your own strengths and weaknesses, and to work with them. Having said that, I have been constantly struck over the years at how certain qualities emerge again and again when I encounter leaders I particularly admire. They may be an extrovert or an introvert, larger than life or self-effacing. They will have taken very different paths to success: some will have taken the entrepreneurial route, starting with nothing to create a world-class business, while others will have

'Be the person you really are. Leadership is very personal and one of the things people sniff out more than anything else is reality. Leaders who are not sincere get found out very quickly'

Justin King, J Sainsbury

been classic professional managers who worked their way up through the ranks of an established company. But they all seem to share certain characteristics that mark them out from the rest, and it's on these characteristics that I want to focus in closing.

The power of passion

The best leaders that I know are passionate about what they do. They know exactly where it is they want their company to be and demonstrate an enormous amount of energy and enthusiasm to get it there. This passion is a key trait. Running a business is not an easy thing to do, and if you don't care sufficiently about it, or don't believe that it's a 24-hour-a-day, seven-day-a-week task until the day you leave, then you're not going to do very well. As I said earlier, there is not a day, not even Christmas Day or family holidays, when top business people are not thinking about their organisation and how they can make it better. Not surprisingly, then, 'enthusiasm', 'passion' and 'commitment' have proved to be constantly recurring words in my conversations with other business leaders. 'I honestly wake up in the morning feeling lucky and

'Good leaders are restless. They are always a bit paranoid, thinking that what they are doing is not enough and worrying about what the next threat is'

Andy Hornby, HBOS

really look forward to my day,' says Carolyn McCall. 'No matter how awful they might be, because some days are always difficult, I just love what I do.'

It's not just about your own attitude to work. If you don't have huge reserves of excitement about your business, then you won't create that feeling in the people around you. Brent Hoberman, co-founder of lastminute.com, is adamant about this: 'Passion shines through in terms of motivating staff,' he argues. 'If you're passionate and excited about the business and are prepared to do everything yourself, then you're fun to work with.' Or as Carolyn McCall puts it: 'Passion is a fantastically contagious quality. People want to work with people who like their job. If the team think that you like what you do and enjoy where you are, it's very energising and stimulating.'

Not surprisingly, perhaps, the word passion occurs especially frequently among entrepreneurs. Not surprisingly – because they have to believe absolutely in what they have set out to achieve; otherwise the inevitable setbacks and disappointments that they will encounter on their way will crush them.

The career of Sir Gulam Noon, founder of Noon Products, offers a textbook example of the need for, and value of, an absolute belief in what you're doing, the 'fire in your belly', as he puts it. Gulam moved to England from Mumbai in 1971 with a 50 per cent stake in the UK arm of Royal Sweets, a small confectionery company his grandfather had founded in India more than 100 years before. Bombay Halwa, the UK company Gulam established, quickly did well, particularly with Gulam's most famous innova-tion, Bombay Mix. But problems inevitably cropped up. In 1980 he made an ill-fated attempt to open a food factory in the United States supplying Indian ready meals to supermarkets. Undeterred, he returned to London, established Noon Products, tried to persuade Birds Eye to distribute his products, and was turned down again and again. He recalls:

> Finally, a brand manager said he would listen to me. I said, 'I know you are a manufacturer and a giant and I am a small businessman, but I have something which you don't have.' I showed him the product, he approved it, we made a deal and he gave me an order worth £2.7 million that day. To have the money to produce the products I had to re-mortgage my house, but I never looked back. Entrepreneurship is all about risk-taking, perseverance, tenacity and hard work.

Noon Products now supplies most of the UK's leading supermarkets, getting through a ton of garlic and chilli a day per factory, and achieving more than £140 million in annual sales.

The story could be repeated a hundred times, but the basic elements are the same: success belongs to the individual who passionately believes in what they're trying to achieve, who doesn't give up and who uses their passion to enthuse others. If you don't have this, then you don't have anything.

'The defining feature of leadership is that you have to seriously enjoy the job. You have to live it, breathe it and jump out of bed every morning at the thought of the day ahead'

Andy Hornby, HBOS

Making decisions, taking risks

Passion implies a certain bloody-mindedness, so it's not surprising that good leaders are decisive. They know that you can't time opportunities – they're always too early or too late. But because they constantly search for improvement, they seize these opportunities quickly when they arise. This, of course, goes hand in hand with taking risks, and the best leaders know that they must lead from the front, often in the face of some fairly vocal criticism from outside.

Few business leaders demonstrate these qualities better than Rupert Murdoch, the media giant who, despite his obvious success, is the subject of constant carping. Rupert characteristically takes the criticism head on. 'Everybody has predicted total disaster for most of the things I've done,' he says. 'I've had to develop a very thick skin.' He's also anxious to explain why making potentially risky decisions is so vitally important to the future of his business:

> Media is changing. It has always been changing, but now it is changing by the week. Our challenge is to understand that and seize the opportunities.
>
> Technology-wise it's a different world from when I started

'Tomorrow's decisions are better than today's. The best decisions are those never made'

Allan Leighton

out. It is developing at such a tremendous pace and the form of distributing news and entertainment is changing all the time. But, if I were starting out on the *Adelaide News* today, I would do the same things. I would ask myself what steps I could take to give me the capital and size to be able to take some big risks.

In truth, the best and the most profitable deals we have done are ones that cost us the back end of nothing. We managed to buy the *Sun* for £500,000. It has never made less than £1 million every week since. When we bought the Fox Network it was very hard work. We had to run three or four stations on the cheap, broadcasting for just one night a week and then two nights and so on. It took a long time to capture the imagination, but now it's number one. As usual, everybody ridiculed us for taking on CNN with our Fox News Channel, just as they predicted total disaster for Sky and the *Sun* too.

It's Rupert's decisiveness and intuition that has built one of the world's most powerful media empires from the basis of owning just one evening newspaper in Adelaide.

Another media head who embraces the need to take risks on a smaller day-to-day basis is Gail Rebuck, the chairman and chief executive at book publishing giant Random House. Her view is that, in her line of work, doing business and taking risks are inseparable. 'When we decide whether or not to publish a book,' she argues, 'we are in the risk business. No one knows how the book will sell. You can't base your decision to spend a lot of money solely on market research. Market research is very useful in helping to develop a regular brand-name author. But what publishers have to do is be ahead of public taste. We are meant to intuit what

> 'Active luck is taking advantage of opportunities. Look at the upside and the downside; if the latter isn't too big, go for it!'
>
> Julian Richer, Richer Sounds

people want to read next, the zeitgeist if you like, rather than do more of the same. If you ask people what they want to read they will simply say something like the last thing they read. That is not very helpful.'

Gail believes in meeting this challenge squarely:

> I always say follow your instincts. As you mature in whatever career you are in, you are going to have unconsciously accumulated a huge amount of knowledge. When you are forced to make a quick decision, close down all the outside influences for a second and try to feel what is right. Then do the checks and all the necessary analysis. Ultimately, the brain is like a computer going through these files of accumulated experience.
>
> In publishing, more so than in any other industry, you do tend to make decisions based on instinct. The publisher just feels it's right. Sometimes a publisher whose taste and judgement I respect says that they've found this new novelist, they've never read anything like it before and they want to spend some large sum of money immediately to stay ahead of the competition. All I try to do is sense whether they are being authentic or not, whether they feel real passion and commitment. If they do, then I normally tell them to go ahead.

It's not only media leaders who feel this way. Sir Ken Morrison, for example, built his entire chain of Morrisons supermarkets on a creative hunch that required taking a huge risk. He'd started out his career selling eggs in Bradford market shortly after the Second World War (he says that his toughness in business is motivated by a 'constant feeling of insecurity' born out of the tough times). In 1960 he decided to swap the markets for a career building a chain of supermarkets. The move coincided with a time when people were just beginning to have a little more money to spend and were becoming more mobile thanks to the growth in car ownership. But, even then, his decision to open the first out-of-town supermarket took considerable nerve:

My first big store was built in a converted cinema out of town. We only got planning permission because the council planning officials didn't really know what it was they were giving permission for. They didn't realise just how much this would change things and, to be honest, nor did I.

At that time the town centres were booming. My motive for the new store was based on the simple fact that I could recognise as a retailer that I needed bigger premises and I could see that times were changing. As a small company with no financial muscle, I couldn't afford to take a lease on a big shop in the town centre. I had to chase cheap property out of town because there was no covenant to cover a loan.

My friends thought I was crazy and told me so. I thought so too at one stage when I looked out on a Saturday afternoon and saw crowds of people heading into town on the buses. I was left looking around for the next customer and hoping it would work out in the end.

As it transpired, out-of-town stores were not a disaster. Ken's farsighted move paved the way for an explosion of out-of-town stores in subsequent years and heralded a revolution in retailing. With the larger stores affording more sales space, retailers expanded their selection of the more lucrative, high-margin, non-food items with goods such as clothes, toys, books and electronic items. They were also able to offer more prepared foods, now an essential to many families where both partners work.

By making his customers' shopping trip as easy as possible and offering the best value goods, Ken's courageous move ensured a three-decade-long growth and profitability for Morrisons that was the envy of many of its rivals. He is anxious, though, to distinguish between risk-taking for its own sake and risk-taking to back an informed hunch. 'I have never regarded anything I have done as speculation,' he argues. 'I have always seen it as backing judgement. If I am going to gamble on something I might as well put some money on the 2.30 at Windsor, but if you are backing your judgement it is quite a different matter.' He believes that, 'having faith and holding your nerve is a great quality', although he rather disarmingly adds, 'the only thing is, you have got to be right otherwise it's a disaster.'

Sir Philip Green, one of the most powerful figures in British retailing, is similarly famous for his decisiveness and willingness

'If one day you'll regret not taking a chance – then take that chance'

Allan Leighton

to take risks. 'I don't want to get tortured over a decision,' he says. 'I want to spend my time where I can make the most impact.'

He takes a pretty dim view of people who aren't prepared to step up to the mark in this way. 'People running public companies don't take risks,' he complains. 'Most of them couldn't even spell risk. Their definition of risk is they have a temporary PA who makes them a cup of coffee who doesn't realise they want a little milk rather than a lot of milk.' This may be a little harsh, but it's true to Philip Green's business philosophy.

Perhaps the last word here should go to Charles Dunstone, founder of Carphone Warehouse. He doesn't simply believe that risks should be accepted, but that they form an inevitable part of everyday business life:

> Risks are a part of the culture of business. The world is becoming so risk averse, so driven by certain outcomes and risk management, in the end no one is going to want to take any risks or do anything. Yes, it might go wrong. But every time you walk off a pavement someone might run you over. That is life. You have to take risks. That is what we are all paid to do, take risks. That is the only thing that moves the world forward.

'I am learning every day. I drive myself hard and want to win every time. You have got to want to get it right and you have got to love it. Every day is a new day'

Sir Philip Green, Arcadia and Bhs

Making mistakes

If you take risks, you're inevitably going to make mistakes. In fact, I'd go as far as to say that it's impossible to do business and not make mistakes. What the effective leader does, though, is not to sweep the problem under the carpet, but to recognise it as quickly as possible, and then learn from it.

In my case, the worst mistake I ever made was at ASDA in May 1993. We had been struggling for months to turn around the business with not a penny to invest in it. Then we sold our stake in the MFI home furnishings business for £73 million. I remember clearly sitting around a table in a pizza restaurant in Leeds with Archie Norman and Phil Cox, the finance director, discussing what exactly we were going to do with the money. It was a huge sum and the business had never had such an injection of cash. Everyone agreed that I could have the money for the store renewal programme. We had been experimenting with different formats for months at our Wolstanton store and we now felt ready to roll out what we had learned. I immediately set out an aggressive schedule of renewing forty stores in the first year, at an average cost of £2.5 million a store. In the initial stage we focused on twenty stores.

The problem was there is a huge difference in renewing one store and renewing twenty. I really didn't know what I was doing. I had no idea of the scale of the task and completely ignored the fact that it had taken six months to get Wolstanton right, with almost full-time attention.

I was working long hours and was so tired I was just ordering people around – saying put this there, that over there and paint that wall in that colour. I was not demonstrating any of the cultural traits or management styles we had worked so hard to encourage. However, I crashed the programme through, and within three months twenty stores were revamped. Then the sales went down. And they kept on going down. I was in despair. I felt like I was living in a nightmare.

The problem was the stores looked nice, but they were difficult to shop in and hard to manage. I had completely forgotten all I had learned about retail, and worst of all I had forgotten that this whole thing was about the customer.

Late one night, on the sixth successive week of sales drops, I went out for a run, then went back to my desk at ASDA's HQ. I was so angry and depressed. Archie came around and asked, 'What's the matter?' I told him the matter was I had really screwed up on those stores. I was going to have to undo them and spend another £10 million redoing what I should have got right in the first place. Archie laughed and said, 'Thank Christ for that. Everybody knows you screwed up. Everybody knows you are going round like a bear with a sore head, but nobody wants to be the one to come and tell you. Just get on with it.'

It was a lesson. We cancelled the next twenty stores, went back to the first group and fixed them. Sales immediately went up. Roll out is the death of innovation. Because I had the money, despite all the stuff I had taught myself, I just spent it. I didn't spend it wisely, though, and then I wasn't prepared to say that I was wrong. I learned the hard way that when a business has money to invest you should act as if you don't have it. It was a vital lesson to learn, and I haven't forgotten it.

In any business the stakes are pretty high. The leader may have risked everything on their venture and invested hundreds of thousands of pounds of other people's money. Consequently, the fear of making mistakes is always there. But as I've already said, if you accept as a given that you're going to get some things wrong, the crucial thing is how you react to your mistakes and what you get from the experience. I have often noticed that entrepreneurs are particularly good at dealing with this aspect of business – perhaps because it has taken them so long to get where they are, and they have suffered a few knocks en route. They seem to be very resilient. Certainly, they bounce back from their mistakes much quicker than many others.

For me, a classic example of this is the way that Charles Dunstone dealt with the toughest challenge of his career at Carphone Warehouse. It was April 2005, and Carphone Warehouse, which prides itself on having high standards of customer care, launched a free broadband service. Within weeks more than 470,000 customers applied for the package, which included phone calls and internet access, and the strong demand caused mayhem. The company received a barrage of complaints from would-be customers. Weeks after launching the offer thousands of people were still waiting to be signed up. Gleeful rivals carped that they would not launch a similar offer until they had given more time to training staff and increased call centre capacity. Charles was forced to issue a painful *mea culpa* and double the number of call centre staff to reduce the queues.

Looking back on the débâcle, he says:

> It has been very tough, but there was a big lesson. I will try and make sure we are better prepared and have more contingency another time. In the past when we have got a bit carried away, or something has got bigger than we thought, we could always fix it quickly if we worked all night for a week. Suddenly, we

had created something so big that, however much willingness there was to do that, we simply couldn't put the capacity in place that we needed so quickly.

Broadband was a mess of our making. But we were trying to revolutionise a market in a very bold initiative which is the Carphone style. We had to make some very difficult judgement calls about taking on new call centre capacity, putting agents in and deciding how much was the minimum training we could give so that they could answer the phone and still know what was going on. Every single day was about rationing resources and making tough decisions.

We were very honest with our customers and our employees, and said we were very sorry. I have agonised about it since, because I think I might have been too apologetic. We were quickly in a position where we were the fastest call centre on broadband – much better than any supplier in the UK – yet we carried on saying 'sorry it is not enough'. The press and our competitors seized on that because it was easy to do.

However painful it was, it was the right thing to do. I would do it again. It is only the people who are really bold that really change things. Sometimes when you do really bold things you get unusual outcomes because you are absolutely in uncharted territory.

Of course, it's not just about learning from mistakes, it's also about your attitude when things go wrong – which, in business, they inevitably do. One of Britain's most respected business leaders, Lord Browne, for example, experienced an *annus horribilis* in 2006 following a series of significant corporate set-backs at BP and an investigation into a fire that killed fifteen employees. 'The unexpected always occurs,' he says. 'While you can look back and see how it has happened, what you can't tell beforehand is how those tiny little segments will one day just create something.'

The test of a leader is how they respond. If they panic, they're lost. In Lord Browne's case he was determined not to be thrown off course:

> What is most important is that, when the unexpected occurs, as has happened many times in my career, you must never lose the plot. Leaders have to have a vision and a purpose for what they are doing. They have to be very disciplined to remember what they are about. You are about making sure the team is with you the whole time, that you treat them well and you respect them.
>
> It would pretty easy to let it all go when something unexpected happens and say, gosh, we have got to change and we've got to get all hands on deck. But then you lose everything. Just remember, things happen. Sometimes there is a reason, sometimes there isn't. Life is about the cut and thrust of human interaction. It is not all about rational business and net present values.
>
> The most imporant thing is to keep the vision and keep everyone aligned with that.

The whole truth

In a world of spin, near truth and the statistical obfuscations of politicians, it is healthy to remind ourselves that, according to all the effective leaders I know, finding and telling the truth is just as important as passion. It is a key leadership skill to build a culture that encourages people to tell the truth. And, as I've already pointed out in an earlier chapter, the proof of this is that, in failed or problematic companies, no one ever tells the truth or, at any rate, the whole truth. To repeat the words of Professor Michael Beer of the Harvard Business School, 'The ability of people to speak the truth to the senior team cannot be underestimated. Once you allow the truth to inform power, things will happen.'

And let's not forget the impact that dishonesty has on the outside world. As Patience Wheatcroft of the *Sunday Telegraph* puts it: 'The greatest lesson for any business or business leader is that there is no mileage in not being truthful. A journalist who has ever been lied to, never forgets.'

Self-confidence means knowing when to listen

People don't enjoy following leaders whose appearance and demeanour give the impression that they're being led into the valley of death. They want to follow leaders who emanate a sense of purpose and self-confidence, and all the people I respect at the top have these qualities in spades. It's important to understand, though, that self-confidence means a positive outlook and an ability to be at ease with yourself. It doesn't mean a leader who thinks they know the answer to everything. Leaders who think this way can actually have a negative impact because their supposed omniscience discourages their teams from ever taking the initiative. And, at its very worst, overbearing self-confidence becomes the business-killer, arrogance.

I noticed once, in the office of Henry Kravis, of the private equity firm company KKR, a sign that said simply: Arrogance kills. I questioned him about this, and he told me that, after many years observing hundreds of companies, he'd come to the conclusion that the leaders he admires are the ones who listen. 'I have seen so many people become so arrogant that they implode,' he said. 'They start making really bad mistakes, because they won't listen to anybody. They think they have all the answers. Nobody, however smart and capable, has all the answers.' He elaborated on his view:

> The leaders I admire have the ability to make a commitment and really stick by it. They also communicate really well. If you cannot communicate what your ideas are to a group, then I don't believe that you can really be a leader. To be a leader you have to have followers, and that means you have to gain the respect and confidence of the people you are trying to lead so they believe in you. Getting people to listen and sign on to what you are advocating is an important feat.
>
> To be a good leader you have to encourage people to speak up. You have to encourage people not to be afraid of you. Leading by fear is a disaster. I see that in certain companies, and to me that is not leadership. Basically, you are just scaring the heck out of somebody so they do what they have to do. That is not real leadership and you will never get people to perform at their peak capabilities.

At its best, self-confidence allows others to make a contribution and also ensures that the leader emanates a sense of optimism, even if times are hard. After all, people look to the leader. The chief executive is like a barometer. A glance at you and the

'A leader is a dealer in hope'

Allan Leighton

team instantly decides which way the wind is blowing and whether it's favourable or not. You need always to remember that, and to be aware of the effect your demeanour has on people, even when you have other pressing matters on your mind.

This doesn't mean that you can avoid the realities of your situation, but what it does mean is that you can always be certain that, with your team, you can overcome the problems and succeed. You're not just the eternal optimist, but a pragmatic and motivating leader who tells it how it is, yet with an air that things will soon be on the up and up. A barometer stuck on 'set fair' won't fool anyone over time. As Val Gooding, chief executive of BUPA, says: 'The role of a leader is to inspire and motivate people. If you can do that in your working day and your people have gone about their job with more self-confidence, then that is probably the biggest contribution you can make.' She chooses as a great role model one of Britain's greatest explorers:

> Leaders might not be inwardly optimistic at all times, but they should never say, 'This is dire, what are we going to do?' If they do, everyone else thinks that if the boss doesn't know what to do they really are in trouble. Even when you don't know what to do, you have to have the approach of the Antarctic explorer [Ernest] Shackleton, declaring that we are going to get through this and come out the other side. We are going to be better and stronger and we will all learn something.

The five principles of Mars

Thirty years ago when I started out at Mars, they introduced me on day one to the five principles of Mars – the guiding framework that sought to build the prosperity of the company through the prosperity of the people (associates) who worked there and by putting the customer first.

- *Freedom* – for associates to work to their full potential, and for the company to generate profit.
- *Efficiency* – through being the most efficient producer, and so being able to pass on great value to the customer, who is king.
- *Mutuality* – everyone was in the company together, everyone had a role to play, and everything done was for the mutuality of the company, associates and customer.
- *Responsibility* – to make the highest quality products, protect the company's assets, to work safely and to deliver the company plan.
- *Quality* – in everything we did.

Leadership is all about such principles, and any leader who creates or operates an organisation along these lines is 'doing the right thing'. Simply put, that's what leadership is all about – 'doing the right thing'.

And remember:

On the darkest days, when things aren't going so well, try to remember that failures don't make you an awful person. Likewise, your company's success doesn't make you a genius either!

Epilogue

Harold Wilson once famously said 'a week is a long time in politics' and this could not be more true of the corporate world. Since this book was first published, much has moved on for everyone involved and, in some cases, there have been significant changes. In October 2007, for example, Mark Thompson announced that the BBC would make a further massive wave of redundancies, following the lower than expected licence fee settlement. Mark has had to defend his stance robustly against widespread criticism, from both within and without, that the reduction in jobs is depriving licence fee payers of the high-quality product expected from the corporation.

James Murdoch has also taken centre stage, with some commentators claiming he is now the most powerful man in Britain, following the announcement he was stepping down as chief executive of BSkyB to head News Corp's European and Asian businesses. The move, which clearly establishes him as a successor to Rupert Murdoch's media empire, puts James in control of the most powerful newspaper group in the UK, the largest pay-TV provider, the dominant player in the key Premiership football market and the fast-growing BSkyB broadband, internet and telephone market.

International expansion, and all the complexities that it brings with it, has also been key for other *On Leadership* contributors. Terry Leahy has led Tesco into the United States with its Fresh & Easy convenience store venture. Rivals carp that it is 'Leahy's biggest ever gamble', but if anyone can succeed where so many other British retailers have failed, it is Terry without a doubt. Likewise, Philip Green has characteristically faced down the naysayers by opening up his first Topshop store in New York on the back of the runaway success of the range designed for the fashion chain by supermodel Kate Moss.

I, too, have seen some tough tests of my leadership skills, perhaps none more so than at the Royal Mail. In the summer of 2007, the Communication Workers Union staged a series of walk-outs over proposals on pay, pensions and working practices. At stake was the future of an institution which is part of the fabric of British society. Since the strike ended with the CWU agreeing to a deal with the Royal Mail that will enable the modernisation drive to continue, the government has announced a comprehensive review of the postal services market. I have agreed to extend my tenure as chairman until the conclusion of this review.

What this massive postal strike, and indeed all the other issues listed here, demonstrates is that the challenges faced by leaders change on a daily basis. These challenges all need to be managed minute-by-minute; leadership is constantly being tested. In just these few examples there are demonstrations of leadership in its various forms. They show that good leadership cannot be a popularity contest; the importance of telling people how it is; the need to be prepared to adjust things as circumstances change; and the value of innovative thought. In fact, all the things that I strongly believed about leadership when I first set out to write *On Leadership*.

So much of leadership is simple common sense. Although, as this book shows, different leaders have different styles and will tackle things in different ways to get to the same point, they all share the characteristics of sound judgement and acres of common sense. Is this all new? Apparently not. Not long ago, while staying at a hotel, I found myself browsing in a grand, oak-panelled library. I chanced upon a small, leather-bound book which rather took my fancy. Called *The First Book of Psychology*, it dated back to the early nineteenth century. I don't know what originally attracted me to this book, but I was hooked in seconds. The titles of the chapters alone encapsulated everything I have been saying here.

There is, for example, a chapter entitled 'The Will and the Rhythm'. In any organisation there has to be a will to succeed, but that collective will is not enough on its own because every business must create a rhythm. How does a rhythm work? Well, people make decisions, they get them right and that gives them confidence. Therefore they make more decisions, which are often even better and give them even more confidence. This creates momentum. When people talk about businesses being on a roll, that's what they mean: there is a will and a rhythm in the business. The task for the leader is to create the will and the rhythm.

Another chapter which attracted my attention is called, rather obliquely, 'Finding the Jewel in the Toad's Head'. Put simply, in every bad company there are good people and good things that happen. Finding the jewel in the toad's head is about discovering what's good amid everything that is bad. For a leader, particularly in a turnaround situation, that's a big part of what has to be done. Then there's another favourite of mine: 'Avoid the Funeral of the Living Corpse'. This is all about having fun. You can either live each day as if it were your funeral, or you can instil the belief, in both yourself and the business, that fun really makes a difference. It's much better to be in an environment where fun is part of the culture.

Finally, there's a chapter heading which, in just a handful of words, reflects what has been the downfall of countless numbers of businesses, 'Don't Mate With Who You Hate'. Forming alliances with people who you don't really like, or people with whom you have competed for years, should not be taken lightly. One of the often overlooked issues about corporate mergers is that they generally involve businesses that have fought against each other for years but that are now trying to work together. Not surprisingly, if you mate with who you hate, the problems caused by the cultural clashes that emerge often outweigh the benefits of the financial synergies.

What does all this really mean? It means that the rules behind effective leadership and creating a sustainable business have not actually changed in hundreds of years. Here is a very clear demonstration that in the nineteenth century people knew what this was all about, and that there's nothing new in any of it. There is no need to reinvent the wheel. Keeping things simple has always been my mantra in business – why would any leader want to complicate matters?

In the end it is just about being focussed, listening, learning, having fun and, of course, it is also about good, old-fashioned common sense.

Appendix

Who's who

Marcus Agius (Barclays Bank)

Marcus Agius trained as a mechanical engineer at Cambridge, but spent over thirty years of his working life at top-drawer independent bank Lazards, rising to become chairman in London, before leaving to become chairman of Barclays in January 2007. He has been dubbed the 'quintessential English banker' and at Lazards was credited with bringing in some of the biggest deals of the day, working closely with Pearson, HBOS, Next and BSkyB, among others.

Dawn Airey (former MD, Sky Networks)

Dawn Airey began her career as a management trainee at Central TV. She quickly rose to become controller of programme planning, moving on to ITV to be controller of children's and daytime programmes. In 1994 she joined Channel 4 to head arts and entertainment, acquiring smash hits such as *ER*, *Friends* and *Frasier* from America. In 1995 Airey was invited to join Channel Five. Despite its tiny budget, the station had a huge impact and Airey took over as chief executive in 2000, moving to Sky Networks in 2003. In October 2007 Airey joined ITV as head of global content.

Surinder Arora (Arora International)

Surinder Arora started his career as an office junior at British Airways while moonlighting as a hotel waiter. He invested all of his family's savings in property, eventually developing a row of houses opposite Heathrow Airport into a large-scale bed-and-breakfast operation. From that, in 1999, emerged his first hotel specifically for air crews. By 2004, when Arora International won the contract for a 600-bedroom hotel at Heathrow's new Terminal 5 development, he had built a hotel and property empire worth £227 million.

Richard Baker (Boots)

After graduating with an engineering degree from Cambridge, Richard Baker decided his chosen career was 'too slow and not very exciting' and joined Mars. After nine years at Mars, his former colleague Allan Leighton recruited him to be business unit director of ASDA, where he progressed up the ranks to become chief operating officer. His success at the grocer propelled him into the job of chief executive of Boots, with the brief to revive the fortunes of an ailing retailer. Baker resigned from Boots in July 2007, following the completion of Boots' £8 billion merger with French Group Alliance Unichem, which created Europe's largest health and beauty retailer with 2,500 pharmacies and 390 drug distribution outlets in 14 countries.

Lionel Barber (*Financial Times*)

Lionel Barber graduated from Oxford University with a joint honours degree in German and modern history. He began his career as a reporter on the *Scotsman* before moving to *The Sunday Times* in 1981 to become a business correspondent. He joined the *Financial Times* as Washington correspondent in 1986. He has been Brussels bureau chief and editor of the *FT* Continental European and US editions. He was appointed editor of the *Financial Times* in November 2005.

Professor Michael Beer (Harvard Business School)

Michael Beer is Cahners-Rabb professor of business administration,

Emeritus, Harvard Business School. His specialisations include strategic human resource management, management development and managing organisational effectiveness and change. He is also a director of GTECH Corporation and a consultant to many companies, including Hewlett Packard, Honeywell, Merck and Whitbread.

Josh Bekenstein (Bain Capital)

Josh Bekenstein received an MBA from Harvard Business School and a BA from Yale University. He is a managing director of Bain Capital, which he helped start in 1984 when Bain raised their first $367 million fund. Today, Bain Capital manages over $40 billion in a variety of private investment funds located in seven cities and five countries around the globe.

Lord Browne (BP)

John Browne graduated from St John's College, Cambridge, with a first in physics and joined BP in 1966. Identified early as a rare talent, he rose through the ranks in a variety of exploration, production and finance posts worldwide, becoming chief executive in 1995. He then transformed BP from a £20 billion company into the £140 billion behemoth it is today. In 1998 Sir John Browne, as he was then known, masterminded what was history's biggest ever industrial merger when BP purchased Amoco for $55 billion. In May 2007 Lord Browne retired from BP.

Alex Brummer (*Daily Mail*)

Alex Brummer read economics and politics at the University of Southampton and went on to do an MBA at the University of Bradford Management Centre. He began his career at J Walter Thomson and Haymarket Publishing, before beginning a twenty-six-year stint at the *Guardian*, starting as financial correspondent, moving on to become Washington correspondent, foreign editor and then financial editor. Alex Brummer became City editor of the *Daily Mail* in May 2000. He has recently written a book on the current credit crisis, *The Crunch*.

Adam Crozier (Royal Mail)

After graduating from Edinburgh's Heriot Watt University, Adam Crozier moved into sales at Mars. He joined Saatchi & Saatchi as a media executive in 1988 and made it to the top – rapidly – becoming chief executive at the age of thirty-one, after the founders left. He moved to the Football Association in 2000, where he made radical and often controversial changes. He became chief executive of the Royal Mail in February 2003.

Guy Davison (Cinven)

Guy Davison read history at Cambridge before joining KPMG and then private equity firm Larpent Newton. He joined Cinven in 1988 and has been involved in deals for CBR, Maxeda, Unique Pub Company and William Hill.

Charles Dunstone (Carphone Warehouse)

After leaving Uppingham School, where he had set up his first entrepreneurial venture selling pens and cigarette lighters, Charles Dunstone took a job with Japanese electronics giant NEC rather than go to university. In 1989, using £6,000 of savings, he opened his first Carphone Warehouse shop in Marylebone, London, with the idea of opening up the fledging mobile phone market to individual tradespeople. The chain is now Europe's leading mobile communications retailer, with more than 1,400 shops in ten countries.

Sir James Dyson (Dyson)

After scraping through A Levels, James Dyson went to the Royal College of Art where he teamed up with his mentor, Jeremy Fry, an inventor who loved engineering, to develop the Sea Truck. James's next successful invention was the Ballbarrow. He then devised the now-famous bagless vacuum cleaner. After fifteen years, 5,127 prototypes and rejection by a string of companies, the product finally got to market. In 2005, Dyson overtook Hoover to become the biggest vacuum cleaner in America, with a 20.7 per cent share of the market.

Jonathan Feuer (CVC)

Jonathan Feuer holds a degree in applied mathematics from the University of Warwick. His first job was at Ernst & Whinney, where he qualified as a chartered accountant. He joined CVC in 1988 from the corporate finance department of Baring Brothers. At CVC he has been involved in several high-profile deals, including car parts retailer Halfords and department store Debenhams.

Sir Christopher Gent (GlaxoSmithKline)

Sir Christopher Gent began his career as a management trainee at National Westminster Bank, before going on to work at Schroder Computer Services and ICL. He joined Vodafone as managing director in 1985, when the mobile phone service was first launched in the UK, and became chief executive in 1997. Under his leadership Vodafone was transformed from a UK-focused business with four million customers, into a global player with interests in more than twenty countries. He retired from Vodafone in July 2003. Sir Christopher has been chairman of GlaxoSmithKline (GSK) since January 2005. He is a non-executive director of Lehman Brothers Holdings Inc, a non-executive director of Ferrari spa, a member of the Financial Reporting Council Limited, a senior adviser at Bain & Co and a member of the Advisory Board of Reform.

Jacqueline Gold (Ann Summers)

Jacqueline Gold joined Ann Summers, then just comprising two sex shops, as an office junior mid-way through her A Level year. She hit upon the idea of selling sexy lingerie and sex toys at private parties because she realised that many women did not want to be seen in the shops and, in so doing, transformed the business into a multi-million pound concern, with a sales force of 7,500 women as party organisers. Jacqueline Gold has been voted Britain's 'most powerful businesswoman' in a number of polls by publications, including *Cosmopolitan*, *Woman* and the *Daily Mail*.

Val Gooding (BUPA)

Val Gooding began her career as a reservations agent for British Airways, working her way up through a number of senior positions, including head of cabin services and director of business units. After twenty-three years at BA, she quit to join BUPA because she felt it was too 'narrow' to spend a whole career with one company in one industry. After two years as managing director, UK operations, Val Gooding became chief executive and has presided over annual double-digit income growth.

Sir Philip Green (Arcadia)

Sir Philip Green's first job was helping his mother with the running of the family businesses following the death of his father when he was just twelve. Leaving school at sixteen, he began buying and selling clothes. At thirty-three he struck gold – selling the Jean Jeanie chain for £3 million, having paid just £65,000 a year before. The bid that subsequently propelled him into the major league was the 1999 joint venture with the billionaire Barclay Brothers to buy Sears. Today, with the Bhs and Arcadia Group, he owns 2,300 shops in the UK and has assets of around £3.6 billion.

Sir Stuart Hampson (John Lewis)

Stuart Hampson read modern languages at St John's College, Oxford, before beginning a career in the Civil Service. He rose to become private secretary to the Minister for Consumer Affairs and then to the Secretary of State for Trade. He joined the John Lewis Partnership in 1982, running the Southampton store Tyrrell & Green and becoming the Partnership's fourth chairman in 1993. He retired from the John Lewis Partnership in March 2007.

Professor Charles Handy

Charles Handy began his business career in marketing at Shell International. He was a co-founder of the London Business School in 1967. A prolific author, Charles Handy specialises in organisational behaviour and management. Among the ideas he has advanced are the 'portfolio worker' and the 'shamrock organisation'.

Lord Michael Heseltine

Lord Heseltine was a Member of Parliament from 1959 to 2001. He was a cabinet minister in various departments from 1979 and Deputy Prime Minister from 1995 to 1997. He is founder and chairman of the Haymarket Publishing Group, the largest privately owned publishing company in the UK. He has written books on Europe and, most recently, his political autobiography, *Life in the Jungle*. In 1998 he was invited to become Chairman of the UK–China Forum. He also served as a Millennium Commissioner. Lord Heseltine is an enthusiastic gardener and is creating an arboretum to house his collection of over 3,500 different trees and shrubs.

Brent Hoberman (lastminute.com)

Brent Hoberman read French and German at New College, Oxford. During a series of post-university jobs in media and strategy, he was constantly thinking of his own business ideas. Turning to the internet, Brent Hoberman decided the service he would most like would be one that would help him do everything at the last minute, and lastminute.com was born. The business became one of the most successful and high-profile symbols of the dotcom boom in the late 1990s and was sold to US online rival Travelocity for £577 million in 2005.

Andy Hornby (HBOS)

Andy Hornby was educated at Oxford University and Harvard Business School. In 1996 he was headhunted by ASDA's then CEO Archie Norman to become director of corporate development and went on to become MD of ASDA's clothing business. Four years later, Andy Hornby got his second big break, when once again the headhunters came calling and recruited him as head of retail at Halifax. In January 2006, aged just thirty-nine, he became chief executive of HBOS.

Sir Tom Hunter

Sir Tom Hunter started his career helping out at his father's grocery shop. Inspired by the growing popularity of training shoes, he borrowed £5,000 from his father and £5,000 from the Royal Bank of Scotland, bought a job lot of shoes and a van, and wrote to every retailer in Britain asking for space. One replied offering him a concession, the business mushroomed and within ten years Sports Division was turning over £260 million and making a profit of £34 million. Today he is Britain's most prolific philanthropist, dividing his time between work for international charities and venture capital companies which invest in retail and property.

Clive Jacobs (holiday autos)

Clive Jacobs's first job in travel was, when aged nineteen, he moved to Israel and got a job as a messenger with a travel company delivering tickets. Returning to England, he set up a series of travel businesses, one of which merged with another larger business with a small car rental section called Cars Abroad. He subsequently used the car rental idea to start holiday autos, which revolutionised the car rental market by becoming the first firm to offer pre-booked, pre-paid, fully inclusive car rental packages. The firm achieved annual revenues of £200 million in sixteen years of growth before being sold to lastminute.com for £43 million in 2003.

Justin King (Sainsbury)

On graduating from Bath University Justin King joined Mars as a trainee, working first in production and then sales. After a brief spell with Pepsi and three years at Haagen Dazs, Justin King joined ASDA, then at the beginning of its recovery process. In 2000 he joined Marks & Spencer as executive director in the food division. Four years on he was persuaded to join J Sainsbury Plc as chief executive to halt the slide in the grocer's market share. Since he joined he has made significant changes to the supermarket, including an aggressive price-cutting campaign, supply chain changes and the recruitment of respected industry figures to the board.

Henry Kravis (KKR)

Henry Kravis holds an MBA from Columbia University. After various jobs in New York City's financial sector he joined Bear, Stearns and Company with his cousin George Roberts and worked under corporate finance manager Jerome Kohlberg Jr. In 1976 the three men left to set up their own investment company, Kohlberg, Kravis, Roberts & Co, which has grown to become one of the world's most prominent private equity firms. The list of companies Henry Kravis has bought and sold over the years include many of the great American brand names, such as Texaco, Gillette, Safeway and Legrand.

Martha Lane Fox (Lucky Voice)

After graduating from Magdalen College, Oxford, Martha Lane Fox joined Spectrum management consultants, where she met her future business partner Brent Hoberman. She was Hoberman's second choice for a partner in his vision to set up lastminute.com – she initially scoffed at the idea of a last-minute lifestyle e-retailer, claiming she was not passionate about technology. Starting out in a 'broom cupboard', Martha Lane Fox's skills at cold-calling airlines, persuading investors and attracting publicity were instrumental in making lastminute.com the internet's best-known dotcom business.

Sir Terry Leahy (Tesco)

Sir Terry Leahy read management science at the University of Manchester Institute of Science and Technology. He started his career as a product manager at the Co-op and joined Tesco as marketing executive in 1979, where he has been ever since. He became marketing manager in 1981, marketing director in 1992, deputy managing director in 1995 and chief executive at the age of forty-one. Sir Terry Leahy has been regularly voted one of Britain's most admired business leaders.

Carolyn McCall (Guardian Media Group)

Carolyn McCall began her career as a history teacher at Holland Park School in London. She joined the *Guardian* in 1986 and rose quickly through the ranks, becoming managing director of Guardian Newspapers in 2000 and chief executive in 2004. She became chief executive of the parent company, Guardian Media Group, in May 2006. Her two biggest triumphs have been the launch of the website Guardian Unlimited in 1999 and relaunching the *Guardian* newspaper in its Berliner format, both of which she calls the 'best decisions of her working life'.

David Mayhew (JP Morgan Cazenove)

David Mayhew's first job after Eton was as a trainee stockbroker at Panmure Gordon. In 1969 he joined Cazenove, becoming dealing partner in 1972 and chairman by 2001. Three years later, with Cazenove representing more than forty of the UK's biggest 100 companies, David Mayhew oversaw a landmark deal with JP Morgan. Cazenove joined forces with the US investment bank, ending 181 years of independence.

Sir Kenneth Morrison (Wm Morrison)

Ken Morrison joined the family grocery business in 1952 after completing National Service. He saw the opportunity to open self-service stores with checkouts rather than traditional counter service and opened his first large superstore in Bradford in 1960. He then transformed the company into the fourth largest supermarket group in the United Kingdom, with nearly four decades of unbroken sales and profit growth. In 2003 Morrisons bought the rival Safeway chain in a hotly contested bid. Sir Ken Morrison retired from Wm Morrison in January 2008 and took on the newly-created role of company president.

James Murdoch (BSkyB)

James Murdoch is the fourth of Rupert Murdoch's six children. He studied in Rome and even considered becoming an archaeologist before signing up for Harvard. At the age of twenty-seven, James Murdoch moved to

Hong Kong to take control of News Corp's ailing Asian satellite service, Star TV. It was losing £100 million a year but was turned around to make a modest profit, thanks to new channels and distribution deals with China, Taiwan and India. He became chief executive of BSkyB in 2003 in a move which provoked howls of nepotism but which has since been viewed favourably in the City. In December 2007, James became chairman and chief executive of News Corp's European and Asian holdings.

Rupert Murdoch (NewsCorp)

Rupert Murdoch read economics at Oxford and his first job was running the Adelaide paper *The News*, which he inherited from his father. He quickly established himself as the most dynamic newspaper proprietor in the country, acquiring a string of titles, before branching out worldwide in the 1960s to acquire titles in London and New York. Today he is the controlling shareholder, chairman and managing director of News Corporation, with assets worldwide in television, film, media and the internet.

Sir Gulam Noon MBE (Noon Products)

Sir Gulam Noon ran the family food business in India for ten years before leaving for the UK in 1969 with £50 in his pocket. His first company, a confectionery business called Bombay Halwa Ltd (Royal Sweets), grew rapidly from a single shop in Southall, London. He moved into ready meals in 1988 after trying a supermarket curry which he thought was 'unattractive, insipid and badly packaged, a million miles from authentic Indian food'. His first factory had a workforce of eleven people. Today, between his two companies, he employs more than 1,250 staff and works closely with the UK's leading supermarkets.

Archie Norman (Aurigo)

Educated at Charterhouse School and Cambridge University, Archie Norman began his business career at McKinsey & Co. He joined Kingfisher as finance director at the age of thirty-three and, from 1991 until 2000, he was chief executive and then chairman of ASDA, spearheading its revival and paving the way for its sale to Wal-Mart. He spent eight years as the Conservative MP for Tunbridge Wells (1997–2005) before returning to business full time, founding venture capital fund Aurigo in 2006.

Robert Peston (BBC)

Robert Peston is business editor of the BBC. From 2002 to 2005, he was City editor and assistant editor of the *Sunday Telegraph*, in charge of its Business and Money sections. Until September 2000 he was the *Financial Times*'s financial editor (in charge of all business and financial coverage) and a member of the *FT*'s editorial board as an assistant editor. At the *FT*, which he joined in 1991, his previous positions were political editor, banking editor and head of an investigations unit (which he founded). Peston is a past winner of the Harold Wincott Senior Financial Journalist of the Year Award (2005), the London Press Club's Scoop of the Year Award (2005), Granada Television's 'What the Papers Say' award for investigative journalist of the year (1994) and the Wincott Young Financial Journalist of the year (1986). He is the author of *Brown's Britain* (2005).

Peter Peterson (The Blackstone Group)

Peter Peterson, whose career straddles both business and politics, is senior chairman and co-founder of US investment giant The Blackstone Group. In politics his most prominent position was as US Secretary of Commerce in 1972, in the Nixon administration. He is chairman of the Council on Foreign Relations, founding chairman of the Peterson Institute for International Economics in Washington and was chairman of the Federal Reserve Bank of New York from 2000 to 2004. He is also the author of several definitive books, including *Running on Empty: How the Democratic and Republican Parties are Bankrupting our Future*.

Baroness Margaret Prosser

Baroness Margaret Prosser is a life-long campaigner for equal rights and is chair of the Women's National Commission and the Women and

Work Commission. She has twenty years' experience as a senior trade union official with the Transport and General Workers Union, working as National Women's Secretary, National Organiser and Deputy General Secretary. She was a member of the TUC General Council for eleven years and TUC President in 1995–96.

Feargal Quinn (Superquinn)

Feargal Quinn opened his first store in Dundalk at the age of twenty-three, with the idea of specialising in fresh food. With the main focus on customer service, he pioneered in-store bakeries, pizza, pasta and even sausage kitchens and eventually captured 9 per cent of Ireland's grocery market. Feargal Quinn has also pursued a successful political career as an independent member of the Seanad Éireann, the upper house of the Irish parliament, since 1993.

Jeff Randall (*Daily Telegraph*)

Jeff Randall read economics at the University of Nottingham. His introduction to journalism was a postgraduate course at the University of Florida and he became city correspondent at the *Sunday Telegraph* in 1986. After six years as city editor at *The Sunday Times* (1989–95), Jeff moved into City PR briefly before returning to *The Sunday Times* as assistant editor/sports editor. He edited *Sunday Business* before moving to the BBC in 2001 as the corporation's first business editor, resigning in 2005 to become the *Daily Telegraph*'s 'editor at large'.

Gail Rebuck (The Random House Group)

Gail Rebuck read Intellectual History at Sussex University. After a brief stint as a European tour guide, she began her publishing career as a production assistant before Century Publishing founder Anthony Cheetham asked her to join him in 1982. Starting with a phone in a small room, they built a business which took over the far bigger Hutchinson, and which was subsequently bought by Random House in a £64.5 million deal in 1989. Gail Rebuck became chairman and chief executive in 1991. Random House was sold to Bertelsmann in 1998 and has recently announced the acquisition of majority stakes in both BBC and Virgin Books.

Julian Richer (Richer Sounds)

Julian Richer opened his first branch of Richer Sounds near London Bridge in 1978 when he was just nineteen. The venture grew into one of the UK's most successful retail operations and boasts an entry in the *Guinness Book of Records* as achieving the world's highest sales per square foot of retail space. His business interests now cover manufacturing, franchising and a property portfolio. His consultancy, Richer Consulting, advises some of the country's largest organisations at chief executive level on cultural change management, staff motivation, customer service, staff communications and staff and customer suggestion schemes.

Simon Robey (Morgan Stanley)

Simon Robey read English at Magdalen College, Oxford. While considering becoming a professional singer, he went along to a Lazards 'milk round' presentation and got a job with them. He joined Morgan Stanley from Lazards and has had a spectacular deal history, including advising SmithKline Beecham on the £47.7 billion merger with Glaxo Wellcome, selling Abbey to Banco Santander for £10.2 billion, advising Pernod Ricard on the purchase of Allied Domecq for 14.2 billion Euros, and selling Scottish Power to Iberdrola for £116 billion. In 2004 Robey successfully defended Marks & Spencer against a hostile 400p a share takeover by Philip Green.

Sir Stuart Rose (Marks & Spencer)

Stuart Rose first joined Marks & Spencer in 1972 as a management trainee, spending seventeen years at the high street giant before joining the Burton Group in 1989. There, initially, he was a director of Debenhams and went on to become chief executive of the Multiples Division, including Dorothy Perkins, Burtons, Evans and Principles. In 1997 he moved on to become chief executive of Argos, where he was unsuccessful in defending the company from a takeover bid by Great Universal Stores, but won respect for securing an increased price for the company. He subsequently joined Booker, which he turned around and then merged with Iceland Plc. He then went on to turn around the Arcadia Group, which he subsequently sold to Philip Green in 2002. Stuart Rose became chief executive of M&S in 2004, successfully fighting off a bid by Philip Green and restoring the fortunes of the chain.

Professor Earl Sasser

Earl Sasser has been at the Harvard Business School since 1969, after completing his PhD in economics at Duke University. He also acts as a consultant to a number of companies in North America, Asia and Europe. Earl Sasser specialises in the field of service management and has co-authored several books, including *Service Breakthroughs: Changing the Rules of the Game,* following five years of research in fourteen service industries. His new book (co-authored with James Heskett and Joe Wheeler), *The Science of Delight*, will be published in autumn 2008.

Stephen A. Schwarzman (The Blackstone Group)

Stephen A. Schwarzman holds a BA from Yale University and an MBA from Harvard Business School. He began his career at Lehman Brothers where he became managing director in 1978 at the age of thirty-one. In 1985 Stephen Schwarzman founded The Blackstone Group with Peter Peterson and a balance sheet of $400,000. Today The Blackstone Group is a multibillion-dollar global financial services empire spanning private equity, real estate, restructuring and corporate advisory work. Since 1987, Blackstone has raised over $80 billion for alternative asset investing.

Lee Scott (Wal-Mart)

Lee Scott's first job was as a salesman for a transport company, but his big break came when he contacted Wal-Mart to negotiate over a $7,000 debt owed to his employer. He was offered a job managing a new distribution centre where it was quickly discovered he had a flair for organisation and 'stripping out costs', which led to his rapid promotion through the ranks. In 2000 he was appointed president and chief executive of the global retail giant.

Fred Smith (FedEx)

At Yale Fred Smith was famously awarded a C for his economics paper that outlined his idea for an overnight delivery service. He went on to found FedEx in 1971 on his return from service in Vietnam, using £2.3 million of his inheritance to help raise £46 million in venture capital. Today FedEx is a $30 billion corporation, handling more than six million shipments a day and employing 250,000 staff in 215 countries.

Sir Martin Sorrell (WPP)

Martin Sorrell read economics at Christ's College, Cambridge, and has an MBA from Harvard University. He began his career at Glendinning Associates in Westport, then worked for Mark McCormack at IMG and the retail entrepreneur Jimmy Gulliver, before becoming finance director for the Saatchi brothers. Sorrell bought a stake in a shell company in Kent called Wire & Plastic Products, which made wire baskets for supermarkets. He joined WPP as chief executive in 1986 and transformed it by buying a string of marketing services companies. In 1987 he stunned the agency world with the hostile takeover of top ad agency J Walter Thompson. Two years later he succeeded in another dramatic takeover, this time of Ogilvy and Mather, so securing WPP's place as one of the major players in the global advertising market.

Mark Thompson (BBC)

Mark Thompson joined the BBC as a production trainee after graduating from Merton College, Oxford. Among various key roles, he was appointed editor of the *Nine O'Clock News* in 1988, editor of *Panorama* in 1990 and controller of BBC Two in 1996. By 2000 he was BBC director of television, but left the corporation in 2002 to become chief executive of Channel Four. He returned to the BBC as director general in May 2004, following a unanimous decision by the BBC Board of Governors which declared he had 'unquestionable public service credentials'.

Rebekah Wade (*Sun*)

Rebekah Wade joined the *News of the World* as a researcher in 1989, rising through the ranks to become deputy editor. In 1998 she transferred to the *Sun* to become deputy editor, returning to edit the *News of the World* just two years later. Her tenure at the top-selling weekly was punctuated by a high-profile campaign to name and shame known paedophiles. Renowned as a consummate networker with celebrities, businessmen and politicians, Rebekah Wade moved back to the *Sun* in January 2003 to become the paper's first female editor.

John Waples (*The Sunday Times*)

John Waples has been a journalist at *The Sunday Times* since 1994. Prior to *The Sunday Times* he worked on the *Harlow and Bishop's Stortford Gazette* and *Estates Times*. He has risen through the ranks from City correspondent through to deputy City editor and was promoted to business editor in September 2005.

Perween Warsi (S&A Foods)

Perween Warsi, dubbed 'Britain's curry queen', began making finger foods in her Derby home in 1986 after becoming increasingly dissatisfied with the quality of Indian food available in British supermarkets. The breakthrough for S&A Foods came in 1987 when ASDA agreed to put some dishes to a taste test. The popularity of ethnic dishes was growing and supermarkets were looking for authentic ranges. S&A Foods is now a £70 million operation, employing 800 staff and making foods for major supermarket chains.

Jenny Watson (EOC)

Jenny Watson started her career as a secretary before taking a degree in communications at Sheffield Hallam University, followed by a master's in history at the University of Westminster. She went on to specialise in the not-for-profit sector, mainly in human rights at organisations such as Liberty, Charter88 and the Fawcett Society. She joined the Equal Opportunities Commission (EOC) Board in 1999 as a commissioner, becoming deputy chair in 2000 and chair in 2005. She was a founding director of Global Partners and Associates, a consultancy focusing on democracy, governance and human rights. In October 2007, the EOC was merged with the new Commission for Equality and Human Rights.

Alannah Weston (Selfridges)

Graduating from Merton College, Oxford, Alannah Weston started her career in journalism, working on an arts supplement for the *Daily Telegraph*. She then moved to Burberry to become international head of press, just as the company was undergoing a revival under Rose Marie Bravo. Alannah, who says retail has always been in her blood, finally succumbed to the family retail empire, becoming creative director at Selfridges in 2004.

Galen Weston (Weston)

Born into the already hugely wealthy and successful Weston clan, Galen Weston's first real test of his business acumen came when he moved to Canada in 1973 and was given full rein over the family's rambling business interests there. He transformed George Weston Limited into a retail empire which is number one in Canada, selling a third of the country's groceries. Along the way he had to dump $300 million of unproductive assets and make a number of acquisitions. Galen's business interests have spread to the United Kingdom, most notably with the purchase of Selfridges in 2003.

Patience Wheatcroft (Barclays)

Patience Wheatcroft was deputy city editor of the *Mail on Sunday* and then edited the business section of *The Times* for nine years before becoming editor of the *Sunday Telegraph* in 2006. She left the *Sunday*

Telegraph in September 2007 and has been appointed a non-executive director of Barclays. She is a regular commentator on radio and television, discussing business and current affairs.

Bob Wigley (Merrill Lynch)

Bob Wigley graduated from Bath University with a business degree and joined Arthur Andersen, training first as a chartered accountant, then as a consultant. He spent ten years at Morgan Grenfell, latterly as managing director. In 1996, Bob Wigley was headhunted to join Merrill Lynch to spearhead the development of its European business on the strength of his reputation as one of London's top corporate advisers. He is now senior vice-president and chairman of EMEA at Merrill Lynch.

Lord Wilson of Dinton

After qualifying as a barrister, Richard Wilson joined the Civil Service as Assistant Principal in the Board of Trade in 1966. He subsequently served in a number of departments, including twelve years in the Department of Energy, where his responsibilities included nuclear power policy and the privatisation of Britoil. He was promoted to head the Domestic and Economic Secretariat of the Cabinet Office under Margaret Thatcher from 1987 to 1990. Then, after two years in the Treasury, he was appointed Permanent Secretary of the Department of the Environment in 1992. He became Permanent Under Secretary of the Home Office in 1994 and Secretary of the Cabinet and Head of the Home Civil Service in 1998. He retired from the Civil Service in 2002 and is Master of Emmanuel College, Cambridge. He has a number of non-executive posts, including chairman of C Hoare & Co and a director of BSkyB.

Index

THE POWER OF READING

Visit the Random House website and get connected with information on all our books and authors

EXTRACTS from our recently published books and selected backlist titles

COMPETITIONS AND PRIZE DRAWS Win signed books, audiobooks and more

AUTHOR EVENTS Find out which of our authors are on tour and where you can meet them

LATEST NEWS on bestsellers, awards and new publications

MINISITES with exclusive special features dedicated to our authors and their titles

READING GROUPS Reading guides, special features and all the information you need for your reading group

LISTEN to extracts from the latest audiobook publications

WATCH video clips of interviews and readings with our authors

RANDOM HOUSE INFORMATION including advice for writers, job vacancies and all your general queries answered

Come home to Random House
www.rbooks.co.uk

Bad Samaritans

Ha-Joon Chang

A radical look by a leading economist at the issues surrounding globalization.

It's rare that a book appears with a fresh perspective on world affairs, but renowned economist Ha-Joon Chang has some startlingly original things to say about the future of globalization. In theory, he argues, the world's wealthiest countries and supranational institutions like the IMF, World Bank and WTO want to see all nations developing into modern industrial societies. In practice, though, those at the top are 'kicking away the ladder' to wealth that they themselves climbed.

Why? Self-interest certainly plays a part. But, more often, rich and powerful governments and institutions are actually being 'Bad Samaritans': their intentions are worthy but their simplistic free-market ideology and poor understanding of history leads them to inflict policy errors on others. Chang demonstrates this by contrasting the route to success of economically vibrant countries with the very different route now being dictated to the world's poorer nations. In the course of this, he shows just how muddled the thinking is in such key areas as trade and foreign investment. He shows that the case for privatisation and against state involvement is far from proven. And he explores the ways in which attitudes to national cultures and political ideologies are obscuring clear thinking and creating bad policy. Finally, he argues the case for new strategies for a more prosperous world that may appall the 'Bad Samaritans'.

'A smart, lively and provocative book that offers us compelling new ways to look at globalization.' Joseph E. Stiglitz, Nobel laureate in Economics, 2001

'Every orthodoxy needs effective critics. Ha-Joon Chang is probably the world's most effective critic of globalization. He does not deny the benefits to developing countries of integration into the world economy. But he draws on the lessons of history to argue that they must be allowed to integrate on their own terms.' Martin Wolf, *Financial Times*, author of *Why Globalization Works*

'This is a marvellous book. Well researched, panoramic in its scope and beautifully written, *Bad Samaritans*, is the perfect riposte to devotees of a one-size-fits-all model of growth and globalization. I strongly urge you to read it.' Larry Elliott, Economics Editor, *Guardian*

'In this more polemical tract, [Chang] adds the spark of personal reflection . . . and some mischievous rhetorical set-pieces.' *Economist*

'This is an excellent book . . . deploys the logical discipline of economics and its engagement with quantitative evidence, but does so in jargon-free prose that sparkles with anecdotes and practical observations.' *International Affairs*

BUSINESS
BOOKS

ALSO AVAILABLE IN RANDOM HOUSE BUSINESS BOOKS

The Crunch

Alex Brummer

The first book to take the lid off the events surrounding the recent turmoil in the financial markets and the near collapse of Northern Rock – and to reveal the potentially disastrous path down which we're all being led.

On 9 August 2007 France's largest bank announced that it had had to suspend trading in two huge investment funds it controlled. The same day three German banks revealed that they were close to collapse. A few days later came the first run on a British bank since the 1860s as vast queues of worried investors besieged Northern Rock. Within weeks, the Government were being forced to bail out this previously little-known bank to the tune of £30 billion, share prices in other mortgage lenders were plummeting, and alarming news about the state of several of the biggest US banks was crossing the Atlantic. What lay behind this series of crippling disasters?

In *The Crunch*, award-winning journalist Alex Brummer painstakingly traces the course of the crisis from its origins in the US 'subprime' market to its explosion on to the international scene. It's a story of greed, mismanagement and dithering in which bankers seeking to make a quick buck, regulators engaged in turf wars and blame-avoidance, and governments paralysed by the sheer scale of the problem all conspired to bring the banking system almost to its knees. It's also a story of victims: the 1.5 million people in the US who have already been thrown out of their houses, the entire population of the UK who have been co-opted to guarantee Northern Rock with £30 billion of public money, borrowers everywhere who are now finding credit more expensive and harder to get. And, as Alex Brummer convincingly argues, it's not a story that has yet played itself out.

BUSINESS
BOOKS

ALSO AVAILABLE IN RANDOM HOUSE BUSINESS BOOKS

The Long Tail

Chris Anderson

The new economics of culture and commerce

With his brilliant theory of the Long Tail – a powerful new economic force in a world where the internet allows access to almost unlimited choice – Chris Anderson has identified an important truth about our economy and culture: that the future does not lie in hits – the high-volume end of a traditional demand curve – but in what used to be regarded as misses – the curve's endlessly long tail.

In this expanded and updated edition, published for the first time in paperback, he examines how niche interests, which make up the millions of misses, have come together in a global network, stimulating innovation on an unprecedented scale. The result, he argues, is a cultural richness in which enthusiasms previously dismissed as 'minority' thrive and everybody everywhere can find something to their taste.

'A smart, timely and oddly inspiring book.' *Time Out*

'It's the Big Idea of 2006.' *GQ*

'*The Long Tail* is an eloquent exposition of a simple idea, but one that has huge ramifications for our media and culture if followed to its logical conclusions.' *Guardian Media*

'Each year produces a book that captures the Zeitgeist . . . This year Chris Anderson's *The Long Tail* has helped to reinterpret our world.' *The Times*

'. . . snappily argued and thought-provoking.' *New Yorker*

BUSINESS
BOOKS

**Order more Random House Business Books
from your local bookshop, or have them delivered
direct to your door by Bookpost**

Bad Samaritans Ha-Joon Chang	9781905211371	£8.99
The Crunch Alex Brummer	9781847940087	£11.99
The Long Tail Chris Anderson	9781844138517	£8.99

Free post and packing
Overseas customers allow £2 per paperback
Phone: 01624 677237
Post: Random House Business Books
c/o Bookpost, PO Box 29, Douglas, Isle of Man IM99 1BQ
Fax: 01624 670923
email: bookshop@enterprise.net
Cheques (payable to Bookpost) and credit cards accepted

Prices and availability subject to change without notice.
Allow 28 days for delivery.
When placing your order, please state if you do not wish to receive any
additional information.
www.rbooks.co.uk

BUSINESS
BOOKS